Schooling the Child

What is a child? How is the concept of childhood defined? This book aims to explore these perennial and complex questions by looking at the way in which society constructs and understands childhood. The authors focus in particular on the school – a key location within which social and cultural notions of childhood are defined and performed.

The book is divided into three major parts:

Part I frames the accepted notions of childhood and schooling, and introduces ethnomethodological analysis as a tool to rethink current versions of the child.
Part II focuses on how school students become members of a category within the institution of the classroom. The authors explore this idea through transcripts of talk between teachers and students, and amongst students themselves in two classroom studies.
Part III looks at the materials of education, concentrating specifically on children's texts: those written *for* children and those written *by* children. The authors examine how such texts portray a notion of the child within the story, and also assume a notion of the child as reader of the story.

This important book shows how much is at stake for children in accepting adults' deep-seated notions of childhood. It will be of great interest to educational researchers and policy makers, sociologists of childhood, teachers and student teachers.

Helena Austin is a lecturer in language and literacy at the School of Education and Professional Studies at Griffith University, Australia. **Bronwyn Dwyer** is a research officer in the Australian Commonwealth Public Service. **Peter Freebody** is a Professor in the Faculty of Education and Director of the Centre for Literacy and Language Education Research at Griffith University, Australia.

Schooling the Child
The making of students in classrooms

**Helena Austin, Bronwyn Dwyer
and Peter Freebody**

RoutledgeFalmer
Taylor & Francis Group

LONDON AND NEW YORK

First published 2003 by RoutledgeFalmer
11 New Fetter Lane, London EC4P 4EE

Simultaneously published in the USA and Canada
by RoutledgeFalmer
29 West 35th Street, New York, NY 10001

RoutledgeFalmer is an imprint of the Taylor & Francis Group

© 2003 Helena Austin, Bronwyn Dwyer and Peter Freebody

Typeset in Bembo by BC Typesetting, Bristol
Printed and bound in Great Britain by
MPG Books Ltd, Bodmin, Cornwall

British Library Cataloguing in Publication Data
A catalogue record for this book is available from the British Library

Library of Congress Cataloging in Publication Data
A catalog record for this book has been requested

ISBN 0–415–26325–5 (hbk)
ISBN 0–415–26326–3 (pbk)

Contents

Acknowledgements

We would like to thank Colin Thiele for the use of extracts from *Magpie Island*.

We also thank the teachers and students of the classrooms we observed and audio-taped. Their generosity in allowing us access to their daily schooling made this research possible. We thank 'Mrs Field', the teacher of '6F', for access to her planning and assessment documents.

Thank you also to Cameron Barnes and Margaret Murphy for their meticulous editing.

The order of authorship is alphabetical.

Transcript conventions

Turns are numbered, the original turn number is used to give a sense of where in the ongoing interaction this extract took place.

T	Teacher speaking
R	Researcher speaking
S	Unidentified student speaking
Ss	Many students speaking together
(. . .)	untranscribable
–	short pause, less than 1 second
—	pause less than 2 seconds
(2)	pause in seconds
/	latched turn, no pause between speakers
//	next speaker interrupts at this point
(*comment*)	transcriber's comment or description of context
. . .	turn continues, or preceding text has been deleted
[	square bracket indicates overlapping talk
CAPITALS	words in capitals indicate the speaker is reading from a written text
<u>Underlined</u>	underlined fragments indicate speaker emphasis
?	a question mark indicates a rising inflection – note that the utterance may not be a question
.	a fullstop indicates a falling or closing tone
:	a colon between two letters in a word indicates that the speaker has extended the sound in speech

Part I
Considering childhood

1 Framing childhood

This book deals with Childhood, a topic about which most readers will know a great deal. This knowledge comes from our having been children for a number of years, even though, for interesting reasons, the precise number of those years may be difficult to specify. It may also come from having become parents of children, or having long-term contact with other people's children. Along with this first-hand, experiential knowledge, we have folk or commonsensical knowledge learned from listening to family members and acquaintances, and from observing their behaviour patterns. We also have access to official knowledge about children, learned from our contact with the child professions (e.g. in health, law and education) and from the social sciences that both study and inform us about these topics. The bodies of knowledge from these sources (consistent, compatible and articulated or not) we hold alongside one another as we go about trying to understand, evaluate and act in the various public and domestic settings that make up our daily lives.

Who could possibly ask 'What is a Child?' What does it mean even to ask this? One of the main points of this book is that these sources of knowledge cannot simply be put to the test against some authoritative definition of Childhood or some final criterion of what, when, and how is a Child. While our personal, commonsensical and official knowledges may be compatible on a number of points, they are called into play at different times and in different settings, made appropriate or irrelevant, powerful or incidental, depending on the practical purposes of the events at hand, events that make some versions of 'childhood' operative and others not so. These domains of knowledge that we can draw on do not operate in isolation from one another. Rather, they inform, support or challenge one another, again, variously in various settings.

So, what is 'a Child'?

> Despite a long commitment to the good of the child and a more recent intellectual engagement with the topic of childhood, what remains perpetually diffuse and ambiguous is the basic conceptualization of childhood as a social practice. Childhood remains largely unrealized as an emergent patterning of action. The child, therefore, cannot be imagined except in relation to a conception of the adult, but essentially it becomes impossible

to generate a well-defined sense of the adult, and indeed adult society, without first positing the child.

(Jenks 1996: 2–3)

Every day, adults and children alike certainly behave as if Jenks is wrong, as if there is nothing 'diffuse and ambiguous' about our conceptualizations of what children are, or about the directness and transparency of our knowledge of what they are. So too do writers of official policies that govern children, and so do most social scientists, who have spent considerable time and effort documenting what children do, say and think – namely, what they are. The contents of this category of person, which we here call the Child,[1] are taken by members of a culture to be unremarkable matters of familiarity.

An example to start: the circularity of definitions

To frame these ideas, we can take, as an instance, the most comprehensive, global declarations about children ever made, the United Nations Convention on the Rights of the Child (1989). Article 1 defines the child as follows: 'a child means every human being below the age of eighteen years unless under the law applicable to the child, majority is attained earlier'. In the Preamble to the articles, the Convention declares the consequences of satisfying this definition thus: 'in the Universal Declaration of Human Rights, the United Nations has proclaimed that childhood is entitled to special care and assistance'.

In the document, many statements and recommendations are made that could and, indeed, do elsewhere in UN documents, apply equally to adults (e.g. freedom from discrimination, from violence, and so on). Only in one place is a statement made that elaborates on and justifies the 'special care and assistance' that is to be afforded members of this category of person, and it is this, again from the Preamble:

> Bearing in mind that, as indicated in the Declaration of the Rights of the Child, 'the child, by reason of his physical and mental immaturity, needs special safeguards and care, including appropriate legal protection, before as well as after birth . . .'

So the straightforward and unexplicated notion of 'physical and mental immaturity' is offered, commonsensically, as the basis of the special needs of persons under the age of eighteen years. While there is nothing necessarily ambiguous about the stance taken in the Convention, on the matter of precisely what it is that constitutes immaturity, the document has nothing more to say. What this means is that the contents of this 'immaturity' and its connection to the need for 'special care and assistance' are taken to be obvious, ingrained, so deeply commonsensical that no further explication is needed.

Our commonsensical versions of Childhood and the social and behavioural implications of those versions are held in place by what is essentially a moral commitment. Historians, anthropologists and sociologists have demonstrated that children are different, have been treated differently in different times, and are treated differently in different cultures (see Chapter 2). Put succinctly, the Child has been found to be enacted in fundamentally different ways in different settings. However, documented historical and cultural variations do not typically lead us to redefine our fundamental notions of children. Nor do they make our own certainties on this matter a conceptual or practical problem. The initial reaction of most members of our culture is to regard differences, when they are mild, as variations on an essential theme of Childhood and, when they are extreme, as the aberrations of a malevolent, neglectful or misguided adult generation (James *et al.* 1998).

Just as the UN Convention commits the signatories to a moral attitude to children and to the institutional manifestations of that attitude, so too our culture's attitude to children is informed by our understanding of their place in the moral order of our society. This place that children occupy we can explicate at length, pointing to their rights, responsibilities and needs, and to the ways in which these are afforded by institutional provisions in our legal, educational and health establishments.

The overall goal of this book is to redefine the ways in which common-sense and professional understandings about children and Childhood reconstruct, reaccomplish and sustain Childhood as a lived experience for young people. The book aims to make a problem of how it is that people display and act on those understandings. In part, we aim to develop a counter-position to developmental approaches, using analyses drawing on ethnomethodology, as outlined in Chapter 4. This examination we conduct from within the institution that manages children's formal education. We present a number of settings that make up and inform classroom life for young people, and develop increasing levels of specificity and detail as we go. We explore whole class teacher-led talk, talk in student groups, a novel written for children and used in school, and how students write in school, examining each of these settings for the ways each builds, reflects and represents what it is to be a child of schooling.

This book extends current documentations and critiques of contemporary theorizations of Childhood by exploring their currency as beliefs for action among a highly significant sector of the adult population, namely, school teachers. As the social service professions expand their purview of activity, become more specialized in their understanding and treatment of children, and accept the requirement to base their work on available research about children, the need to document variations in enacted theories about the Child and to explore the implications of these variations becomes more important. There is a clear need to engage in a fundamental way with daily enactments of the concept of the Child, and the period described as Childhood, as one of our culture's most consequential categorizations of persons – a categorization that has extensive implications for the ways in which young people are treated and for the nature of their participation in social life and cultural experience.

Until only recently social science research approaches to the study of children and Childhood have generally been developmental, that is, based on common-sense propositions that children are people in the process of developing (Speier 1971, 1976), and that the attributes of children are thus to be properly considered in relation to adult socio-cultural functioning. Children are primarily taken to be persons heading for adulthood. These propositions have in common premises about the distinctiveness of children *vis-à-vis* adults, and about Childhood as a specific cultural condition. Such premises have remained largely taken as read, rarely considered to be either problematic or objects of study – rarely anything but resolute, unexamined resources for institutional and public practice, including research.

As a concomitant of this, Childhood has come to be understood in terms of predetermined cognitive, emotional, physical or moral continuums or staged sequences. Contemporary education, for example, draws upon developmental continuums in formulating teaching and learning theories and in setting curricular content, scope and sequence. Theories of pedagogy have, in the course of the last century, drawn upon Skinnerian, Chomskian, Piagetian and Freudian theorizations of the Child and Childhood, derived, in turn, from behaviourist, linguistic, information processing and psychodynamic accounts of human functioning, with adult functioning as the implicit model of normality (Luke 1991). Every one of these theorizations presents children as the focal points of study, construes what is important about children within the terms of the given theory, and assesses them along a continuum. Each theory, therefore, is premised upon and endorses a particular version of the Child. Each version of the Child, in turn, calls forth and endorses socio-cultural and institutional practices that explicitly refer to and assemble a particular inflection of the Child. Theoretical propositions play out in policy and practice, often in ways that retrospectively validate those propositions so that they seem to have had objective status in the first place.

However, the challenge presented in Jenks's claim to specify Childhood as social practice has not gone unnoticed. Certain lines of research have addressed this through an engagement with Childhood as a cultural and historical construct. Such research, a facet of the 'new sociology of childhood' (James *et al.* 1998), has recognized that, while Childhood has biological bases, it is clear that the ways in which adults have recognized and acted on these bases throughout history and across cultures have been varied, leading to variations in the role in socio-cultural life played by children (Baker and Campbell 2000; Baker and Freebody 1989a; Corsaro, 1997; Jenks 1996). This research tradition has drawn on various accounts of the Child throughout history, across cultures and in various folk and official discourses (e.g. Ariès 1962; Cleverley and Phillips 1988; de Mause 1976; Jackson 1982; Jenks 1982, 1996; Polakow-Suransky 1982; Tyler 1993).

In pursuing these lines, some researchers have also recognized the need to examine the patterns of interaction that define and enact the Child in key everyday socio-cultural locations. For example, some studies (as reported in Goodwin 1990; Hutchby and Moran-Ellis 1998) have documented the inter-active competencies of children. While we discuss these lines of work in later Parts of this book, the point to be made here is that such research has implications for our commonsensical and professional understandings of the Child and, thus, in turn, for the acculturation, education and care of children.

Research of the kind reported in this book amounts to an examination of Childhood as actively accomplished in and through the social experiences of the actual participants (i.e. by children and those with whom they interact) rather than as a predefined stage of life. Such research critiques the notion, usually assumed, that children are beings whose activities are comprehensively explicable in terms of the imperatives or, less strongly, the normativities of the life cycle.

In this book, we document:

- the extent of reliance on official contemporary theories of the Child (e.g. from variants of social learning theories and developmental psychology) evident in classroom talk and the materials used in schools with, for and about children;
- the ways in which official contemporary theories of the Child are manifest differently within the institutional context of schooling;
- variations in interpretive accounts of the Child available in different social configurations used in classrooms;
- the extent to which the participants call on common-sense accounts of their own childhood experiences in accounting for the contents of Child;
- the consequentiality for practice of these enacted understandings, including possible ways in which these understandings support or undermine stated institutional goals.

Framing schooling

It is partly through our contact with the activities of the institutions that traverse and shape our public lives (e.g. institutions that deal with the law and health, or the domains of school, family and church) that we learn about the categories into which we might be and are grouped (e.g. Lawyer, Nurse, Teacher, Mother, Sister, Child). Of interest to us here are the categories assembled in school, one of the significant social locations in which each generation has assembled children and has enacted, both for and with them, its versions of them as a category.

A second quote from Jenks provides a backdrop for our consideration of the critical place of schooling in contemporary generation formation:

> The idea of childhood is not a natural but a social construct; as such its status is constituted in particular socially located forms of discourse . . .

the child is assembled intentionally to serve the purposes of supporting
and perpetuating the fundamental grounds of and versions of man [*sic*],
action, order, language, and rationality within particular theories.

(Jenks 1982: 23)

Schooling, while clearly not the only cultural site within which categories of
persons are constructed to support and perpetuate cultural order, constitutes
a particularly relevant site with respect to the Child. As with understandings
of Childhood, our knowledge of schooling comes not from a single, conceptually unified source that lies somehow beyond our experience of public life.
Our knowledge of schooling is informed by propositions from a range of
sources, among them our knowledge of how education is currently conducted,
perhaps by or with us, and how it was conducted with us in earlier years. These
knowledges are not merely collections of factual propositions about children
and school; rather, our common-sense understandings are held in place,
given durability and ascribed importance as moral and cultural resources in
our public and domestic lives.

The social and cultural activities conducted in schools by, with and for
children themselves accomplish particular versions of the Child and have implications for the acculturation, education and care of children. And indeed,
schooling and school activities have been closely observed and theorized as
social practice. As discussed in Chapter 3, the enacted purpose and function
of schooling – as well as the function of classroom talk, curriculum and
resources – have been the subject of much contemporary critical research.

In this book, we take the work of Jenks and others *vis-à-vis* Childhood as a
challenge to make less diffuse and less ambiguous understandings of both Childhood *and* school by documenting the ways in which schooling can be seen as an
important source of knowledge about Childhood, for children. We show how
educational practices not only set about providing children with specifications
of the category to which they belong, but at the same time rely upon children's
already competent enactments of this category. One of the significant
hindrances to addressing Jenks's challenge to study Childhood as social practice
is that, apart from and potentially against the experiences that derive from our
personal histories, there does in fact appear to be a reasonably unified and conceptually coherent field of research and theory to which we can turn to learn
about 'what children are' – the field of 'development': developmental psychology, developmental sociology, developmental linguistics, and so on. These
research domains have conceptualized the Child as a set of ontological propositions; propositions often about social practices but rarely derived from detailed
analysis of everyday social practice, and never by incorporating children's own
knowledge production as part of the cultural context of growing up.

In a comment directly applicable to our understanding of children, Dorothy
Smith described these mainstream social sciences, including schooling, as
providing

a consciousness that looks at society, social relations, and people's lives as if we could stand outside them, ignoring the particular local places in the everyday in which we live our lives. It claims objectivity not on the basis of its capacity to speak truthfully, but in terms of its specific capacity to exclude the presence and experience of particular subjectivities . . . A mode of ruling has become dominant that involves a continual transcription of the local and particular actualities of our lives into abstracted and generalized forms. It is an extra local mode of ruling . . . We are ruled by forms of organization vested in and mediated by texts and documents, and constituted externally to particular individuals and their personal and familial relationships. The practice of ruling involves the ongoing representation of the local actualities of our worlds in the standardized and general forms of knowledge that enter them into the relations of ruling . . . Forms of consciousness are created that are properties of organization or discourse rather than of individual subjects.

(Smith 1987: 2–3; see also Smith 1999)

Within this framework, official knowledges about children function not as neutral guides to social practice but, rather, as forces colonizing local actualities with more standardized forms of thinking compatible with certain public interests. This frame enables a more political reading of Jenks's position that 'the child is assembled intentionally to serve the purposes of . . . particular theories' (Jenks 1982: 23). Specifically, propositions about children become organizing principles, systems of interpretation that overwrite other ways of considering people and interpreting their actions. They similarly provide normative specifications that serve as evaluative criteria for the behaviour of people at different points in the life cycle. To meet these norms, in our case to do well at school, students must, among other things, briskly discover what the adults' theories of children are and how they, as teachable students, might enact important features of those theories.

The structure of the book

The ideas outlined above form the theoretical and practical backdrop to this book. This book takes these as challenges to our professional and common-sense understandings and practices, and addresses them in three Parts. In Part I we explore the significance of schooling in the assembling of Childhood and, then, conversely, the significance of particular versions of Childhood in the production of schooling. We draw together theoretical perspectives and empirical research from psychology, sociology, and history and reframe their relevance to our problem within an ethnomethodological perspective, a position that provides both theoretical and analytic procedures for reconsidering the relationship between social structure and everyday social practice. We demonstrate that this perspective enables research to go beyond subjectivist theories of Childhood that rely on the variegations of individual intentions and the personal constructions of identity, and also beyond deterministic approaches that start with the internalization of norms and proceed to document the quasi-autonomous structural forces that shape children in and for school.

In Parts II and III, we use the tools of ethnomethodology to analyse two broad data sets which, taken together, comprise eight subsets of data. The various analytic passes we make through these data sets contribute to the project of critiquing Childhood, not by reining in the category Child and revealing its finite or essential attributes but, rather, by showing that the Child, like all categories of people, is locally driven and, as such, is whatever participants enact it to be within the various cultural membership categories available in any institutional location.

In Part II, we examine the institutional practices of schooling that give shape and content to students' social practices in school. We detail a range of contexts in which children are instructed in the various interactive rights and responsibilities of the schoolchild. We demonstrate the different ways the students are constituted as Children for School, showing the artfulness of the students' operations as they work within and adapt versions of the Child and Childhood. We highlight students' sensitivity to the varying social and organizational features that they encounter in lessons.

In Part III, we document some of the specific curricular contents attributed to Childhood and drawn on as sources of knowledge relevant to the conduct of lessons. To exemplify these processes, we investigate primary school lessons in the area of English language and literature. We analyse a novel for its use of particular versions of Childhood, and show how these versions permeate literacy and literature lessons and the teachers' assessments of students' work. We also document the ways in which interpretations of the novel and of Childhood are conjointly produced by teachers and students, and then are drawn on as part of the criterion for assessment that the teacher deploys when examining the students' written products. Finally, we examine the written pieces and document the ways in which students comply with, resist or challenge the versions of Childhood that are made 'official' through classroom experiences.

Parts II and III conclude with a review of the analyses and discussion of the implications of the findings. Part IV then steps back from the analyses to reflect on how they have contributed to our question – 'What/when/how is a Child?' – and reviews the implications of our findings in terms of research, policy and practice that have consequences for actual children.

2 Rethinking children and childhood

Introduction: the common-sense Child

Society can be described as comprising those who are children and those who are not. Categorization of an individual into one or the other group, at any moment, requires recourse to the society's definitions and understandings of what a Child is for that interactive or social moment. Various scientific and social disciplines have provided us with terms for labelling and understanding the defining features of children. For example, the work of psychology enables children to be defined as immature but developing with physiology and psychology working in tandem to define developmental milestones. Psychology can be used to define children as cognitively, linguistically, emotionally and socially precompetent, but developing toward key sets of competencies.

Children in contemporary societies, ordinarily, have their lives organized by those who are deemed to have already achieved competence and thus are its bearers and models. These people are, for the most part, adults. For example, adults make decisions about the level and type of education a child receives, where children live and with whom they reside, the immunizations given to children and the types of leisure activities in which children may engage. Such decision-making is driven by theories of the Child, in particular, theories of children's rights, wants and needs. Such theorizations also drive commerce. Assumptions and beliefs about children and Childhood inform the design of toyshops, merchandise, fun parks, movies, books and food outlets. Those commercial enterprises that view children as a component of their clientele work, however implicitly or explicitly, with theories of the Child in the production, promotion and sale of their products.

Associated with the common-sense understanding of children as deficient but developing is a state of affairs in which many and, indeed, most decisions consequential for children's lives are made without consulting children. For example, decisions regarding school attendance and child protection laws, as well as theme park attractions and children's merchandising, are made almost exclusively for children by adults. Although they may sometimes entail consultations with children, decisions about children's rights and responsibilities are finally the rights and responsibilities of adults.

At various points in time, debates arise regarding what is right and proper for children. Many of these debates are familiar to us and the ongoing presence of border disputes points to the longevity of their contentiousness. Examples include the nature and extent of children's access to paid work, their engagement in dangerous physical labour, proper discipline in schools and in homes, the toys and diets that are appropriate for children, their access to alcohol and nicotine, the age of sexual consent, punishment for those who abuse and/or neglect children, limitations on children's television viewing and their access to the Internet, the availability of assisted suicide to young people, and all the rest. Such issues become and remain contentious insofar as propositions about what is appropriate for children conflict with one or another theory of the Child. The more a proposition grates upon a given theory, the more inappropriate that proposition may be understood to be, the more persistently it might be pursued by opponents, and the more striking becomes the silence of young people in the debate.

Child, quite simply, is an organizational category that is consequential for social practice. Incumbency in this, or any category, makes certain activities, behaviours and emotions available – or not – to a person. Child is an organizational category in much the same way as Woman or Person of Colour, which have received attention in recent times in terms of how the use of such categories shapes societal practices and attitudes. But compared to other organizational categories, Child is one of the least explicated and theorized (Luke 1991; Prout and James 1990). As will be discussed later in this chapter, Child has only recently received critical attention in terms of the way it, as a category, organizes and shapes societal attitudes and social practices.

Like many other cultural organizational dimensions, Childhood can be described as having biological bases. Yet, throughout history and across cultures, the ways in which this biological difference has been recognized and acted upon has varied, and therefore the role in the social world that the category Child fulfils has differed. There is a considerable body of theorizing about the various versions of the Child that have existed throughout history, across cultures and in different discourses as well as about the essential nature of the Child. It is to this broad body of theorizing that we now turn.

The children in history

Here we do not attempt to review in any depth or detail the various histories of childhood and their methodologies, or provide a definitive summary. Rather, we merely acknowledge the field to present a working overview that provides some context for the studies presented here. An important starting point is the contribution of the social historian Phillipe Ariès (1962). While his thesis has often been debated, Ariès is generally credited with bringing childhood as an historical subject to the fore and his work is often cited as the seminal text in the field of childhood history (Luke 1989). Based primarily on an examination of art and literature, but also including some audit of dress codes, toys, diaries, memoirs, and inscriptions on statues and tombs, Ariès argued that the production of Childhood as a separate and different state of life is a relatively recent move in European history. He argued that in medieval society infancy ended with weaning, somewhere between the ages of three and seven years, from which time the Child became a participating member of adult society. In the seventeenth century, the male children of nobility and the middle class were segregated by dress, separated from the rest of society, and sent to school. Childhood, then, was initially class- and sex-related as well as age-based; the first children were the sons of the middle class (Polakow-Suransky 1982).

Since Ariès, the histories and debates about Childhood can be summarized to describe a 'received view' or historical 'myth' (Graff 1995: xii, 2; Pollock 1983) of Childhood. This myth postulates that there was no concept of Childhood before the seventeenth century and that the concept of Childhood appearing during the seventeenth century followed a renewal of interest in education, developments within the family, the rise of capitalism, and the increasing maturity of parents. The myth continues that, in the eighteenth century, children existed in formal parent–child relationships in which parents were distant, unapproachable beings and children something inferior, whose demands and needs were not met. This received view has it that, up until the eighteenth and early nineteenth century, children were often brutally exploited but that after this time, the concept of Childhood developed until 'the child was accorded a central role in family life and his [*sic*] rights were protected by the state' (Pollock 1983: 262).

But many have disagreed with this 'received version' of the history of Childhood. There has been argument among childhood historians centring on issues such as the selective quotation of sources to sustain certain theories, failure to consider the historical context of evidence, the drawing of spurious conclusions, mistaking the absence of a contemporary Western concept of Childhood for no concept at all, factual inaccuracies in data, wilful misinterpretation of evidence and generalizing to society as a whole from class-specific data (Graff 1995; Luke 1989; Pollock 1983; Wilson 1984).

Our task here is not to settle these debates but simply to note that, broadly speaking, the notion of Childhood has changed over time. The concepts of the Child and Childhood that existed in the past have moved and changed, at times, more or less recognizable to our current theorizations. It is adequate to our purposes here to note an evolution from a perspective that, to us now, may look like an ignorance of Childhood, 'medieval adultism', through to class- and sex-based images of the Child in the eighteenth century, a centring of the family around the child in the nineteenth century, and to the twentieth-century's scientizing of Childhood, in which societies have become 'obsessed with the unqualified separateness of this period of life' (Polakow-Suransky 1982: 7–8). Within the terms of this evolution, the concept of Childhood becomes progressively more concerned, first, with the recognition, definition, development, and evaluation of the Child, and subsequently with interventions that might facilitate or enhance that development (see also, Polakow 1989).

This history has seen the enactment of many versions of the Child, including the innocent in need of protection, the noble in need of gentle civilizing, the inherently wicked in need of training to suppress or exorcise a natural propensity towards sin, the immanent (James *et al.* 1998) neither good nor evil but charged with potential, and the object of scientific study in need of both physiological and psychological monitoring and tutelage, either to guide its natural development or protect it from mismanagement and damage to its development (see also Cleverley and Phillips 1987; Halperin 1986; Luke 1991; Polakow-Suransky 1982). Many of these theorizations currently co-exist, with contemporary traces of each played out in our personal and institutional practices in various, more or less shadowy ways (James *et al.* 1998). The Child, and its Childhood as a lived experience, are created by our social, historical and theoretical conventions (Polakow-Suransky 1982: 6). The Child has been both assumed to be, and shown to be, sinful, wilful, selfish, gentle, loving, innocent, pure, irrational, intellectually, socially and morally self-oriented, a blank slate, and most things in between. Whatever the theorization, however, we see the persistence of a category of person in need of something. A feature of Childhood in our culture is that it always signifies a dependence relationship (Freebody 1995b), such as adult–child, parent–child, teacher–child. In Jenks' words, Childhood is realized in terms of its 'contingency' (1989: 3–4). As a case in point, Baker has noted that in classroom literacy events, students are invited not only to 'situate themselves within the imaginative narrative boundaries of a "child" appropriate story' but also to situate themselves 'within the cultural relation, child-adult' (1991a: 176).

This all too brief and selective review of the history of Childhood serves simply to bring to our attention the proposition that Childhood is an idea with a history, and that this history is one of both research and contest. What we take to be the Child has a history of material, conceptual and moral victories and defeats.

The contemporary Child

Current versions of the Child: development and precompetence

Concurrent with this or that version of the Child and Childhood, of course, is the notion of a 'proper' Childhood and the 'proper' Child, bringing with it the idea that some children are 'better' at being children than are others. The twentieth-century's increasing institutionalization of the Child through law, education, health, social work and the rest, provides a forum for gauging the individual child according to its degree of fit with prevailing theorizations. For example, Tyler (1993) demonstrated how the spatial arrangements in the kindergarten, together with the techniques of surveillance made possible by those spatial arrangements, were central to the production of the 'better child' who made 'appropriate' use of space. The 'problem' child, for example, the hyperactive or solitary child, made 'inappropriate' use of space. Specifically, the hyperactive child made 'too little' use of secluded space while the solitary child made 'too much' use of the same area. Tyler concluded that the good or proper child was socially produced, the space itself designed 'to permit the child to be the child that child psychologists had determined the child would be' (ibid.: 38–54).

This leads us to consider what it is that the contemporary Child, the one under scrutiny here, is taken to be. The 'taken-to-be-ness' of the Child is relevant to us on several fronts, within everyday common sense, within schooling, the institution we here investigate, and within research that studies the Child. We consider the question of 'what is the contemporary Child?', first, within research that has studied the Child and Childhood.

In a recent review of such studies, James *et al.* (1998) have described models of Childhood and the approaches to child study that group around these models. They drew distinctions between what they called pre-sociological approaches, transitional or socialization approaches and sociological approaches to child study. James *et al.* described pre-sociological approaches as 'the dustbin of history' (ibid.: 9) and as having become part of conventional wisdom, informing both contemporary analytic and everyday understandings of the Child and Childhood. The authors included in pre-sociological discourses historical versions of Childhood rehearsed above: innocent, evil and immanent as well as the naturalizing and universalizing colonization of Childhood represented in developmental psychology (i.e. Child as a 'potential' within clearly defined stages of growth) and psychoanalysis (i.e. Child as the history of the Adult).

According to James *et al.*, transitional theorizing employs the concept of socialization, closely paralleling developmental psychology's concern with cognitive maturation. But it is concerned with the process by which children mature to conform to society's norms. Speier (1971) had earlier noted that sociology from this perspective considered the Child only within wider analyses of the school or family, for example, and always treated Childhood as a preparatory phase before entering the everyday activities of that site as a fully fledged member, that is, Adult. He noted that within adult sociologists' investigations of children's behaviour 'the child is treated as a special kind of social actor who is continually in need of learning how to participate in society' (Speier 1976: 98) and argued that sociologists' investigations of childhood were premised on the following: children are adults in the making; they are socialized or 'made' into adults; they progressively develop into competent social members; they are defective social participants by virtue of precompetence or incompetence at behaving appropriately, and their development can be either successful as they grow up through stages of life or it can be deviant anywhere along the way (Speier 1971). This sort of sociology, then, neatly warrants itself by taking children, essentially, to be socialization's raw material (see Jenks 1989: 1).

We take up James *et al.*'s (1998) third model or approach to child study, the sociological approaches, below, but we here dwell a moment with Speier. Moving away from studies of the Child and Childhood, we note that, while now about thirty years on, Speier's noticing of the essential taken-to-be precompetence of the Child is one that still bears considerable force in both common-sense and professional sense reasonings of the Child. The notion that the Child is precompetent and developing towards competence is current and implicit in common-sense as well as educational, scientific, biological and medical discourses in western liberal democratic societies (Tyler 1993). The Child's membership of this special category of person lacking 'the capacities necessary for full functioning as a citizen' (ibid.: 35) is taken to be by virtue of the Child's very nature. The Child is seen as essentially lacking, essentially inadequate, imperfect in relation to the category that shows adequacy, that is, the Adult (Jenks 1989; Freebody 1995b). This precompetence has been seen to play out in many ways in actual social settings. As a case in point, using transcripts of school-based and home-based literacy events, Freiberg and Freebody (1995) demonstrated that there are several facets to adult notions about children's precompetence evident in the interactive work that participants do to accomplish precompetence in and for school. These include: the adult wish for children to display an interest in 'domestic fantasy' such as a flying bed or talking dog (see also Baker and Freebody 1989a); an adult belief that strategies that promote 'guessing' or 'suspense' about the plot will act as motivation for children; and the imperative that children display 'trying' or 'striving' in literacy tasks (see also Freebody 1995a and taken up here in Part II).

Similarly, in an investigation of the gendered nature of the writing of primary-aged schoolchildren, Poynton (1985: 36) has argued that a version of the Child as 'innocent, biddable, ignorant of death, destruction and human misery, and generally unwise in the ways of the world' was in operation and that student writing displaying such characteristics received teacher approval.

Adult concern for the provision of children's needs, reflexively creating and sustaining a dependence relationship, relies on notions of precompetence and incompleteness. Moreover, such adult concern is designed to address incompleteness so that children develop those as yet missing capacities and become complete or adequate, that is, Adult (see especially Tyler 1993). Interventions with children are expected to have consequence for the quality of that person's completeness – their adultness. Neglect of certain interventions is also taken to have consequences for the future adult, thereby justifying the assumption that what adults do to, with, or for children is in the best interests of their development towards adulthood.

Precompetence, with its implicit promise of competence, and development are concepts that reflexively buttress each other in theorizing about the Child. Development is an essentially temporal notion, conflated in our culture with 'other pervasive contemporary social metaphors like "growth" and "progress"' (Jenks 1989: 2). Childhood precompetence is transitory. To be sure, Childhood itself is a state of development: 'a child's purpose is . . . not to stay a child; any signs of entrenchment or backtracking (like play) may be interpreted as indicators of a failure to "develop"' (ibid.: 2).

As with the notion of the 'proper' child, development must also follow the 'normal' route, both physiologically, as defined by the discourses of medicine, and cognitively/morally/emotionally as defined in discourses of developmental psychology, routinely translated into education (Luke 1990, 1991). Jenks suggested that the concept of development does not signify a 'natural' process, but rather, it 'makes reference to a socially constructed sense of change pertaining to the young individual' (1989: 3). This sense of change is encoded in the everyday world and in specialist discourses concerning the Child, for example, education and medicine, as a series of benchmarks pertinent to that discourse. A child's 'becoming' or development from the state of lacking or precompetence into a state of adequacy and competence depends upon reference points within normative structures that are 'conventional in the adults' world' (Jenks 1989: 4). The experience of a child in developing into alignment with these conventions is articulated variously – in many sociological models, as the individual succumbing to a process of 'standardization and entrapment' in social structures (ibid.: 6) and in some educational models, as a 'flowering' or 'unfolding' – indicating some sort of ambivalence, contradiction or conflict in our culture's engagement with children's competence and development.

Indeed, precompetence itself neatly reflects a paradox at the heart of our culture's dealings with children (MacKay 1974: 190ff). Children are participants in constructions of themselves. Children must know what adult expectations of Childhood are in order to participate according to those versions. In the context of schooling, for example, MacKay demonstrated with transcripts how a teacher at once treated a group of school children as deficient, according to the normative sociological view of Childhood, and relied on their interactive competence to achieve the lesson, that is, relied on the students interacting according to the teacher's enacted theory of their interactive capabilities. MacKay argued that often the sense of the lesson relied on considerable student competence. For example, in a typical classroom question–answer session, any particular student must be able to ascertain from the interactive features whether his/her answer is correct, and then, if not correct, the reason it was not, and why another answer was correct is left to the student to deduce (ibid.: 188).

Adults supply children with a language with which to talk about and experience themselves and their world, and thereby provide children with a version of what adults perceive the nature of Childhood to be. In everyday encounters in talk with adults and texts written by adults for children, children come face to face with adults' views of how children *are*: how they 'speak, act, and perceive the world', not only as a reflection of the organization of the culture's age relations, but also as a site for its construction (Baker and Freebody 1987). Adults, then, attribute precompetence or deficiency to children and, as MacKay noted, create situations for its manifestation (1974: 190). For example, in classrooms, children's requests for permission function as displays of adult competence in decision-making and knowledge, thereby confirming the adult identity of being askable in the first place and confirming the Child as permission seeker in relation to the Adult (Baker and Freebody 1986).

Both MacKay's paradox and the interrelationship of development and precompetence are important ideas underlying the work presented in this book. The analytic tradition within which we work embraces both the teachers' *and* the students' work in mutually and interactively constructing the categories relevant to the classroom. Our interest, at the outset, was to interrogate school for the versions of Child enacted without pre-empting what those versions might entail. We found one of the relevances oriented to by the participants was children's precompetence and its often unspoken partner, child development. This is perhaps unsurprising because 'not being yet competent in some way' and 'developing towards that competence' are underlying premises in the logic of education generally, and many of the practices and procedures of schooling in particular. The detail of how precompetence was enacted in our data sets and its apparently contradictory reliance on the students enacting particular sorts of competence, especially in accomplishing themselves as precompetent, are the topics of Parts II and III.

Researching the socially constituted Child

As described above, James *et al.*'s (1998) review of studies of the Child and Childhood demonstrated that interest in understanding the 'what' and 'how' of children and Childhood has preceded us. Their third group, the sociological approaches, includes studies that explored both 'the agency of children and their present social, political and economic status as contemporary subjects' (ibid.: 26). James *et al.* described the various ways research within sociological traditions conceptualized Childhood, and in characterizing the 'new sociology of childhood' identified sociological approaches that shared both the determination to make the Child itself the object of concern (rather than subsuming the Child under some other topic, such as family or school) and the basic premise of the fundamentally social character of the object of study – the Child.

Whether or not considering themselves part of the 'new sociology of childhood', several researchers have interrogated different cultural and community contexts, such as classrooms (Austin 1997; Christensen and James 2001; Simpson 2000), school texts (Baker and Freebody 1989a, 1989b), historical texts (Luke 1989), television (Luke 1990), popular culture (Frakenberg 2000; Luke 1991), kindergarten (Tyler 1993), pre-school (Danby and Baker 1998), childcare institutions (Polakow-Suransky 1982), the family (Alanen 1998; Zeiher 2001), the home and school literacy lesson (Freebody *et al.* 1995), and home and health care contexts (Mayall 1994, 1996; Place 2000). These studies did not pre-empt the discovery of a particular sort of Child, nor did they seek to discover an essential Child, rather each sought to study the social practices which defined and delimited what Childhood was taken to be within a particular culture and language community. Each reported versions of Childhood constructed in particular sites and showed the manner in which suppositions about the nature of the Child were enacted.

Several of these studies have taken the issue of precompetence head on, questioning the assumed sequential progression from childhood precompetence to adult completeness and demonstrating, instead, children's competence. Some have focused upon tensions that arise in adult–child relationships over the questions of what children can and cannot do, and who gets to be the arbiter in these contests (several are published in Hutchby and Moran-Ellis 1998). A recent collection pertinent to our work (Alanen and Mayall 2001) examines child–adult relations in various local and social contexts. The studies in this collection focused on generational issues, finding again some contest or 'gaps and conflicts between young people's experience of their lives and the adult assignment of characteristics to them' (ibid.: 2).

While, as noted above, the concept of precompetence is central to the analyses presented in this book, it is not because we decided it so or believed the Child to be essentially precompetent, but rather because in fulfilling our task of mapping the Child achieved 'on the scene', we found joint enactments, contests and negotiations taking place around the whole business of being a Child (and a Student), and that many of the competences and contests turned upon the achievement of precompetence.

Conclusions about the Child

One important and distinctive issue in studying Childhood is that Childhood is available largely, and some would argue, solely through adult theories. According to Speier, investigations of children are generally undertaken in much the same way as

> colonial administrators who might be expected to write scientifically objective reports of the local populace in order to increase their understanding of native culture, and who do so by ideologically formulating only those research problems that pertain to native behaviours coming under the regulation of colonial authority.
>
> (1976: 99)

More recently, Mayall reflected upon the question many sociologists might ask themselves: 'If one is not a child, can one and should one attempt to convey what children's experiences are?' (1996: 1). The possibility that Mayall's question is even asked suggests that Speier's (1976) work did not go unnoticed, and we find that a great deal of recent work has faced this issue decisively (Christensen and James 2000; Greig and Taylor 1999; James and Prout 1997; Lewis and Lindsay 2000). Hutchby and Moran-Ellis (1998), for example, collected a range of studies that are within what they call the 'competence paradigm'. This paradigm, suggested by Prout and James (1990), and named and developed in Hutchby and Moran-Ellis (1998: 8), sought to 'explicate the social competencies which children manifest in the course of their everyday lives as children'. Such work engages seriously with the issue of how analysts find the Child's experience. We cannot, as researchers and analysts, cease to be aware that it is adults who theorize Childhood (Luke 1991: 115) and adults who act towards, with, and upon children according to those theories. Adult contact with children is mediated by adult theory about children (Polakow-Suransky 1982: 13). It is adults who theorize Childhood because, according to adults, 'children in any historical era do not have the authority and status, or "cognitive" and "literate" maturity to write from the position of authorized speaker for and about themselves' (Luke 1991: 115). It is adults who 'define and enforce both the needs and nature of children' (Baker and Freebody 1989a: 3, 203–4). Hence, children are vulnerable, they are 'dependent on those authorized to speak for them' (Luke 1991: 115). And adult constructions of reality may, in fact, be misrepresentations of the child's experience (Polakow-Suransky 1982). Analysts and theorists of Childhood therefore must be aware that:

> We appropriate [children's] everyday life experiences from the child, distort them from the social context in which they originate, and, by this appropriation, construct an extensive body of theoretical data and generalization, alienated from the original life-world of the child actors themselves.
> (Polakow-Suransky 1982: 22)

The colonization of the Child's reality is most clearly evident in confrontations with idealized representations of the Child. In literature for children and in purpose-written early school reading materials, for example, children are presented with idealized representations of themselves and their social and material worlds. Although these adult versions of child reality may be benevolent in intent, Baker and Freebody (1989a) demonstrated the by no means disinterested socializing and acculturating functions of these representations. The force of these idealizations in the common sense of the community is evident when, with each wave of debate on matters to do with our society's provisioning for children's work (e.g. education) and leisure (e.g. television), we see teachers, community leaders, policy-makers and parents accusing the cultural form in question of destroying their idealized version of the childhood innocence of the past (see also West 1988).

The aim here, in the light of the discussion in this chapter, is not to find a better definition of a Child, one more 'true' to children themselves, more 'untainted' by adulthood, or a more accurate, more functional or even more ideologically palatable list of essential features. It is rather to argue for and illustrate a particular orientation or attitude to the Child as a categorization that is given its contents and moral significance by the local, purposeful daily activities of people of all ages. The pursuit of that aim is a documentary task, and one apparently obvious starting point for this documentation is the constellation of institutional practices that take their prime brief to be the acculturation of young people – schooling.

3 Rethinking schooling and classrooms

Introduction: schooling as cultural and institutional practice

We begin this chapter with an historical perspective on the development of schooling as a publicly organized practice. In the twentieth century, many nation–states attempted to embody their members' daily needs in terms of a set of programmatic provisions. People came to invest their domestic and public aspirations in institutionalized programmes: health became heard as medical service, justice as legal service, community support as welfare, even tending the dying as palliative care, and so on. And acculturation and education came to be heard as schooling. The extent to which nation–states transformed themselves into service states by providing programmes for living became a hall-mark of their modernity. The adequacy with which they sustained these pro-visions became a predictor of their political credibility and stability.

Taking on increased educational responsibilities brought with it organiza-tional imperatives. Governments centralized the public administration of schooling and regulated it with legislation for managing and funding schools, training teachers and providing materials and procedures for accounting for the institutions' performance. The fact that governments legally compel chil-dren to spend ten to twelve years in schooling does not astonish us now only because so much of the duty of acculturating the young has been thoroughly transferred to public administration. Among other things, this process entailed installing and regulating a standard, administrable model of the clientele, of the Child. This, in turn, involved attending to the question of who and what were 'the young', what were their needs and what did societies need from them? What was this object of professional, governmental education? How did governmental systems describe it in ways that made it both amenable to bureaucratic administration and compatible with public understandings?

The purposes of schooling became tied to the logic of economic, national, community and personal development. Schooling as public practice invested heavily in increasingly refined versions of the Child, in particular, standard versions that institutions could act on. The policies governing schooling came to place increasing torque on acceptable descriptions of the nature of children, their needs, how they learn, what materials they learn from and how that might be assessed. Chronological age was a central organizing principle for these considerations, not least because age has both common-sensical and organizational appeal. As schools assembled children into grades by age, teaching settings, materials and assessment practices became age-tailored, and those theories of Childhood and development that drew on age as a correlate and potential explanation of 'development and learning' became productive instruments of policy for schooling:

> Psychology . . . in the guise of developmental psychology, firmly colonized childhood in a pact with medicine, education and government agencies . . . Developmental psychology capitalizes, perhaps not artfully but certainly effectively, on two everyday assumptions: first, that children are natural rather than social phenomena; and secondly, that part of this naturalness extends to the inevitable process of their maturation.
>
> (James *et al.* 1998: 17)

Naming, grading and taxonomizing the sub-categories of the Child thus became reasoning practices that legitimated and advanced the prosecution of schooling. Through its teaching, assessment and reporting mechanisms, schooling reflexively validated its age-based organizational principles. The performances of children, documented against a staged, age-based curriculum, served partly to legitimize the ongoing processes of naming, grading and taxonomizing.

Schools simultaneously took upon themselves increased responsibility for providing children with technical skills, a sense of civil responsibility, personal development, mental and physical health, cultural awareness, and all the rest. Sex education, drug education, road safety education, relationship education, personal development and so on – a hundred years ago, people and communities, if they thought of them programmatically at all, did not typically take such topics to be the responsibility of the school. By the end of the twentieth century, it had become commonplace to expect schools not only to provide settings conducive or, at least not antithetical to learning about such things, but moreover actually to have programmes – syllabuses, assignments and assessments – in these areas.

Along with the scope of its interventions, schooling's mandate grew as well in its demographic catchment. More and more children from more and more diverse backgrounds came to be the responsibility of the school. Schooling increasingly needed to serve people from diverse cultures, diverse languages, and diverse ideas about what constituted the Child, about where the Child was headed, and about what schools could and should do about that. In responding to these demographic complexities, however, rather than attempting to decentralize or communalize the management and practices of schooling, administrative systems came to offer communities an expanded set of expectations for the school system as a whole. The centralized management of this expansion of offerings was attached to notions of equality of provision and thus of opportunity. Through their syllabuses, regulation of social behaviour and accountability and assessment routines, schools announced that their institutionalized provisions were both directly relevant to, and comprehensive for, the production of young people who were fully-fledged – intellectually, emotionally, morally, socially and culturally – in all of the communities of the nation–state. Thus the school child became representable as the 'Whole Child'. Life tasks were made into standard programmes that often had only a tenuous or rhetorical relation to the communities in which children lived and into which they grew:

> So self-sustaining did the governmental, managerial bases of schooling seem by the latter part of the twentieth century, so comprehensive and rarely challenged the separation of the social, intellectual, moral and ideological meanings and materials of schools from those of the everyday activities of the communities they purported to serve, that entire communities can now be described as 'failing at education' – as bizarre a notion as imaginable from the vantage of a cultural account of education.
>
> (Freebody 2002: Preface)

But how to rank these calls on the school in the relative expenditure of time and resources? Many current debates about theoretical and pedagogical approaches are based on the premise that schools have, or at least should have, a single major function in society and in the lives of children. Hunter (1993) has argued that schooling, since its development, has had many intersecting and simultaneous functions – pastoral, skilling, regulative, human-capital, individual expression, cultural-heritage and democratic – and that the balance of the contest is determined partly by contemporary economic, cultural, and social discourses. These discourses have at their core preferred ways of thinking and talking about intergenerational relations – how children and adults are and should be differentially positioned as members of a society. Each function of schooling has implications for what constitutes the specialist knowledge that relates to schooling – for teachers, teacher educators and parents (Keogh 1999) – and each embodies a particular Child of the Curriculum: the supported Child, the Child skilled and regulated for vocational life, the Child performing up to standards, the self-expressing Child, the democratic-citizen Child, and so on.

We can recognize all these priorities in public and professional debates about schooling. Their relative importance has been a topic of ongoing debate, and these debates have moved with the changing political, economic and cultural imperatives of the time. Contests over priorities have never been resolved in any final sense, each cyclically invoking its opponents, simply because all of these functions reflect what communities have come to expect of schooling.

At a more overtly ideological level, it has become common among professional educators to think of four competing positions that describe the proper purposes of schooling. These are termed corporatism, traditionalism, progressivism and transformationalism. Traditionalism takes the functions of schooling to be primarily related to the transmission of the culture's heritage. Schooling is about cultural conservation. This heritage again is variously construed as intellectual, scientific, moral, and/or aesthetic.

Progressivism proposes that humanistic values be the central context and the main point of the experience of schooling – free expression, autonomous conduct, and materials that are drawn from and enhance the experiences of the local community. Education is about growth. Since the late 1960s, progressivism has had a significant impact on the practices and policies of schooling, particularly in English-speaking countries. Its supporters have pointed to the benefits of focusing on growth and 'natural' acquisition over instruction, on the liberation of schools' work from decontextualized and repetitive drills, and on genuine engagement with the personal meanings and significances of the curriculum.

Transformationalist approaches to schooling view educational experiences as arenas through which to challenge the entropy of the cultural, economic and political formations that education, unless it is explicitly aimed at transformation, will inevitably support. Such approaches arise from a range of critical perspectives including Neo-Marxism, anti-masculinism, anti-racism, anti-classism, and anti-ageism. A premise typically shared by transformationalists is that the institutions of schooling make it difficult for the outcomes of schooling to result in challenges to the moral, economic and political organization of society. Schools are seen here as reproductionist mechanisms in a society, recreating the dimensions on which goods and services are unevenly distributed among sectors of the citizenry.

In assuming responsibility for mass and extensive schooling through their attendant centralized bureaucracies, governments defined educational practices in terms of various moral, economic, political, and procedural operating principles consonant with their own managerial logics and *métiers*. The centralization and formalization of curriculum amount to the setting of an idealized scope and sequence of knowledge acquisition for the whole of each generation. In the bureaucracies' and thus in the schools' considerations, decreasing prominence comes to be given to the knowledges, ways of communicating and dispositions that grow indigenously in the home cultures and communities from which the clients of schooling come. The life of the school becomes an autonomous domain of experience – a training ground for both the conservative and innovative urges of a society. While all of these functions and purposes speak to administrative procedures, they raise as well fundamental questions about the nature of everyday teacher–student activities in classrooms. What does this training ground look like? What is schooled 'into' children? What are the daily activities that could respond to such a rich collection of expectations? At issue is the extent to which these activities constitute training in the social formations that lie in wait beyond the years of schooling, and the most pressing problems that those years hold in store. So a primary task is to develop ways of describing the activities that make up 'daily school life'.

Classroom talk

Whole class talk

How do we describe the activities conducted in schools? It is now common-place to start with the observation that the ways in which people behave in classrooms are recognizably different from the ways in which people behave in other social, interactional situations (Cazden 1988; Edwards and Westgate 1987; McHoul 1978; Mehan 1986). The activities and the talk in which they are embodied need primarily to serve their own particular schooling purposes. This entails both adults' and children's behaviour. It involves acculturation into particular ways of acting in public. A major theme of this book is that these ways of acting draw largely on resources that can be described as 'theories of child-hood'. These theories are not incidental, but rather central resources for under-standing school activity and for appreciating its significance for the maintenance of social order in and out of schools.

When we view the ways in which teachers of young children work hard to model and explicate the school's special forms of activity (Willes 1983), we see an acknowledgement of the distinctiveness of these ways of interacting and an indication of how different they are from children's lives out of school. In this section, we outline some of these special ways in which teachers and children in school act together. Initially, our discussion is about the particular structural regularities of teacher talk and student talk in whole class talk. We then briefly review research findings that focus on the material effects of these regularities.

There is now a large body of research from a variety of traditions that has addressed the issue of the prevalent features of classroom talk in contemporary western societies. For instance, teachers have been found to take more and longer turns at talk (Bellack *et al.* 1966; Edwards and Westgate 1987; Payne 1976) and to ask lots of questions (Brice-Heath 1983; Flanders 1970; Sharan and Sharan 1992). The literature on classroom talk has overwhelmingly identi-fied a three-part sequence[1] as the traditional pattern of teacher–student inter-action in classrooms (e.g. Alton-Lee *et al.* 1993; Bellack *et al.* 1966; Heap 1982, 1985; Mehan 1979, 1986; Payne 1976; Sinclair and Coulthard 1975). This three-part sequence restrains students' opportunities to speak. Although students have been found to initiate talk (Heap 1992b; Mehan 1979), student talk is usually in response to teachers' talk (Delamont 1976; Flanders 1970). Students speak when invited to do so (Heap 1985). Student contributions to whole class talk are only rarely questions (MacLure and French 1981) and further, students' answers to questions are often presented as questions them-selves, spoken with an interrogative intonation, as if provisional, and awaiting teacher validation (Baker 1991a, 1992). We examine the consequences and implications of many of these features of classroom talk below and in Part II.

These features of classroom interaction have been identified as constructing a closed questioning technique and reflecting high levels of teacher-directedness. The place of student knowledge in such an interactive setting is ambiguous,

Edwards and Westgate concluded that: '[classroom talk] is certainly not conducted normally on a basis of shared knowledge. Its outstanding characteristic . . . is one participant's claim to all the knowledge relevant to the business at hand' (1987: 124).

Students' knowledge then is little used, valued, or developed in such interactive settings. The teacher governs the ownership, scope and breadth of knowledge production through the question–answer–response pattern. Such conclusions might imply traditional teacher-dominated schooling sites. Many of the classrooms studied, however, have not appeared, at least on the surface, to be so. For example, in a study of open plan schools, Bennett *et al.* (1980) found that, in individualized teaching, most talk was initiated by the teacher, and that the teacher frequently interrupted students' talk with corrections, advice or disapproval. They argued that, while these teachers appeared to hold to a belief in open, Socratic-style teaching, their talk to students amounted to a collection of winks and nudges to put the students on the right track. Similarly, Hull (1985) noted that the teachers he studied, while apparently 'non-directive', used question–answer sequences to produce a set of predefined conclusions. Hull described the students' main task as providing contributions to the teacher's 'resumé-to-be' for the lesson (see also Wells 1985).

Freiberg and Freebody (1995: 198) described classroom interaction as sequences of directives and compliance through which the classroom participants work 'interactively toward the visible completion of [the] task' through the production of answers. In this directive–compliance sequence, the teacher gives a directive and selects a student as respondent, the student responds, and, the teacher denotes whether or not the response complies with the directive (Heap 1992a). The cycle continues, with the directive understood to be still in operation regardless of whether it is repeated (see also Payne and Hustler 1980) until compliance is publicly acknowledged. This formulation expands the three-part question–answer–response formulation by allowing that tasks, and components of tasks, are completed as the result of successive teacher directives that project student compliance. This model allows that tasks can include question–answer completion, but does not restrict itself to such. A lesson can thus be redescribed as a knitting together of related directive–compliance sequences. Other sequences, which provide either conceptual resources or logistic information for engaging in the task at hand, may be inserted[2] into directive-compliance sequences (Freiberg and Freebody 1995).

Participants in the whole-class interaction do not just talk for its own sake, but 'speak to get things done' (Heap 1985: 249). What 'gets done' in the course of classroom talk has been documented in studies that viewed classroom talk as a *practical activity* and a *local accomplishment*. These are ideas that require some elaboration here. By practical activity, we mean that the work of classroom participants, teachers and students alike, is directed to getting something done – something publicly known and understood. So classroom activity, including talk, builds propositional knowledge about some topic in the world, some content. It does this through the use of certain procedures for talking and learning that are made acceptable in classrooms, some of which we examined above – when to talk, how to express propositions, and so on. What counts as classroom knowledge, or in other words a 'propositional lesson corpus' is produced and displayed in and through the ways in which teachers respond to various student answers. Teachers build and fine-tune this corpus by elaborating on, or writing on the board or the screen, or reformulating and repeating, for example, particular components of student responses. Such actions function to underscore what it was that was important in what a student just did or said (Baker and Perrott 1988; Heap 1983).

To count as knowledge, answers in classroom talk need to be not only accurate however. Classrooms – for whatever age group and however formal or informal – have been shown to be places in which an accurate answer needs also to be displayed in an appropriate way to be accorded 'correctness' and accepted into the propositional corpus of the lesson. Close attention is given in classroom talk to what counts as knowledge *and* what is required in the way of reasoning and presentation of an answer (Baker and Freebody 1993; Breen 1985). So while the propositional corpus can be thought of as the 'academic' or factual lesson knowledge (Heap 1985), it includes as well the cultural logic in use in the display of those facts, and the expected ways of behaving and acting in the classroom (Baker and Freebody 1993; Mishler 1972). Teachers model, and students rehearse, the required conventions and routines (Baker and Freebody 1993; Freiberg and Freebody 1995).

Insofar as the production of the propositional corpus is public, the force of a lesson is that students can be held accountable for remembering (MacKay 1974) and, more specifically, displaying the propositional corpus (Baker 1992; Baker and Freebody 1993; Mishler 1972). That they can be held so accountable is, in itself, a proposition that is part of students' knowledge of schooling.

To describe all this as locally accomplished means that teachers and students are not simply acting out predetermined scripts, but rather that they are attending to the immediate context of what has just been said, heard and understood, in the light of certain taken-for-granted background understandings, about the world, how to interact, knowledge, learning, and so on. What we present in this book is an elaboration of the point that a crucial plank for these understandings and thus the activities of classrooms is the constitution of Students as a particular category or type of person, and of students as different types of people – primarily as Children, as that is commonly and institutionally understood (Breen *et al.* 1994; Heap 1985; Freiberg and Freebody 1995; Sharp and Green 1984; Walker 1991). Insofar as such findings tell us about what the Schoolchild is like, they are relevant to the question of how schooling builds a tailored version of childhood, and what kinds of displays children need to understand and work with if they are to be successful at school. That is, a vital topic for students to learn about in schools is the school's acted-out theories of them as children and, more specifically, as Schoolchildren.

The constitution of children as Students and students as Children

The relationship between the categories of Student and Teacher is an aspect of schooling that neither teachers nor learners can somehow ignore. As we examine classroom activities in detail in later sections, we see that the construction of this relationship is a visible consequence of the structuring of classroom learning. In schools, students form a particular category of person with distinctive rights and responsibilities (McHoul 1978; Payne 1976). Baker (1991a) has argued that 'being children' is one particular attribute of students which is enacted clearly in whole class talk. Indeed, we find that much of the distinctiveness of classroom activity, as summarized above, manifests a key intersection of the Student and the Child, that is the concept in the sociology of childhood: 'precompetence' (first outlined by Speier 1976 and developed in Baker and Freebody 1989b; Freebody 1995b). We met the notion of precompetence as linked to the category Child in Chapter 2, touching upon, also, its intimate relationship with the concept of 'development'. We revisit precompetence here because, as Freebody (1995b) and Freiberg and Freebody (1995) have argued, precompetence is an attribute relevant to the classroom, necessarily displayed by students who wish to take part successfully in classroom activities.

Students' precompetence is jointly produced by teachers and students in and through the normative systems of talk (as we elaborate in detail in Parts II and III) surrounding, for example, teachers' directives to 'wait and see,' and 'try your best'; students' 'attempts' to do classroom activities, and in the case of students who are children, students' interest in common-sense child interests such as animals and fantasy. The 'provisionality' of students' utterances has been identified as a critical feature of precompetence. Both teachers and students routinely orient to students' actions and utterances within classroom talk systems as provisional (Baker and Freebody 1989a). A provisional utterance is an utterance for which the status of correctness or validity is uncertain, awaiting confirmation. The accomplishment of a speaker's turns at talk as provisional – for example, in the design of answers to questions as questions themselves (Baker 1992) – thus accomplishes that utterance as awaiting the affirmation of a subsequent speaker, and therefore accomplishes that first speaker's knowledge base as partial in relation to another speaker's full knowledge.

Students' precompetence is also jointly produced in the ways that teachers and students interact around and with the materials of the curriculum, the things they read and the writing they produce. Students' precompetence is demonstrated in the very nature of the materials they are given to read, the conversations that take place around those materials, the nature of the writing tasks they are given, their writing and the teacher's assessment of that writing as 'the writing of precompetent writers'.

Students are a group, that is, a cohort. Being 'cohorted' has been shown to be another attribute of students constituted in whole class talk in classrooms (Baker and Perrott 1988; Breen 1985; Breen *et al.* 1994; Payne 1976; Payne and Hustler 1980; Perrott 1988; Willes 1983). Payne and Hustler (1980: 50) made a close study of whole class talk and argued that one outcome of the organization of that talk was the constitution of the students as 'a class, as a collectivity, as a cohort'. They identified a number of management strategies used in classrooms that made the students relevant as a class as opposed to as individuals. These strategies included setting up the interaction as two-party talk (see also Hammersley 1990); providing the students with the resources to hear the current talk as another occasion of some previous talk and thereby to hear the group as a resumption of a past group (see also Payne 1976); naming the group as 'we' (see also Baker 1992; Payne 1976; Mishler 1972); directing the students to carry out the same actions, and drawing attention to students who 'are not with the others' (Payne and Hustler 1980: 63).

Payne and Hustler (1980) concluded that such strategies continually make available to students their 'identity' as members of a class and enable the teacher to physically and metaphorically 'move' *all* students through the classroom activities. What this means is that a student will often be heard as speaking 'for' the cohort: as we document in Part II, when an answer is confirmed as acceptable in whole class talk the teacher typically does not continue scouring the group for any students who might not have produced that answer. Instead, the teacher proceeds as if all the individuals in the room *can* proceed. These and other locally managed strategies and interactional formats serve to allow the construction of the propositional corpus of the lesson to proceed smoothly, but they may well do so at the expense of the heterogeneity of students' understandings, dispositions and attitudes to the topic at hand. We can consider this as a 'homogenizing' practice, not only assuming that students are roughly 'at the same place,' but publicly displaying that to the students themselves and showing it as a precondition of their ongoing, productive participation. Homogenization, then, can be seen as a resource to get done certain jobs at hand.

What sort of student? The categorization of Students

But, of course, parents and researchers know that students are different; this is part of what teachers see everyday, and what is perhaps most loomingly relevant to their work. So the question becomes: in what ways are students different, specifically in what ways that are relevant to the work of school? Studies of whole class classroom talk have shown that the category of Student can itself be further ramified insofar as given students are constituted, through whole class talk, as particular and different types of students. Furthermore, this categorization is consequential to the day-to-day experience of the student in the classroom. For example, studies have found that talk in classroom contributes to the constitution of students as gendered (Clark 1989, 1990; Davies 1989, 1993; Davies and Banks 1992; Gilbert 1997; Gilbert and Taylor 1991; Kamler 1993; Kamler *et al.* 1994; Singh 1995; Walkerdine 1990); as members of either middle or low social class groups (Anyon 1981; Bernstein 1990; Sharp and Green 1984; Turner 1973); as members of particular racial or ethnic groups (Epstein 1993; Freiberg and Freebody 1995; Malcolm 1979), and as either good students or not so good students (Baker and Freebody 1993; Cazden 1988; Freiberg and Freebody 1995; Leiter 1976; Pollard 1984).

Both Sharp and Green (1984) and Freiberg and Freebody (1995) examined classrooms using frameworks that recognized how differences between students were interactively accomplished and enacted in and through everyday classroom interactions. They also showed how the accomplishment of these differences had material effects on the interactive and learning opportunities of students. Sharp and Green (1984) studied differentiations made between students on social class lines in three classes in an infant school. They observed that, as the result of ordinary classroom talk and interaction, students in each of the classes were able to be differentiated. In particular, students were able to be categorized as 'peculiar' and 'abnormal', as 'normal' and 'mainstream', or as 'ideal students' (ibid.: 128).

Sharp and Green drew on a distinction made some time ago by Schutz (1964) to summarize the processes by which a person may be publicly positioned as 'like me' or 'not like me'. Their argument does not centre on the 'teacher's consciousness' but puts it that stratification of students was the result of the match, or otherwise, of particular children's behaviours with teachers' 'background expectancies' (1984: 125). In particular, students whose behaviour remained within the parameters of expectancies were constituted as normal students. Students whose behaviour clashed with the expectancies and who were difficult to get through to, were understood as 'difficult' students and were known only via typifications, that is, as 'types' of student rather than as individual people. Moreover, routinely in classrooms, for the 'normal' student, a learning difficulty or mistake was perceived as temporary, while for the 'peculiar' or 'difficult' student, an error or problem was routinely seen as further evidence of that student's abnormality. Sharp and Green (1984) concluded that the stratification of students is necessary in order that teachers maintain order and distribute scarce resources. They argued that stratification takes place in classrooms regardless of the particular socio-economic designation of the classroom, and that all students play a significant part in the interactive constitution of themselves as particular sorts of students.

In their comparative investigation within a larger study, Freiberg and Freebody (1995) identified a number of differences in the construction of students in designated disadvantaged and non-disadvantaged early childhood classrooms. They found that in classrooms categorized as disadvantaged, the students' behaviour was routinely interpreted as disruption, the students' knowledge of behaving and working was marked as deficient and that students' behaviour was not made consequential to the completion of the classroom activities:

> In 'disadvantaged' classrooms disorderly behaviour and student-to-student interactions are treated as though they are the fuse of an explosive device set to ignite in a situation that is always on the brink of revolution,

chaos, and violence; so that even a small deviation from order and controlled behaviour occasions major comment.

(Freiberg and Freebody 1995: 209)

Moreover, according to Freiberg and Freebody, in the disadvantaged classrooms
such potential or actual problems were attended to in public and were therefore
shared by the cohort and had consequences for that cohort. By comparison,
in the categorized non-disadvantaged classroom, the regulation of individual
students was demonstrated to be collaboratively constituted as the domain of
each individual student.[3]

They found, as did Baker and Perrott (1988), that in the designated non-
disadvantaged classrooms, the familiar classroom convention that 'student turns
are projected by teacher turns' was not consistently accomplished, and that the
teacher did, at times, engage in student-initiated topics and develop student self-
selected turns at talk. In those classrooms, students were found to be routinely
heard as contributing to, rather than disrupting the activity at hand, and teacher
directives were shown to be both shorter and routinely about the task or activity.
There were also fewer and shorter behavioural directives which, when given,
were made consequential to the engagement in the classroom task. They
argued that the under-specification of directives denotes a form of the 'etcetera
procedure' (see also Cicourel 1974) which holds that participants 'will gloss
topics about which they believe the interactants already have some knowledge
or understanding' (Freiberg and Freebody 1995: 206) and marks the speakers as
intimate, culturally congruent or, at least, 'like' each other (see also Payne and
Ridge 1985).

Freiberg and Freebody concluded that students in disadvantaged schools were
typically constituted as unmotivated, not interested and uncultured, while their
counterparts in designated non-disadvantaged schools were constituted as motivated, interested and cultured, and that such attributions had material effects on
the learning environments and the students' concomitant opportunities and
experiences. However, they argued that, rather than deriving from essential
differences between the sites' students, differences were the result of the fact
that 'similar student actions were taken to signify very different things simply
because they were enacted in different socially defined locations' (1995: 209).
Furthermore, they emphasized that the contrast in the students' attributions
was interactively accomplished in and through everyday classroom interactions.

Student group talk

Much of the interaction that occurs in classrooms is between students (Cazden
1986; Webb 1982). However, the bulk of classroom research has focused on
teacher–student interaction in a whole class setting. As a consequence,
student–student interaction has been a relatively neglected area of research
(Cazden 1986, 1988; Johnson 1981; Mehan 1979; Speier 1976). The relative
scarcity of investigations into student–student interaction has been attributed

to difficulties in collecting data (Corsaro 1981; Webb 1982), and to the propensity for researchers to go no further than to categorize student–student interaction as 'off-task' (Alton-Lee *et al.* 1993; Haas-Dyson 1987). Common-sense ideas about childhood in which, as we discussed earlier, children are viewed in relation to adults rather than in their own right (Corsaro 1981; Watson 1992) are also implicated.

With this view, it is not surprising that there has been a lack of sustained research interest in the 'unofficial world of [student] peer culture' (Cazden 1986 : 451), that is, what schoolchildren do and say while not under the direct guidance or gaze of a teacher. Nonetheless, student–student interaction has been the focus of some investigations in early years classrooms (e.g. Haas-Dyson 1991, 1992; Garnica 1981) and primary schools (e.g. Cox 1988; Cree and Donaldson 1996; Gumperz and Field 1995; Lyle 1996; Smith 1988). However, many of these, as well as other studies from across the K-12 range, have focused on assessing whether features of student–student interaction have a positive effect on learning outcomes and achievements rather than on the processes of interaction themselves (see for example, Calkins 1983; Cazden 1986, 1988; Haas-Dyson 1991; Emans and Fox 1973; Finney 1991; Fleer 1992; Johnson and Johnson 1992; Lawlor 1974; Sharan and Sharan 1992; Webb 1982; Weeks 1990). This observation adds weight to Speier's (1976) argument that young people's actions and attitudes are not of interest *per se*, but are of primary interest in terms of their dealings in the world of adults.

A common conclusion of such studies is that student–student interaction is beneficial to student achievement – an inherently 'good thing' – (Cazden 1988; Duin 1986; Finney 1991; Johnson 1981; Johnson and Johnson 1985, 1992, 1994). More specifically, student–student interaction is understood to enhance student self-esteem and to foster the generation, exploration, modification and clarification of ideas (Alton-Lee *et al.* 1993; Reid *et al.* 1989; Sharan and Sharan 1992). Consequently, classroom teachers have been urged to organize for more student–student interaction (see Daniels 1994; Kerry and Sands 1982; Reid *et al.* 1989; Sharan and Sharan 1992, 1994).

However, such recommendations come with warnings of practical problems associated with student–student interaction in classrooms. These include disruption, high noise levels and the problems of the cleverer students being 'held back' and the less clever students being 'left behind' (e.g. Daniels 1994; Kerry aand Sands 1982; Reid *et al.* 1989). Webb (1982) showed that student–student interaction includes 'listening or talking to another student concerning topics that are not relevant to the task' (Webb 1982: 426) and showing no discernible involvement in the set task – observations that would probably not shock most teachers. Although Alton-Lee *et al.* concluded that off-task behaviour had a 'relatively minor role in inhibiting learning' (1993: 58), it has been more generally concluded that 'being off-task' and 'doing nothing' have a negative impact upon student achievement (Webb 1982).

That particular features of student–student interaction might reduce student achievement has contributed to the argument that organizing for student–

student interaction is neither a guarantee of learning, nor a panacea for class-room problems (Gilles and van Doven 1988). However, insofar as reduced achievement is generally attributed to improper organization and the idio-syncrasies of students (Cazden 1986), studies routinely state the argument that properly organized and executed student–student interaction is beneficial for student achievement. In later sections of this work, we step back from the issue of recommending such activity in classrooms, and take a closer look at what actually goes on when students work (or don't) with one another and how it is that they organize those activities. Again, we will show how particular inflections of a notion of the Student are important resources for the students themselves in the accomplishment of this work, and in their dealings with the problems that arise in its course.

Those studies of student–student interaction that have not considered how students systematically organize their talk (Cazden 1986, 1988), focusing instead on the academic benefits of peer talk, generally offer little to our under-standing of the attributes and orientations of the category Child as enacted in school. One exception is Heap's (1992a) consideration of collaborative com-puter editing (and see also Payne and Ridge 1985). Heap (1992a) videotaped the talk-in-interaction of pairs of members in a combined year one/two class as they collaboratively edited stories written by one of the pair. His main aim was to clarify the normative order of such interactions, that is, the prevailing rights and responsibilities involved in computer editing, as they are enacted in the members' talk. Heap (ibid.: 130) also found that the students' talk differed from 'task-independent' talk, or in other words, from ordinary ('off-task') con-versation: for example, students' talk did not necessarily orient to a prior turn at *talk* but could refer to some prior *action*; and students' questions routinely projected an *action* rather than a turn at *talk*. Heap therefore proposed that collaborative computer editing exemplified what he called 'discourse-action machinery'. This refers to the machinery, or organization, of talk that is task-oriented and, therefore, elicits action as opposed to ordinary conversation. Heap concluded that in working jointly with other members of the classroom, learners orient to the conditions of joint work. These conditions include each member's rights and responsibilities as well as the system of talk in which talk projects action and action projects talk. Moreover, of significance for our interests, Heap proposed that by examining the talk and action provided by people who are collaborating, the normative orders oriented to by those people are made available.

We have reviewed above various lines of research that have been developed to study and theorize the interactive patterns found in classrooms. In doing this, we establish the proposition that certain features of interaction have been found in a range of educational contexts that distinguish classroom talk from other kinds of talk. In Parts II and III we examine these features closely asking what work they do in terms of describing the school student, specifically, the attributes, behaviours, dispositions of a member of the category Child–Student.[4] Such categorization work has consequences for individual students. Part III of our study is particularly interested in the consequences of the categorization work that is achieved in school, not only in the talk, but in the reading, writing and assessment practices of the classroom setting.

Conclusion: how to think about these questions

We argue that cultures accomplish versions of childhood and that, as part of that, schools bring off, among other things, versions of the categories Teacher and Student. This is a significant part of the school's cultural work. To study how this happens and to explore its consequences in any particular society, we need a theory and a set of attendant analytic methods that take these processes to be their prime point of interest. We need an approach that neither pre-empts the contexts and workings of childhood, nor even presumes that describing the essentials of Childhood as stand-alone attributes of a person is its main task or outcome. We also need a way of interpreting what we find in school classrooms that does not simply regard the participants in those activities as being pulled along by institutional imperatives – 'that's just how teachers and students behave' – but rather, takes people's behaviours to be 'reasonable', not necessarily acceptable to us, but rather as 'having reason', accountable then and there among the people who brought off the events under study, as those events occurred.

The approach that fits this set of criteria, and that we adopt in the descriptions and interpretations that follow, is drawn from ethnomethodology. Ethnomethodology is a discipline that has developed within sociology specifically with the relationship between social structure and daily practice in mind. It is a domain of enquiry that has as its central interest understanding how people's methodical everyday activities construct and reconstruct social order and social structure. It offers a distinctive understanding of social experience, based on a set of core propositions, some of which we sketch in Chapter 4.[5]

4 Reconsidering social action and social structure

The problem

This book takes a particular theoretical stand on how best to understand the processes of acculturation – how children become students, adults, workers, citizens, and so on. The problem here is that we all take it that we know what children are and what growing up entails. All cultures have strong ideas about the nature of children, and their members act on the basis of those ideas in the particular material and social circumstances in which they live. These ideas are part of what people know in common as members of cultures – part of what makes them cultures and not just people who happen to live near one another. The problem therefore is this: these ideas about Childhood, and the practices to which they relate, are all matters to be studied. They are not the analytic starting points from which to study acculturation; they are *topics* rather than resources for analysis and theorizing.

Introducing ethnomethodology

One theory and analytic method that gives purchase on understanding how people make sense of themselves and each other in everyday life is ethnomethodology. As our task is not to train the reader as ethnomethodologist, we here give a highly selective account of ethnomethodology, aimed at framing the reading of Parts II and III.

Ethnomethodology has developed a set of core, programmatic propositions about how to theorize the nature of social action and its relation to social structure. First, the understandings and practices of members of a culture are inherently and resolutely social – concerted and mutual (Jayyusi 1984, 1991) – and accomplished by multiple parties (Boden and Zimmerman 1991; Drew and Heritage 1992). People's social actions are culturally reflexive. Members of a culture perform certain social activities to accomplish an event and at the same time to provide one another with an account (description, explanation and warrant) of that event (Boden and Zimmerman 1991; Button and Lee 1987; Hester and Eglin 1997).

Furthermore, the accounts of cultural practices that members provide one another, generally through their talk, by which social order is constructed at all points of daily practice (Schegloff 1995), are contingent, that is, accountable primarily in the local terms of the practices themselves, then and there. This is so even where these accounts explicitly involve descriptions, explanations, and evaluations that people draw in from outside the local event (Schegloff 1991). One way of considering this is that in our everyday dealings with people we do both 'social' and 'sociological' work: 'social', in that we get the day's business done through activities coordinated with other people; 'sociological', in the sense that the ways in which we do this business show at the same moment how our joint actions are accountable in terms of the local (and maybe the institutional or cultural) expectations we hold in common with others.

So the orderliness of commonplace actions needs to be discovered 'from within' the actual settings of their occurrence as ongoing accomplishments of those settings and the participants (McHoul 1978). Therefore, it is not satisfactory to investigate, describe, explain, or evaluate features of organized cultural practices, such as classroom lessons, by invoking a rule or a research generalization obtained from outside the setting of the practices, no matter how much that importation may at first make the activities appear more recognizable, coherent or planful (Garfinkel 1967; Heritage 1984). If a rule or generalization *is* relevantly invoked, it is the participants in the events under study who invoke it.

Ethnomethodology treats social interactions such as classroom lessons primarily as organized interactional events, rather than as screens onto which, for example, cognitive processes, linguistic choices or the personality, cultural, and demographic attributes of the people are somehow projected. The goal of ethnomethodology is to explore how people coordinate their everyday courses of action in and through the routines of their talk, without pre-empting what the structure of those routines might look like (Lee 1991). Ethnomethodology takes cultural practices such as we see in schools to be embedded in and built by courses of everyday action, the argument being that this is how members of a culture encounter them, rather than as somehow externally determined: 'Social interaction is the primordial means through which the business of the social world is transacted, the identities of the participants are affirmed or denied, and its cultures are transmitted, renewed, and modified' (Goodwin and Heritage 1990: 283). For instance, no matter how obviously relevant the apparent dominance of the teacher's position may seem in classrooms and how comprehensive the implications of this for how the various participants behave (e.g. teachers give directions), as analysts we need to recover the co-ordinated interactional features that, in our culture, make up events in which teachers attempt to impart learning to learners. As young children progress in their learning, they learn as well, as both a consequence and a precondition, how to participate with increasing efficacy as learners-in-school.

How to make sense of how people make sense?
The documentary method of interpretation

Ethnomethodology proposes that, in making sense of the social world, members do not sequentially categorize objects and actions in terms of what they really are known to be. What an object 'is' is rather an 'accomplished' phenomenon, in the sense that it is actively constituted through the talk and work of the members (Cuff and Payne 1984). People's accomplishments of what objects, actions or utterances are, or mean, take precedence over notions of predefinition or predetermination. This approach to making sense of interaction and action was called by Mannheim, the prominent classical sociologist of knowledge, 'the documentary method of interpretation' (Mannheim 1952, in Garfinkel 1967).

Within this perspective, in order to perceive a particular school lesson as a usual school lesson requires that the person's knowledge of a 'normal school lesson' is adjusted to her or his knowledge of 'this school lesson'. Knowledge of normal social structures thus informs any current situation. Moreover, what happens in a particular lesson becomes part of a participant's knowledge of 'a school lesson'. Thus, current situations themselves inform a member's knowledge of normal structures. Furthermore, future occurrences of the same or similar situations will elaborate what that previously current scene 'was'. Therefore it is, as well, through accomplishing future interactions and events that members come to know what it was that previously happened. This is not to suggest that misunderstandings, mistakes and disagreements do not occur (Coulter 1979a; Lee 1987). Indeed, it is through the reflexive processes of the documentary method of interpretation that problems or troubles are oriented to, understood and made to 'be'. According to Heritage (1984), it is only as a result of these reflexive processes that actions and circumstances are able to be negotiated, understood and engaged in by members. Reflexivity is, therefore, pivotal to the documentary method of interpretation and central to a theory of action (Atkinson 1988; Garfinkel 1967).

One crucial further point is that, in managing circumstances and courses of action through the documentary method of interpretation, members simultaneously accomplish those very scenes as accountable, as normal (Heritage 1984; Taylor and Cameron 1987). Actions and events are accomplished as recognizable and usual by members as they talk and interact in the world.

What makes a particular way of acting, in a classroom for example, available to the members as alternative or different for that group is in the normative accountability of that action (Lee 1987). For example, *if* students climbing on the desks is outside of the normativities and moral order of the classroom, that action will be accounted for and thus made visible as a breach of ordinary classroom interaction. The designation as normal or otherwise therefore occurs *in* actual interaction, it does not precede it. It is often through the visibility of alternative actions that the norms of the social organization of that group are made conspicuous: 'breaches of norms are commonly more revealing about the attitudes, motives and circumstances of other people than is conformity' (Heritage 1984: 116). Thus, even though the accomplishment of a scene as ordinary reveals that group's norms, those norms are frequently most visible in their infractions.

A major focus of this investigation is the documentation of what it *is* to be a child for school in different classrooms. Ethnomethodology provides a framework with which to understand that recognizable, usual and 'right' ways for given schoolchildren to act are accomplished in the workings of normative accountability. In other words, they are accomplished in and through the actions of those particular schoolchildren and their associated classroom interactants.

The methodology of ethnomethodology

Ethnomethodology is premised upon the fact that social structures are locally produced and locally maintained through the interactive, practical activities of members (Garfinkel 1967). It attends to the interpretive procedures through which members are able to make continuous sense out of everyday activities as they occur. For ethnomethodologists, members' methods, that is, their utterances, practices, interpretations and accomplishments, are necessarily foregrounded in investigations of social organization. What this means for this study, as well as for ethnomethodological research in general, is that the theoretical apparatus of ethnomethodology proposes a particular theory of *data*.

What counts as data?

One feature of ethnomethodology is that its data are the material of specific and actual instances of human interaction or action (Coulter 1979b). As Heritage stated, analytic data are 'the primary data of the social world – the raw material of specific, singular events of human conduct' (1984: 235). In ethnomethodological studies, people's *reports* of what they did or did not do and say in a particular situation cannot be substituted for *what* they did or did not do. Similarly, interviews of interactants about a particular incident cannot stand in the place of observations, recordings and transcriptions of the incident. This is not to say that reports and interviews are not potentially interesting data *per se*. For example, in the case of interviews of teachers about classroom practices, the interviews would count as data in the question of what teachers say in interviews about what they do in classrooms, but they would not count as data that answers the question of what those teachers do in classrooms.

Nor can specific instances of interaction be substituted with invented or hypothetical examples of interaction (Goodwin and Heritage 1990; Hilbert 1992; Watson 1992). Invented material can in no way capture the complexity of human interaction, and as it comes (as it must) out of a given analyst's or researcher's head, it necessarily presents typifications of the way in which human interaction occurs. As data, invented material would count as 'the way analysts represent the world of action when they are inventing material about what people do' but would not count as 'what people do'.

In addition, the data of ethnomethodological studies is collected in naturally occurring occasions of everyday interaction (Coulter 1979b; Psathas 1995). Therefore, in the present investigation of social action in classrooms, of prime interest are the interactions that usually, unremarkably and easily occur between the classroom interactants, including interactions that take place through written text, in this case a novel and the students' own writing. Within this framework, the compilation of pre-coded observational schedules and checklists is viewed as inadequate and unsatisfactory data collection. As stated earlier, within ethnomethodology, data comprise the raw materials of interaction or action. Consequently, visual and/or auditory recordings of what the interactants do and say comprise ethnomethodological data. For talk as data in particular, once it is recorded, it is transcribed to facilitate analysis. It is noteworthy that the resultant transcripts are considered to be transcripts *of* the data, rather than the data themselves (Psathas 1995).

Finally but importantly, the data of ethnomethodology comprise every action that occurs in a given research site. This is because ethnomethodology understands that all action is consequential to its circumstances and this is unable to be classified *a priori* as irrelevant to those circumstances. For the purposes of the present study, data include teacher 'asides' to students, as well as students' 'chat' about, for example, Christmas presents, playground games and weekend activities, students' writing and teacher comments about that writing, be that written on the student's text, in talk to the student or to the researcher.

What counts as having 'found something'?

The analyst may well ask what counts as having 'found something' in any corpus of data: that is 'what counts as a warrant?'. The concise answer is that any claim about a particular interactive site's social organization must arise from 'defensible analysis – analysis which departs from, and can always be referred to and grounded in, the details of actual occurrences of conduct in interaction' (Schegloff 1991: 48; see also Drew and Heritage 1992; Wilson 1991). According to Schegloff (1991), such analysis is made possible if the issues of 'relevance' and 'procedural consequentiality' are attended to.

Relevance

In making sense of situations and in apprehending objects, people and situations, social actors orient to what is, for them, relevant about the given object, event or person. Analysts, as members themselves, also make sense of situations and people in this way. The issue of relevance, in the context of methodology, relates to the issue of ensuring that 'who' people consider themselves or others to 'be' correlates with 'who' an analyst determines or 'finds' them to 'be'. In other words, the issue relates to ensuring an analyst does not merely find participants to 'be' what she or he 'pre-interprets' them to 'be', to the exclusion of that which those subjects accomplish themselves as relevantly being then and there.

For any interaction to proceed, members must establish their relevant identity, or membership category (Hilbert 1992; Sacks 1972; Wilson 1991). However, for any one person, many membership categories can generally be applied (Cuff and Payne 1984; Sacks 1972). For example, one individual in a school classroom could be each of the following: Schoolchild, Protestant, Son, Stamp Collector, Blonde, Asian, Netball Player. Such categories occur as collections of like categories within membership category devices, henceforth MCDs (Eglin and Hester 1992; Sacks 1972). These devices are 'collections of categories which "go together", initially in the sense that when a category from a certain device is correctly applied to a person, it can be heard to exclude them from being identified with some other category from the same device' (Cuff and Payne 1984: 172). For example, Schoolchild, Teacher, Cleaner and Principal are arguably categories which belong to the MCD 'occupation for school'.[1]

It is in interaction with other members that a member is *oriented to* in the terms of the category relevant to the particular circumstances of the talk. For example, in talk at home a person might be oriented to as a member of the category Son (from the MCD 'family') while in talk at school that same person might be oriented to as a member of the category Student (from the MCD 'occupation for school'). Furthermore, members use common-sense methods in order to apprehend and accomplish members as incumbents of particular categories (Eglin and Hester 1992; Leiter 1980; Speier 1971). Jayyusi (1984, 1991) argued that incumbency in a particular category may be achieved by members in several ways, perceptual availability (someone who looks like a woman); behavioural availability (someone who behaves like a woman); first-person avowal and third-person declaration (someone who says she is a woman or someone who someone else says is a woman); credential presentation (someone displays some proof of their incumbency in the category, say, a birth certificate), and, ascription (someone has actions ascribed to them that accomplish particular attributes, and therefore, categorizes them, for example, someone is described as doing something that might ordinarily be taken to be the actions of a woman, say 'having her nails painted'). The categories that cluster together in a MCD also pair in Standard Relational Pairs (SRPs), for example, Boy/Girl, Mother/Father, Sister/Brother such that to ascribe attributes to one is to implicatively *not* ascribe them to its pair (Eglin and Hester, 1992: 244). So, for example, to say that the category Girl has the attributes 'sugar and spice and all things nice' is to implicatively say that the category Boy does not.

In terms of the current question of what counts as having actually found something in data, the issue here relates to ensuring that the principles of relevance and the concomitant membership categories oriented to by the participants in any scene under investigation correlate with those 'found' or claimed by an analyst. Therefore, the task of the classroom analyst, for example, is not to merely adequately describe the identities of the participants in terms of what they observably *are* (Schegloff 1991). The analytic task is to elucidate the relevances upon which a given interactive situation is accomplished and to show, from the details of the data, which category, out of myriad possible membership categories, is accomplished for a given classroom interactant in any moment. The warrant for the claim that a particular person is a member of the category Schoolchild is not that the analyses show that that is what that member's category *could possibly and correctly be* but that the analyses demonstrate, for the participants in the interaction, that that is what that member's incumbency *is* then and there. Similarly, when analysing texts with Membership Category Analysis (MCA) the task of the analyst is to demonstrate what categories are relevant to sense-making in the text and how the text assembles category attributes in describing those categories, for example, is the category Sister assembled as wise, caring and protective or as foolish, frivolous and spiteful?

Procedural consequentiality

The issue of relevance is applicable to claims about the contexts of events in much the same way as it is applicable to the claims about membership categories (Schegloff 1991). Schegloff has argued that, just as many categories may be feasibly *correct* for a member, so too are many contexts correct when describing the place or situation in which some event occurred. A conversation may be correctly described as occurring 'in a school', or 'in the principal's office', or 'in the middle of the night' or 'in Scotland'. It follows therefore, that just as an analyst cannot, within ethnomethodology, settle the issue of *who* a participant relevantly is, in a given interaction, in terms of *who* or *what* they look like, nor can an analyst settle the issue of what the context of talk is with a casual observation of the loomingly obvious context (Hilbert 1992). The warrant for making claims about context is in the establishment that *where* an analyst determines members to be, correlates with *where* members, in their talk, accomplish themselves to be.

However, Schegloff argued that the relevance of context extends beyond members' mere recognition of the fact that they are, for example, 'in a classroom' to what he calls the 'procedural consequentiality' of their being in a given site or context. Procedural consequentiality refers to the idea that an analyst has a warrant for making a claim about the context of an interaction only insofar as she or he can document the ways in which the setting or context has 'determinate consequences for the talk' (1991: 53).

The concept of procedural consequentiality provides analysts with a principled way to engage with the idea of context. It is apparent in common-sense terms that setting and context do not reside in physical or geographical features of the world. To be sure, classroom talk, with its concomitant categories Schoolchild and Teacher, can be recorded within a classroom. However, it can also be heard to occur outside of the physical institution of school, for example, on a bus, in a park, and so on. The obverse is also commonsensically available. That is, as well as happening outside of classrooms, non-classroom talk can also occur in the physical space of a classroom – between two cleaners about brooms and mops, between a teacher and a schoolchild who also happens to be that teacher's biological child, and so on.

One way in which the procedural consequentiality of any context for the talk can be gauged is through the analysis of the 'speech exchange systems' that are engaged in by interactants within that setting (Schegloff 1991). That is, in the systematic ways in which participants talk in given sites, identifications are set up for the participants and, as a consequence, the setting is accomplished as a particular one (Hilbert 1992; Schegloff 1991). For example, the 'classroomness' of the talk in a classroom is accomplished in and through the speech-exchange system in play. Insofar as some people routinely ask questions of a particular type and other people routinely answer those questions in a particular way, the talk *itself* accomplishes the setting *as* 'classroom'.

Of course, as we said, classroom talk can proceed in a variety of physically non-classroom settings. The argument of procedural consequentiality would hold that if the speech-exchange systems engaged in by the speakers set up the classroom identifications, it would also accomplish the context as 'classroom' even if it were visibly, say, at the beach. For instances in which non-classroom talk is conducted in classrooms, the argument of procedural consequentiality would hold that the speech-exchange systems engaged in by the speakers would determine the relevant context, for example, as 'work colleague talk' or 'family talk' and maintain the concomitant membership categories. Therefore, the warrant for a claim by an analyst that what is being dealt with, in an investigation, is a particular setting (for example, a classroom) is not that the analyses show what the setting *observably is*. Rather, the claim is warranted in analyses that show that, in the speech-exchange systems of the participants, that setting or 'context' was procedurally consequential for the talk and interaction.

An analyst working with an ethnomethodological perspective cannot settle the issue of 'who' participants relevantly are, or what the context of an inter-action is, on the strength of casual observation of or intuition about the situa-tion, or through some institutional predetermination of their identities. By the same token, an analyst (as a research designer) is precluded from common-sensically assuming that sites and interactions that look the same are, for analytic purposes, 'the same', and, similarly, is barred from assuming that features 'found' in a site are peculiar to that site. The issue of warrant, therefore, limits the claims made by analysts to information that is defensively and analysably available in the data. These concerns are of particular significance in this book in that we compare and contrast members' work in particular locales within classroom sites, both in talk and written text, in order to elucidate the topic of the enact-ment of Childhood for school.

Analytic methods

Ethnomethodology aims to engage with theories of social order and organization that contend with the methods used by members as they interact. From the traditions of ethnomethodology we draw some general guidelines for our research, and these are listed below:

- We studied records of actual interactions, rather than idealized, intermixed, stereotyped, invented, speculative, possible or remembered interactions. This is because of a belief in the particular value of understanding actual educational practice. We did not rely on substitutes for actual, naturally occurring interactional data such as: what we were told in interviews; what we coded or summarized from observations; intuitively invented instances of possible interaction; or artificially produced data, such as role plays or laboratory simulations. In these less than satisfactory methods 'the specific details of naturally situated interactional conduct are irretrievably lost and are replaced by idealizations about how interaction works' (Heritage 1984: 236).
- We viewed interactions as structurally organized through turns at talk. Everyday activities, including educational activities, are organized in some way or another. Interaction is not just an additional feature of human activity that helps the organization of daily life; rather, interaction is itself a major part of the action, and interactional events are organized in recognizable, structured ways. It is the nature of the structures that reflects and at the same time constructs the nature of the activity in the world. Talk is action; action is organized.
- We viewed the classroom interactions as mutually accomplished. We understood the interactions we taped and observed to be brought off by the various speakers and listeners involved, even in a highly structured and 'stage-managed' event such as a classroom lesson; they were not accomplished, or even 'mainly accomplished', by one of the speakers alone.
- We held the view that how something is heard – the work it is taken to do in the talk – is available, while the intent of the speaker is not. While we may believe we recognize a teacher's or learner's intent, analysing talk does not equate to describing purposes. We need rather to look at how the participants themselves display explicit clues to what they take to be going on.
- We viewed sequences of talk as they are used by the speakers – *as* sequences and *in* sequence. We took seriously the ethnomethodological position that:
  - any utterance has the potential to be heard in many ways, and may be taken to have potentially multiple functions and hearings in a sequence of interaction;
  - the work done by an utterance, then and there, depends on *how it is heard* in sequence – its location in the course of jointly produced action; indeed, an utterance can be heard as projected by previous turns at talk, from the other speakers and from the speaker in question;

- a speaker's analysis, understanding, and/or appreciation of a prior turn at talk will be displayed in that speaker's current turn. Thus, speakers publicly display and sustain an updated shared, intersubjective understanding of what is going on and how they may contribute;
- a description of an utterance that is warranted is one that takes account of the point at which any utterance occurs within a sequence of talk;
- there is an overriding assumption among speakers that everything said is pertinent to the business at hand – 'sustained relevance' – unless explicit markers to the contrary are evident in the talk. Thus, insertions that may appear to be tangential or irrelevant, however embedded and extensive, are heard by participants as being within the frame of sustained relevance, unless otherwise indicated by the participants themselves;
- therefore, no interactional detail can be dismissed in advance as digressive, irrelevant, disorderly, or accidental.

Similar guidelines have been associated with a great deal of detailed analysis of talk-in-interaction, manifesting a particular analytic terminology. The mechanisms used by social actors as they engage in mundane talk-in-interaction have been well documented (Goodwin and Heritage 1990; Heritage 1984; Sacks *et al.* 1974; Taylor and Cameron 1987; Watson and Seiler 1992). Therefore, these mechanisms of mundane talk-in-interaction are available as methods for the detailed analysis of mundane talk-in-interaction. Of interest to the present study of classroom talk is Drew and Heritage's argument that, given the systematic variation of 'institutional' talk on the features of mundane talk, the conventions of mundane talk-in-interaction 'constitute a kind of benchmark against which other more formal or "institutional" types of interaction are recognized and experienced' (1992: 19). In this book, the features of mundane talk-in-interaction are used as analytic tools with which to interrogate talk in classrooms (see Appendix I for further details of the analytic features specifically referred to in Parts II and III).

The analyst as ethnomethodologist

According to Schegloff, the basic task of the ethnomethodologist is 'to convert insistent intuition, however correct, into empirically detailed analysis' (1991: 66). Lee's (1991) five principles of ethnomethodology summarize the analyst's position as taken in this study. First, an ethnomethodologist suspends belief or acceptance of social relationships between categories of people (Hilbert 1992; Psathas 1995). For example, matters of cause and effect relationships or power relationships are set aside until such time as those relationships are made relevant and accomplished by the members themselves as they interact. An ethnomethodologist understands that members continually display the 'lived' reality of their relationships and their world to themselves and to others (Brandt 1992). Therefore, in the present study, it is inappropriate, as well as unnecessary, to privilege traditional sociological theories of classroom relationships, because the classroom members will assuredly display to the analyst the 'lived' realities of their classroom, as they accomplish them.

Second, the ethnomethodologist's task is to treat interactive situations as scenes that are jointly and sequentially produced by all participants. Mundane talk-in-interaction occurs within a framework that assumes 'that utterances which are placed immediately next to some prior are to be understood as produced in response to or, more loosely, in relation to that prior' (Heritage 1984: 261). Therefore, what a turn at talk *is* (for example, a question) is ascertained in how it is heard as the sequence of talk continues, hence its joint and sequential accomplishment.

Third, the ethnomethodologist sets aside formats of talk or interaction that given participants *would* or *should* use in favour of the structures of talk and interaction that they *do* use (Cuff and Payne 1984; Psathas 1995; Schegloff 1995). The aim of the present study, then, is to document the coordinated and/or non-coordinated courses of action that the classroom members *do* routinely accomplish, rather than analytically or theoretically pre-empting what those courses of interaction would look like.

Fourth, the assumption that the orderliness of social structures and social organization is achieved in the day-to-day ordinary activities of members and will, therefore, be available in the details of everyday events, is maintained by the ethnomethodologist. In the present study, the analytic focus remains on the mundane everyday work of the classroom members, both in talk and text. It documents what the members orient to as normal, unremarkable and, to use Garfinkel's (1967) description, 'unnoticed'. The fine-grained analyses of defensively 'normal' classroom talk and text in each research site, therefore, illuminate the organizational structure, that is to say, the moral order within which that site operates.

Finally, and following on from the point above, the ethnomethodologist understands that, for members of a society, that society's traditions, customs and mores are not sequestered from the talk and interaction, nor do they limit and constrain what those members do and say. Rather, a society's culture is embedded in and built by everyday courses of action. Therefore, for the purposes of the present study, both schoolchildren and teachers are understood to accomplish themselves and others as participants in reasoned sequences of action that develop in particular directions, and that make relevant particular categories of members.

Conclusion

Here we have presented a discussion of the bases and tenets of ethnomethodology and considered the practical application of ethnomethodology to research sites and empirical data.

This chapter provides purchase on how we aim to address the central task of this book. The focus of our investigation is on the enactment of Childhood in and for schools: we ask what are the attributes of the membership category

Schoolchild in classroom sites, are there comparisons between sites and are there comparisons or contrasts within one site? We take our questions to three different classrooms and to different talk-in-interaction sites within those classrooms, namely, whole class talk and student group talk, and to different textual sites: talk, students' written text, teacher planning and the materials of study – in this instance, a children's novel. In each of these strands of our data pool we adhere to the tenets of ethnomethodology, applying the tools of Conversation Analysis and Membership Category Analysis to track a particular and selective path through this data as we pursue the enactment of Childhood in school.

Part II

Respecifying the institutional child

One way to describe our overall project is that we use the framework of ethnomethodology to explore the educational respecification of children as members of the category Child–Student. In particular, we detail attributes of the category unremarkably accomplished in and through different classroom moments. Our interest in Parts II and III, therefore, is to provide empirically warrantable answers to the question of 'What (and how and when) is a child?' 'Child' and 'Student' are to all practical purposes used as interchangeable terms in schools, and in Part II we develop our use of the term Child–Student to capture a sense of the individual's childness in the student context. In Part III, however, we go on to demonstrate how the attributes of Child and Student are *simultaneously* relevant, actually working together, and against one another, to produce, rather than an interchangeable descriptor, the category Child–Student. In Part III, the category Child–Student describes a double incumbency that is consequential for all the categories collected by the concept School. Parts II and III, then, inform our project in complementary ways, each taking a particular course through a large data pool, here deliberately juxtaposed to highlight the breadth and significance of our major points.

Earlier we drew on ethnomethodology to claim that social order and social phenomena are accomplished in and through the everyday interactive and interpretive processes of people, and are made to stand as socially real through those very same processes. The analyses reported here recognize that the category Child–Student is an accomplished phenomenon. In one sense, we aim to point to the intricacies of the accomplishment of this category rather than to expose any simple, essential or universal Child–Student. As pieces of analysis, each of the three chapters within each Part may be read independently of the other two chapters as stand-alone findings about the attributes of Child–Student as accomplished, for example, in small group talk or within a novel. When read in combination with the other two chapters in the relevant Part, however, the chapters together then read as relevant components of an answer to our overall question 'What is a child?' Similarly, Parts II and III each stand alone as a position informing our overriding question *and as well* combine with the other Part to allow new insights into the category Child–Student.

Part II focuses on how students become members of the category Child–Student within the institutional procedures of the classroom. Here, we interrogate some of our data to explicate the accomplishment of Child–Student as a multi-faceted category that we show to be a function of what students were able to bring to bear on any configuration in their classroom work.

We use one corpus of whole class and student group talk collected in two year three classrooms (7 and 8-year-old students) over a two-month period. By whole class talk, we mean talk conducted in sessions in which students interact with the teacher in whole group discussion, direct teaching situations and situations in which the teacher reconnoitres students' performances while they work in small groups. By student group talk, we mean talk that occurs – without the teacher's direct guidance and gaze – between up to six students who are engaged in either a group task or in individual work while seated in a group. This corpus of data comprises audiotapes and transcripts of sixteen whole class sessions and fourteen student group sessions.

In Chapter 5, we treat the whole class talk collected in the two sites as one data set to show comparisons on the matter of the attributes of the category Child–Student. We then further detail the category Child–Student in Chapter 6 as we separate the whole class talk from each site and contrast one with the other to document the distinctive attributional work that is done in each site. Finally, we add another dimension to the exploration of the educational respecification of children as members of the category Child–Student by documenting in Chapter 7 the inflections of the category made visible when students work in small groups without the teacher's direct gaze or guidance. In that chapter, we treat the student group transcripts collected in the two sites as one data set and contrast this set of student group talk with the whole class set that was the focus of Chapter 5. In Chapter 7, we also briefly contrast the attributional work done in the student group talk in each site.

Our analyses focus on what was routine and unremarkable for the participants. We have less interest in what was frequent or infrequent, and more interest in turns at talk that are marked by the participants as within or beyond the normativities of that group for that moment. What might be described within other research traditions as inconsistencies in the attributional work done in one or another locale is not taken here to expose any finding as necessarily erroneous. We are able to comprehend apparent contradictions as highlighting the breadth of mundane interaction and, furthermore, we use them to enrich our understandings of the accomplishment of the category Child in the classroom.

In each chapter there is a concluding descriptive summary statement of our findings. Each summary statement highlights that chapter's particular contribution to current understandings of interaction and talk in whole class and student group configurations. Chapter by chapter, we establish the following:

- the Child–Student of whole class talk is precompetent and accomplished in cohorts (Chapter 5);

- matters of distinction between the sites' whole class talk range around the normativites of the cohort (Chapter 6);
- student group talk differs systematically from whole class talk and the manner of cohorting is a point of distinction between sites (Chapter 7).

It must be noted, however, that central to this Part are the contrasts between the various data sets (whole class, student group) that are detailed. The contrasts show that in interaction with teachers, students ordinarily enacted particular constellations of themselves which made them look like they were somewhat 'incomplete' in relation to those teachers – that, as a cohort, they needed the gaze and guidance of the Teacher – while in interactions between school-children, they were routinely accomplished as competent people. That is, we find that the category Child–Student is a locally driven category, that classroom participants use multiple reasoning practices to enact the category in different sites and different work configurations, and that students and teachers are artful in the kinds of interactive options they exercise in those different locales.

Part II demonstrates the capacity of students in two classrooms to enact their status as members of the category Child. We also provide evidence, however, of another set of behavioural capabilities and resources, apparently more adult-like, that students can draw upon in getting tasks done. The following three chapters, taken together, therefore demonstrate the forcefulness of MacKay's (1974) point, articulated in Chapter 2, that children have to marshal their knowledge about adults' theories of childhood and their own interactive resources in order to participate in interactions with adults. In short, they must collaborate in adult theorizations of the Child in order to participate successfully in adult–child interactions. How these and other insights made available by the contrasts inform our overriding question of 'What (and how and when) is a Child–Student?' is pursued in the discussion that concludes this Part.

The additional insights into the attributional work done in classrooms and into the concomitant category Child–Student made available by considering *together* the findings of Parts II and III, are discussed in the Conclusion. It is our contention that most contemporary theorizations and conceptualizations of childhood are unable to accommodate the different enacted clusters of attributes of the category Child–Student detailed in the following six chapters. Ways forward from here for theorists, teachers, policy-makers and researchers are taken up in the Conclusion.

5   The schoolchild

Introduction

In this chapter, we introduce two of our focus classrooms: year three at Aralia College and the same year level at St Luke's School. The transcripts taken from these classrooms are indicative of the everyday talk that occurs in a vast number of schools in Australia and in comparable societies. They are, to all intents and purposes, normal Australian classrooms – neither was selected because of any novel features, notable inadequacies, particularly outstanding students or particular excellence in teaching. Their inclusion here was based on the view that the interactions and talk we would be able to collect as data in these two classrooms were ordinary.

Our purpose here is to document and contrast attributes of the Child–Student accomplished by the teachers and students in these classrooms. It is important to note that this chapter does not provide an exhaustive list of all the attributes of the category Child–Student that the transcripts might support. Further analyses, or other sorts of analyses, may reveal other attributional work done in and through the classroom talk of either site. For the purposes of showing comparabilities, however, we will, for the moment, dwell on two locally driven attributes that were available in the whole class talk in these two classrooms. The first of these was *precompetence,* and the second, being a member of a *cohort.* When describing the enactment of the category Child–Student we find a nexus in the accomplishments of precompetence and cohorting. First, then, we will consider the attribute of precompetence.

The Child–Student is precompetent

Students, apparently, are neither incompetent nor competent. In the classrooms we studied we found that it was unremarkable in whole class sessions for the students to be seen as talking and acting in ways that were not incompetent and not fully competent but, rather, as *developing into or toward* competency. As described in Chapter 2, others have referred to this achieved development into competence as the attribution of precompetence (Baker and Freebody 1989a; Speier 1976). This precompetence is not passively acquired nor is it enforced. It is accomplished in classrooms in several ways, detailed in the sections that follow: participants (teachers and students) persist in orienting to students as existing in the realm of 'trying', they orient to students' interests and dispositions as distinctive, and they do these things in unremarked and unremarkable ways. Although the achievement of precompetence is, by and large, unremarkable, we show that students negotiate the precise definition of the precompetence operating moment by moment in the classroom; that is, that they show awareness of their assignation as precompetent. At times they demonstrate, as well, considerable interactive skill and delicate understanding of the nature and policing of the boundaries of their competence as not only 'students' but as 'children' in school.

Child–Student: not incompetent but not yet competent

Precompetence through displays of competence in trying

We found that students spent much of their time 'trying' – that is, trying to spell, to write creatively and to think. In both teachers' responses to students' requests for assistance and in teachers' introductions to classroom activities, it was usual for students to be directed to 'have a try', 'have a go', 'try your best', and to 'just do the best you can'. What was unremarkable, then, was the accomplishment of student action as a display of 'trying to do', rather than actually doing activities. We begin with an example concerning spelling.

Extract 5.1

246 Pr: = Is this how you spell village?
247 T: Perre, um, if you would like to have, no, sit down, Perre. If you have one go, have a look, do you think that is correct?
248 Pr: No
249 T: Right, well, have another try
250 Pr: But there's no room
251 T: Well, have another try, that's all right, do it down here. Right, now it doesn't matter if it's exactly right or wrong, does it? What you have to do is, have a try. And then have another try. And if you're still not sure, you can have another try if you like! Then pick the one that you think is the best and put it in your rough copy. If you're still not sure, put a circle around it. That'll tell me, I think that's how you spell it but I'm not sure. And then you can go on to the next word.

Throughout this sequence of talk, Perre is said to be neither competent nor completely incompetent in the matter of spelling the word 'village'. He is oriented to as capable of identifying his own spelling errors (247–248), making continued attempts at spelling and, finally, evaluating the attempts and selecting the best (251). Note, however, that in Turn 251, the teacher oriented to the idea that although Perre would be able to *try* many times, he would be unable to actually *spell* the word (given the number of attempts needed), and although able to identify incorrect attempts, he would ultimately require the assistance of the teacher. Perre, then, is demonstrably precompetent; that is, at some point between incompetence and competence. This example neatly exemplifies the paradox of children's competent and seamless enactment of childhood as identified by Mackay (1974) and described in Chapter 2, insofar as the teacher at once treated Perre as deficient *and* relied upon his competence in enacting the pedagogy, part of which entailed his competence in identifying his own mistakenness.

Precompetence through provisionality

Students' talk was generally 'pending approval'. That is, it was usual for the students' turns at talk to be heard as awaiting the teacher's confirmation. This was most routinely achieved in orientation to the students' answers to teachers' questions as questions themselves (see also Baker 1992; Freiberg and Freebody 1995).

Extract 5.2

68	*T:*	. . . I'm, oh, when am I writing this letter? When am I writing the letter?
69	*S:*	Today?
70	*T:*	Today. So what do I need on it?
71	*Jl:*	The date?
72	*T:*	Today's date . . .
88	*T:*	. . . Dear Daniel, double check where you're going to write it. So we have (*writes*) DEAR capital 'd', DEAR DANIEL. And then I have?
89	*Be:*	A comma?
90	*T:*	A comma. DEAR DANIEL and a comma.

Turns 69, 71 and 89 were all offered and heard as *possible* answers to the teacher's questions in Turns 68, 70 and 88, respectively. This hearing is available in the students' use of an interrogative inflection and in the teacher's unmarked acceptance of answers designed in this way. In this almost ritualized design and hearing of students' answers as questions, the students and teachers together accomplish such answers as provisional – that is, as awaiting designation as valid by the teacher – thereby accomplishing the students' precompetence.

Precompetence through the provisional knowers' knowledge displays

Part of what a student knows is that it is not sufficient simply to have the right knowledge, one must also know how to present or display that knowledge. The following extract shows the work that is done by classroom participants to ensure both criteria are met in the course of everyday classroom talk.

Extract 5.3

92	*T:*	Begin writing my letter. I wonder where I'm going to begin writing my letter?
93	*So:*	Underneath
94	*T:*	I wonder?
95	*So:*	Underneath
96	*T:*	Underneath where Sophia?
97	*So:*	Underneath DEAR DANIEL
98	*T:*	Whereabouts underneath DEAR DANIEL?
99	*So:*	Um starting from the very edge?
100	*T:*	Starting from the very edge. Over here. (*writes*)

In this sequence of talk, Sophia's original answer in Turn 93 was retrospectively audible as essentially correct; and we could fashion a teacher response that displays this, for example, 'Underneath. Right underneath and right over near the edge'. However, the teacher continued to nominate Sophia's answer as incorrect until it displayed this particular information in a particular form. Note that throughout this sequence, the participants achieved through their talk a particular display of knowledge and the display of a particular sort of student – the provisional knower. In the next example, in Turn 123, the teacher explicitly states the relevance of the design of a turn to successful classroom participation.

Extract 5.4

114	*T:*	Okay, so let's pretend William has written to his friend dear Daniel
118	*T:*	. . . So what's he going to do? Perre?
119	*Bt:*	From your best friend Perre
120	*Pr:*	From your best friend?
121	*T:*	Okay, could say, from your best friend
122	*Be:*	Yours truly William
123	*T:*	Would you put your hand up please instead of calling out? I can't hear you when you call out. Beatrice?
124	*Be:*	Yours truly William?
125	*T:*	Yours truly William

The student turns of interest here are Brittany's Turn 119 and Beatrice's Turns 122 and 124. Turn 119, with no interrogative intonation was, seemingly, ignored while Turn 122 audibly projected the teacher's naming of the trouble caused by students' calling out answers – specifically, she is unable to hear them. Note that following the teacher's selection at the end of Turn 123, Beatrice provided the answer that she had previously uttered as Turn 122, how-ever, as Turn 124, that answer was designed as provisional insofar as it was delivered with an interrogative inflection. It is this turn that is repeated and thus validated by the teacher.

The classrooms we studied, then, were places wherein a student's answer, to be accorded correctness and admitted to the propositional corpus of the lesson, must be accurate in content and must be displayed in an appropriate way. Such classrooms can be understood as places that are as much to do with attending closely to what counts as knowledge and what is required in the way of reason-ing and presentation as they are with knowing *how* to do something or what an accurate answer *is* (Baker and Freebody 1993; Breen 1985). Neatly exemplified, especially in Extract 5.3, is the fact that students are knowledgeable about the normativities of classroom life and are very well practised at collaborating in the maintenance of those normativities. Students become good at enacting the precompetent student.

The Child–Student: a predilection for pretending and serendipity

In the classrooms we examined students and teachers routinely made fantasy (see also Baker and Freebody 1989a), pretending and make believe relevant to the business of undertaking school work. We see in the example above the use that teachers made of the school students' facility with imagining or, in this case, pretending (Extract 5.4, Turn 114). Given that no speaker remarked on such directives to pretend, such turns were accomplished as routine ways of organizing interaction in the classroom. A test of recipient design can be applied: 'Would this be unremarkable in an adult class? Could this interaction ordinarily have taken place with an adult student?'

Serendipity also played a part in many aspects of the lessons we studied. That is, the students were routinely accomplished as succumbing to the suggestion that classroom events were the result of unexpected good fortune rather than any amount of teacher forethought or planning.

Extract 5.5

72 *T:*   Today's date, today's the?
73 *Ss:* Twentieth of October
74 *T:*   (*writes*) Twentieth, straight underneath again. Straight down, in the middle of the page, twentieth, capital letter. Oh just as well we learnt how to spell October in our spelling isn't it? Capital 'o', TWENTIETH OCTOBER
97 *T:*   . . . Give these out Yena. Lucy take one and pass the others along that row. Gemma pass them, sitting in rows makes it easy doesn't it Gemma. Three boys there. Lan and Andrew

Turns 74 and 97 are examples of the routine way in which the participants oriented to situations that arose in the classroom as opportunistic and serendipitous rather than matters of design.

The Child–Student: a proclivity for excitability and being kept in suspense

Students, it seems, are also susceptible to being kept in suspense. Teachers use wait-and-see techniques in the course of routine classroom talk (Baker and Freebody 1989a; Freebody 1995b; Freiberg and Freebody 1995). Students are ordinarily kept waiting until the moment the teacher reveals an activity, worksheet or book for all to see. Such situations effectively accomplish students as precompetent people by ensuring that they 'do not know what might be made pertinent at any moment, nor can they know what, more generally, the nature of the learning is supposed by the teacher to be' (Freiberg and Freebody 1995: 322). In having to wait-and-see, then, the students' knowledge base was achieved in these lessons as partial and precompetent in relation to the teacher's competent, complete and authoritative knowledge (Baker and Freebody 1989a).

Extract 5.6

1 *T:* . . . I want you to listen to this very carefully and I want you to think very hard. Because when we finish talking about this I'm going to ask you to go and um do something in a group.

3 *T:* . . . Right. I have something very interesting for you to do later. But, now listen, will you take out a pencil please

In these excerpts, the students were constituted as having to wait until later to see what the activity was to be. By the same token, the talk also accomplished the teacher as not having to wait-and-see because she already presumably knew what the 'something' was. Such reference to activities that are known only by the teacher are usual in many primary classrooms and were certainly unremarkable features of our data corpus. In Turn 3 above a further layer of the students' unknowing is demonstrated. At times, students might not know when the actual moment of revelation might be, except in the most general terms, for example, 'later'. That is, they do not know how long they will be asked to wait, in readiness, for the point to be revealed.

Another wait-and-see technique is the public wondering of the teacher, which will be recalled from Extract 5.3 and is reproduced below.

92 *T:* /Begin writing my letter. I wonder where I'm going to begin writing my letter?

93 *So:* Underneath

94 *T:* I wonder?

In both this example and the one below, such wondering was accomplished by the teacher, as well as by students, as unremarkable and routine.

Extract 5.7

239 *T:*   Now, I wonder when we'll be ready to perform our plays?
240 *Lm:* Tomorrow?
241 *Jf:* Monday? Monday or Tuesday then?
242 *T:*   I wonder?
243 *Ss:* (*various*)
244 *T:*   Aahm? Gemma?
245 *Gm:* Friday. On next Friday?
246 *T:*   Yes. How about we make a date for next Friday. That gives you a week

The students here were accomplished as having to wait-and-see what day the teacher nominated as the performance day. Although we cannot argue that the teacher knew all along that the answer was Friday, we can see that she decreed that Friday was the answer and therefore, for one brief moment, knew before the students that it was the answer. In this example, the teacher demonstrated arbitration rights in relation to the students' right to suggest, but not decide, what day the play would be performed. This transcript provides a clear example, as well, of the work of suspense in everyday classroom interaction in focusing students' attention and encouraging participation in activities.

Excitement was another child-like concern that both students and teachers oriented to as relevant to the business of primary education. For example, at the beginning of the lesson on personal letter writing, the teacher oriented to the cohort as excited,

Extract 5.8

7 *T:*   . . . Now I know you're excited about all of this

as needing to have that excitement curbed,

7 *T:*   . . . But can you just listen please . . .

and, as having an interest in exciting things.

7 *T:*   . . . I might already know because I've decided to write to a friend and I want to tell him something exciting . . .

Routinely in our whole class data set, the teachers oriented to and therefore made relevant to the business at hand, the proclivity of the students to be excitable and excited and to the concomitant need for the students to be settled.

Extract 5.9

  34 *T:*   . . . (17) Excuse me, I'm sure you're very excited about what you're doing, but the noise is a bit much

563 *T:*   . . . Right, could you people come and sit on the floor, we are not going to computer until you're settled. So come and sit on the floor. We're going to have a little bit of our story, and when you're settled, you'll go to the computer.

In these examples students participated in the accomplishment of themselves as excitable insofar as they displayed the projected settling down. In other situations, students accomplished themselves as excitable simply by unremarkably providing chorused or individual 'Ooh aah' responses to teacher projections of exciting activities.

Extract 5.10

17 *T:*   Now, this week, I mean, you acted in plays last week. This week we're going a bit further. This week you're going to write a play.

18 *Ks:* Ooh aah

19 *Jo:* Wow

20 *Ky:* Yeah!

In responding in this way, the students revealed themselves as the type of people who would find writing a play exciting. Considering that such writing tasks are routine in classrooms, with perhaps the only novelty being the text type, a play, the type of people who would find play writing exciting are people with limited life experience, that is, children, who have a proclivity for finding everyday things *exciting*.

    Thus far, we have detailed the documentable ways in which precompetence was consistently made relevant to the business of being both a child and a student in a primary school classroom. In the matter of precompetence, our data showed the Child–Student:

- was not incompetent but not *yet* competent;
- possessed a predilection for pretending and serendipity;
- possessed a proclivity for being excitable and kept in 'suspense'.

These three facets combined and complemented each other in reconfiguring the students as precompetent in the course of ordinary classroom interaction. Recall that precompetence was only one of the locally driven attributes we found in the whole class talk data set. The second attribute of the category Child–Student available in our data was that of being cohorted.

The Child–Student is cohorted

In the classrooms we viewed, students were talked and listened to as one party to the talk – as one body of persons associated in a common organization and acting under a common direction. To use a term coined by Payne and Hustler (1980) they were accomplished as a 'cohort'. So, although our classrooms contained up to 30 interactants at any one moment, whole class talk was routinely audible not as the multi-party talk of all these participants but as the two-party talk of one cohort (of students) and one other party (the teacher).

As with the accomplishment of precompetence, this second attribute was accomplished in and through the interactive work of *all* of the participants – specifically, in their continued unmarked orientation to the students as a collective with a name and a particular relationship with the teacher and in their orientation to the students' common purpose, knowledge and trajectory.

Extract 5.11

9 *T:*   Right, what happened to silent reading? Where's Simon?
10 *El:* He had to [get the
11 *T:*   [Oh to get that, oh yes. Is everyone here today?
12 *K:*   Yes
13 *T:*   (4) Excuse me. Emilia, read the book in silence please. (3) Who is that! Emilia, go and sit by yourself /
14 *E:*   / Jennifer
15 *T:*   Anyone with fifty cents for a raffle ticket, go out onto the verandah and buy it please. (4) Who is still mutttering? Isaac? (5) Ngoc, oh who are our messengers? Come here please Lan. Go and ask Mrs Hardy in the library (. . .) and ah Ari. You can go down to Mrs Oates and (. . .). You go to Mrs Hardy and you go to Mrs Oates. Someone is still muttering aren't they? Ngoc ah Cuong? Isaac. Isaac? Put the book down. Thank you. (5) Who is still talking? (180) Right put your books away and come and sit here. We're going to have to find a solution to that book shelf problem. Our shelf has just about fallen fallen to bits hasn't it? Right, would you come and sit close up here where you can see those sheets very clearly.
16 *Js:* Whose is this?
17 *T:*   Who owns the ruler Joshua is holding up? Lachlan, can you just sit on that chair please because I really don't feel we can have any more marks on the floor. (*S re-enters the room*) Ah, Simon, come out here please. Anyone else who feels they can't sit here on the floor without making marks on it please go away. Now, this week, I mean, you

acted in plays last week. This week we're going a bit further. This week you're going to write a play

18 *Ks:* Ooh aah

Extract 5.11 illustrates, in a compact way, how the students were reconfigured as cohorted in the course of ordinary classroom interaction. These will be explained below, but briefly, we see in the talk the following:

- particular generic interactive options available to the students within a two-party system of talk;
- the whole class of students named as a cohort;
- the engagement in synchronized actions of students;
- the marking of one or some students as being not members of the cohort;
- the whole class as a particular and current group;
- students as accountable for displaying cohort knowledge.

These facets combined and complemented each other to sustain being a member of the cohort as an attribute of the Child–Student across the sites.

The Child–Student: particular and generic interactive options

Throughout Extract 5.11, the teacher oriented to herself as having particular interactive options. In her first Turn (9), she oriented to her right to address the students as a single hearing unit and to provide a commentary on the classroom proceedings. As the sequence proceeded, she made relevant her right to do the following:

- interrupt another speaker's turn at talk (11);
- direct the talk through questioning (9, 15, and 17);
- make use of pre-topic shifts, such as 'Right', to enable a topic shift from classroom management to the planned activity (9, 15 and 17).

The teacher's own participation in the talk organized and sustained the participation of the other interactants. Indeed, according to Payne and Hustler 'in taking our own identities we are also telling others what identities to take' (1980: 54). This is what we can see in this transcript. Notably, the teacher's participation differed from that of the other interactants. For example, within the system of talk, the students were accomplished as having the responsibility to do the following:

- accept interruption (10 in which El is interrupted);
- attend to the teacher's topic shifts (9, 15, and 17);
- answer her questions (9, 15, 17);
- not interrupt her long turns at talk (15 and 17).

Throughout the segment, the students were accomplished as having reduced control over the sequence of talk in that their turns were limited, in a sense, at the direction and 'by the leave' of the teacher's turns. Above we see the students' turns to be controlled in form (answers), topic, placement and status (student turns are interruptable). Further, the students' turns were routinely relatively short, and addressed to the teacher.

This is not to argue, however, that one interactant's orientation to particular relevances or, in this case, particular interactive options, enforced a particular social organization. Indeed, the students designed their turns as short, they routinely addressed their turns to the teacher, and they routinely reacted to being interrupted unproblematically.[1] They, therefore, both created and sustained the teacher's right to initiate and terminate talk; all participants, in a sense, choreographed the turn-taking system. Just as the accomplishment of the teacher's participation organized the students' participation, so too did the accomplishment of the students' participation organize the participation of the teacher. This is what it means to say the students and teachers *interactively* accomplished the interactive options of each category of person – *together* they accomplished certain and different options for each category of person.

It is notable that inherent in the achievement of the students' interactive options as different from the teacher's was the achievement of those options as the same as each others. Furthermore, any *one* student's bid to answer will count as the answer provided by all the students. Note throughout Extract 5.11, that although the teacher addressed the students as a cohort she received answers from single speakers. Turns 11 to 13, reproduced below, demonstrate that such answers were routinely heard by all participants as the answer of the cohort.

```
11  T:   . . . Is everyone here today?
12  K:   Yes
13       (4)
```

In this example, the teacher's question was answered by one student. We can hear that the answer in Turn 12 was demonstrably heard by all participants as the answer of the whole class insofar as no other student answered as well, no other student displayed after Turn 12 that they heard that it was remarkable for one student to answer for all of them, and the teacher did not take a third turn to similarly display the unusualness of one speaker answering for everyone.

The students interact within a set of particular and generic interactive options in which the turn possibilities available to them are different from those available to the teacher and the same as each other. Integral to this is that a turn taken by any one student can count as the turn of all the students. Later we demonstrate not only that such turns count as the turn of the cohort but that each student is accountable to displaying the content of such turns as part of the knowledge of the cohort.

The Child–Student: within a named cohort

The bulk of classroom research (and those with any experience in ordinary classroom talk) concludes that it is not unusual for students to be addressed as a cohort, using for example, the class name, year level or some other collective term. We found this practice in our data; in each site, the cohort was customarily and routinely named using a variety of terms (see the emphasized terms, below).

Extract 5.12

  11 *T:* [Oh to get that, oh yes. Is **everyone** here today?
    1 *T:* All right, thank you **year three** (*claps*) listening, please . . .
163 *T:* Right, **children** . . .
    1 *T:* Come and sit down the back, please **3M**
563 *T:* Right, could **you people** come and sit on the floor . . .

In each excerpt and routinely in the whole class talk, insofar as no third turn was used to remark upon such naming, naming the students as one collection was an unremarkable way of referring to the students.

The Child–Student: engagement in synchronized action

Another commonsensically recognizable feature of classroom life is that teacher talk often elicits some physical action undertaken simultaneously by all the students. Quite differently from one student acting *for* the group of students, say, in answering a question as discussed above, it often happens also that just as the cohort is addressed, the cohort acts. Such coordinated action makes salient the groupness, that is, the common purpose and the common interactive options of the students.

Extract 5.13

  1 *T:* All right, thank you year three (*claps*) listening, please. Right, sit down, please. (*puts hands on head*)
  2 *Ss:* (*put hands on heads*)
  3 *T:* (*takes hands off head; Ss take hands of heads*) Take your hands off your head now, Kieran. In our laps please, down by our sides. We don't need to open our study skills books at the moment

13 *T:* Could I just have quiet for a moment please? Still waiting. Still waiting. (*raises hand into the air*)
14 *Ss:* (*hands raised – no talking*)
15 *T:* Thank you, put your hands down. Do not start to talk again. Listen. You're there to write a play

In Turns 2 and 14 above, the students act as one; they synchronize, such that together they act upon instruction, notably, instruction to the cohort and for the cohort, not for individuals within that cohort. In Turn 3 above we see that not acting in a synchronized manner with the cohort serves to mark one out of the cohort and has consequences. Students who breach the expectation are held accountable. Being marked out of the cohort is taken up further below, but here we note that Kieran has not lowered his hand together with his peers and is instructed individually to do so.

Students also synchronized their talk in response to explicit orders or directives.

Extract 5.14

19	*T:*	FOOD AND WATER, BECAUSE? THEY WILL GROW STRONG AND HEALTHY. Say it all together
20	*Ss:*	HAPPY ARE THOSE WHO?

482	*El:*	Elephant
483	*T:*	Elephant. And you can tell it, what order is it arranged in?
484	*Jo:*	Alphabetical order
485	*T:*	Thank you. Everyone say it. It's arranged in what order?
486	*Ss:*	Alphabetical order
487	*T:*	Right . . .

In the first excerpt, the teacher read aloud a line on the chart and directed the students to 'say' the next line on the chart 'all together'. In the second excerpt, the teacher explicitly directs the cohort to repeat the previous turn (485). In both examples, compliance occurred and was unmarked.

We also find coordinated responses to solicitations; specifically, in the teacher design of the turn as an unfinished sentence,

Extract 5.15

68	*T:*	A bear. What are they all?
69	*Ss:*	Animals
70	*T:*	They're all?
71	*Ss:*	Animals
72	*T:*	Right, they're all animals . . .

or in the use of intonation that suggests a relevant or correct answer.

Extract 5.16

105	*T:*	All right? Does everyone agree with that? We'll start with the characters?

106 *Ss:* Yes
107 *T:* Right, your job is to think up interesting characters . . .

It is the upward intonation at the end of 'Does everyone agree with that?', 'We'll start with the characters?' and 'They're all?' which audibly solicits the given answers. An approximation of what these excerpts sounded like will be easily fashioned in the mind of most teachers and students. Note again that student compliance was unmarked.

The unproblematic realization of teacher projections of synchronized action (both action and talk as action) in the ways detailed above was a common feature of our whole class corpus. Students' compliance with these directives accomplished them as one coordinated body. That no turns at talk marked the synchronicity as out of the ordinary allows us to assess that the achievement of the students as one cohort through synchronization of the students' actions is routine.

The Child–Student: orientation to some as not members of the cohort

The student cohort exists in particular times to enact a particular range of activities. Appropriate membership of a cohort is a matter of concern to the members on the scene in that attributes which mark an individual as outside the cohort are noted and made the subject of further action. In some circumstances, then, individual students are oriented to as acting outside of the cohort's purposes and duties. The unremarkable orientation to some students as not being members of the cohort accomplished those students as not-cohorted and, as well, the other students *as* cohorted.

In Extract 5.11, presented earlier, the teacher provided a running commentary on the progress of the silent reading session in terms of breaches of the normalized activity by either someone unknown (for example, 'Who is still muttering?'(15) and 'Who is still talking?' (15)) or by someone in particular (for example, 'Emilia, read the book in silence' (13) and 'Isaac. Isaac? Put the book down' (15)). These students were audibly oriented to as breaching the activity of silent reading and were accomplished as acting outside of the common purpose of the cohort. They were thereby named as not being members of the cohort. By the same token, those students *not* muttering and *not* personally named were achieved as operating *as* a member of the cohort.

To be not-cohorted is troublesome and, further, needs repair. We know this because being not-cohorted was oriented to in the talk as in need of restoration to the usual 'being' a member of the cohort. The accomplishment of Emilia as not-cohorted in turn 13 in the same example provides an illustration of this.

13 *T:* Excuse me. Emilia, read the book in silence please. (3) Who is that! Emilia, go and sit by yourself . . .

At the beginning of Turn 13, Emilia was accomplished as not reading silently insofar as she was accomplished as the person whose action had projected the teacher utterance, 'Excuse me'. Her action was nominated as troublesome in the directive to 'read the book in silence', in other words, in the directive to make relevant her membership of the cohort (who were reading silently). However, just three seconds later, Emilia audibly – from the teacher's perspective – doubly refused to read in silence and was physically distanced from the cohort. Such ejection highlights this student's non-cohort behaviour and underlines her non-member status for this moment. Furthermore, insofar as other students *remain* in the group, they are sustained *as* members of the cohort.

The Child–Student: member of a particular and current group

The student cohort is *particular* and *current*. It is not just as *any* group but is particularly *this current* group. If we continue from the end of Turn 17 in Extract 5.11, above, we find the participants orienting to the current talk as a resumption, or another instance, of the group being the particular group that they are.

17 *T:*   . . . Now, this week, I mean, you acted in plays last week. This week we're going a bit further. This week you're going to write a play.
18 *Ks:* Ooh aah
19 *Jo:* Wow
20 *Ky*   Yeah!
21 *T:*   And of course when you've written the play, you can act in it. Last week you acted very very well. And next door thought your plays were great, didn't they? They really liked them.

In Turn 17, the teacher oriented to a specific previous activity and established the link between 'then' and 'now' (i.e. 'we're going to go a bit further'). The teacher's orientation to the activities was not displayed as remarkable by either the teacher or the students, the participants interactively accomplishing the current situation as a resumption of the current group's interaction and, as such, as another instance of the group being this current group. Note that as the teacher continued her turn at talk, she accomplished a 'move' from 'last week' through 'this week' and into the future, 'when you've written the play you can act in it'. She thereby oriented to the members of the cohort as having a shared trajectory, that is, as history, present and future. In the orientation to their shared future, the students were prospectively provided with the resources to hear the projected future interaction as a resumption of *this current* group.

In our data, such resuming talk routinely oriented not to specific individuals but rather to the students as a category, as a cohort of students. Payne and Hustler argued that this provides for 'the non-consequential absence or presence of any *one* of them on this occasion' (1980: 56). And we saw precisely this in our data – the accomplishment of the current group as 'last week's group' as well as 'the future group' glossed over any changes to the actual composition of the group. Consequently, the possibility that one or some students who were in the group last time may not currently be present, or who were not in the group last time may currently be present, or who were currently present may not be present in the future, or who will be present in the future, may not be in the current group was largely irrelevant to the accomplishment of the current group as a single set.

The Child–Student: accountable for displaying cohort knowledge

The many facets of cohorting of the Child–Student are drawn together in the accountability of each individual student to displays of the class's cohort knowledge.

Extract 5.17

33 *T:*   Exactly, you had to read the script, and how did you know when it was your turn? (2) Well, come on, you've all read the script. How did you know when it was your turn to say something
34 *Ma:* It had the name of it?
35 *T:*   It had the name . . .

In this example, the teacher heard the pause in Turn 33 as a missing answer which the current group, with the known experience of reading the script, accountably knew and, thus, were able to display. Therefore, the ascription of an activity as something the cohort had experienced accomplished the students as being accountable for having *had* the experience and for being able to display their knowledge of that experience. In such an environment, inability to display this knowledge might, predictably, be encountered as troublesome.

Extract 5.18

5 *T:*   So, let's say our poem together. You ready? See if you can say it with expression and remember how we used to say it. One, two
6 *Ss:* (*various*)
7 *T:*   [Oh stop. What did we forget already?
8 *Br:* We didn't say the title
9 *T:*   We didn't say the title and we didn't say? Who?

This example shows the routine way in which such trouble in displaying cohort knowledge was recast as a problem of memory rather than knowing. Throughout our whole class data, the relevance made of remembering reinstated the group as the current group and allowed a trouble-free orientation to the accountability of the students for knowing the cohort knowledge. 'Remembering' might also excuse any particular individual who was not present at the time from being accountable to the cohort knowledge.

Child–Student – different inflections

We have seen, thus far, how the Child–Student attributes of precompetence and being cohorted were ordinarily accomplished in whole class talk. Although we make a detailed review of the enactment of the Child–Student at these sites, we do not suggest that these two were the only relevant attributes of the student participants on this scene; nor do we argue that the attributes of Child–Student accomplished in and through talk in even one primary classroom are necessarily internally consistent. As with any ethnomethodological analyses, our aim is to document what is routine and unremarkable rather than what is most frequent. Ethnomethodology does not find inconsistency troublesome and makes no attempt to iron flat the data to produce one wrinkle-free answer. With this in mind, we now briefly consider the idea that different inflections of the precompetent, cohorted Child–Student can be invoked for different students in virtually the same teaching moment.

In the following two examples, taken from one site, we see the routine enactment of distinctions between students. The distinctions were drawn between students on what turns out to be quite usual grounds – namely, polarizing one or another student on the grounds of his/her productiveness with respect to the activity at hand.

Extract 5.19 (a)

173	*T:*	Right what happened for 'c'?
174	*Ln:*	COMET
175	*Gm:*	CRATER
176	*Mi:*	CONSTELLATION
177	*Jo:*	COSMONAUT
178	*Ha:*	COLLISION? (*pronounced coll-ish-on*)
179	*T:*	What are you talking about?
180	*Ha:*	When two things crash together
181	*T:*	Collision (*correct pronunciation*) When two things bash into each other you have a collision, and they seem to have a lot of those out in space, don't they? Yes, good word. Anything else?

Extract 5.19 (b)

296	*T:*	. . . Right Lachlan you start
297	*Ll:*	He has um? =
298	*T:*	= Um who are you starting with?
299	*Ll:*	Super?

300 *T:*   Yes, superant, yes?
301 *Ll:* He has ten eyes?
302 *T:*   But why is that a problem?
303 *Ll:* (*shrugs shoulders*)
304 *T:*   See, we're talking about the problem they're having. We're not talking about what they look like. All right? Jennifer?

In these sequences of talk, very different work is done by the students and the teacher with the answers of Hoa and Lachlan. In (a), in Turn 180, Hoa displayed that she heard the teacher's question (179) as a real question, that is, as a request for more information. In Turn 303, however, Lachlan did not display a hearing of the teacher's question as a request for more information. Lachlan did not, for example, provide an account of why having ten eyes would be a problem for Superant. In response to Hoa's answer, the teacher, in Turn 181, sustains Hoa's hearing of the question as demonstrated in her answer at 180, treating Hoa's answer as troublesome but repairable, that is, she corrects Hoa's pronunciation and repeats Hoa's definition, with a minor change. In Lachlan's case, however, the teacher's response, at Turn 304, to his answer at Turn 303, while sustaining Lachlan's hearing of the teacher question, that is, hearing Lachlan's shrug as an answer to her question rather than, say, a non-hearing, treats his answer as irreparably troublesome, that is, as evidence of trouble beyond the scope of his answer, in this case, evidence he has not understood the task itself.

In the space of just a few moments, then, two students were attributed as being different types of student. Hoa was credited with knowing what the task was and being able to understand and talk about her approach to the activity. Lachlan, however, was credited with neither knowing nor understanding what the task was and as being inarticulate on the matter of his approach to the activity.

Although the example is here from one site, it was routine in our data that students whose actions were accomplished as productive of the set task were unremarkably attributed with being productive students. By the same token, students whose actions were accomplished as counterproductive of the set task were unremarkably attributed with being counterproductive students.

Our main point here is that in comparing the two excerpts, both 'What are you talking about?' and 'But why is that a problem?' are audible either as real questions requesting more information *or* as queries about the relevance of the answer to the original question. Therefore, there was a structural move by the participants to accomplish Hoa's answer, 'Collision?', as problematic yet relevant to and therefore productive of the current group activity. There was also a structural move by the participants to accomplish Lachlan's answer, 'He has ten eyes?', as problematic, irrelevant to and counterproductive of the current group activity. Note that the point here is not Lachlan's intent, that is, whether he really was or was not providing a description or a problem. Our point is about the work that is done by all participants to hear answers in different ways.

Conclusion

In examining the category Child–Student as accomplished in classrooms, we found the Child–Student of whole class talk to be both precompetent and cohorted. We detailed the achievement of precompetence in terms of the interactive accomplishment of the following:

- students as not incompetent but not yet competent (e.g. in the orientation to student action and product as displays of 'trying' or as pending teacher validation as correct);
- students' predilection for pretence and serendipity (e.g. in the routine direction for students to pretend, and in routine orientation to classroom situations as the result of unexpected good luck);
- students' proclivity for being kept in suspense and being excitable (e.g. in the use of wait-and-see techniques as well as explicit references to the students as being too excited and needing to be settled).

We also detailed the achievement of cohorting in terms of the interactive accomplishment of these elements:

- particular interactive options for the students as a group (e.g. the routine way in which the teachers directed the classroom talk while students complied);
- the whole class as a named cohort (e.g. the unremarkable naming of the students as a collection of people using names such as 'year three' and 'you');
- student synchronized action (e.g. teacher directions for all students to stand or raise their hand);
- some students as non-members of the cohort, (e.g. the orientation to students' breaches of the normativities of the group and/or the physical removal of a breaching student from the gathered group);
- students as members of a particularly 'this' group, (e.g. the enactment of resuming practices which enable the students to view themselves as having a shared history, present and future);
- students as accountable for displaying cohort knowledge, (e.g. the enactment of students forgetting rather than not knowing given information).

Although, as indicated earlier, attributional work is not necessarily done by and for all students in a unitary way, our analyses show that there were comparabilities between the two sites on the matter of this attributional work. Moreover, our analyses indicate that the orientation by participants to the relevance of the attributes of precompetence and being cohorted ensured that the students enacted Child–Student in the course of whole class talk and interaction. Across the sites we found consistent features in the whole class talk that directly inform the institutional shaping of the Child. It is worth re-emphasizing that these features were always jointly produced: That is, the students themselves routinely took active part in the accomplishment of specific features of childhood in their concerted efforts to 'bring off' lessons. There were, however, other features of the interactive rights and responsibilities pertaining to classroom life that distinguished the classrooms we studied, and it is to these that we now turn.

6 The classroom child
Variations on a theme

Introduction

Some presuppositions about being a school student were explored in Chapter 5. We documented the twin accomplishments of precompetence and cohort membership ordinarily and routinely oriented to in whole class talk in the two schools we studied. Here we examine the whole class corpuses separately comparing the category work done in the two sites and documenting the distinctive attributes of the Child–Student operable in each school. Classroom interactions revealed a distinction between the attributes of the category Child–Student in terms of what was interactively achieved as the normativities of the cohort. In particular, what the students were accountable for knowing, their interactive options *vis-à-vis* the teacher, what counted as working and, what counted as being a worker were defined and achieved differently in each school. This chapter moves between the two sites, between St Luke's School and Aralia College, to document each site's particular inflection of the Child–Student.

Classroom Child–Student: distinctive knowledges

Summary statements articulate what it is that everyone now knows.

Extract 6.1

1 *T:* What, in your opinion, is really important in life? What things are really important? What things do you think in life are really important? For instance, is chewing gum important?

2 *Ss:* No

3 *T:* You don't think chewing gum is important? How about? Having parents to look after you? (*raises hand*)

4 *Ss:* (*hands raised*)

5 *T:* Is it? (*lowers hand*) Okay. So obviously you've all got some ideas about what you think's important. Because you certainly knew one thing that you did think was important and you thought another wasn't

Such statements provide a neat précis of what the participants in the talk are normatively accountable for knowing. When not refuted, they stand as the accepted version of events. In this example, the students were accomplished as accountable for knowing what was important and what was not important.

We can examine what it was that students were taken to *not* know by turning our attention to what was explained in great detail, that is, procedures or knowledges that were over-specified, in the classroom. We found that in the teacher talk at St Luke's, the strategies students should or could employ to properly use their brains received a great deal of attention,

Extract 6.2

1 T: First of all. To do this you have to do some imagining and if you're imagining you have to sit very still. Your body has to be still to give your brain has a chance to hear the work. Sometimes when you're trying to imagine it's very helpful if you close your eyes, because that allows you to concentrate better. If you don't want to close your eyes, sometimes it's a good idea to look down into your hands or something. So that what's happening around you doesn't stop your brain from concentrating on what you want it to think. You really need to get this picture in your mind if you're going to do this activity

as did working properly in a group.

Extract 6.3

1 T: Because when we finish talking about this I'm going to ask you to go and, um, do something in a group. And you know what it's like in a group. It's important in a group that everyone in the group knows what they have to do and helps as best they can . . .

5 T: Now, one person in the group can write, remember the writer writes what you tell them to write . . . But I do want you to take time to write down everything that someone in your group thinks is important. Okay? If someone says, oh look, I think this is important, and you say, oh that's not important! Is that the way to go about it?
6 Ss: No
7 T: No, it's not. Now make sure everyone does get a chance to say what they do think is important. And to write down the things that everyone in the group thinks are really important in life. Now I'd like everyone to really try.

Over-specification audibly simplifies and amplifies situations, one hearing being that the over-specification is designed such that those with limited experiences and capacities can understand. In the over-specification, here, of details of thinking and of working in small groups, the teacher accomplishes the students as having limited knowledge of how to do these things. Again, consider the test of recipient design: 'Would this level of specification be provided to someone who knows how to think and how to work in a group?'

So the Child–Student of the St Luke's classroom was accomplished as knowing *about* the topic of the set task but requiring precise and lengthy instructions on how to organize their bodies in order to use their brains, how to think and how to work cooperatively with other students.

The Aralia College Child–Student was also accomplished as knowledgeable about the topic of the set task.

Extract 6.4

116　*T:*　But what I'd like you to do is think of some animals that you could use to write another verse for this song
117　*So:*　I know one
118　*T:*　Now there's lots and lots [of animals
119　*Jl:*　[Snake (. . .)
120　*T:*　I'm not going to write them all on the board, I want you to think of them for yourself. The other thing /

124　*T:*　. . . The other thing I want you do to, is to write down something that that animal could be thankful for. So you're going to end up with two lists. One list, that has the animals, and beside that, the word or whatever it is that animal could be thankful for. It could be a part of their body, a naming word. It could be an action that they can do. Okay something that they can do, that makes them (. . .)

Throughout the talk in this example, the students were accomplished as able to think of animals to be inserted into the verses of the song. They were also accomplished as knowing and being able to write down positive characteristics of their chosen animals. Essentially, they were oriented to as able to fulfil the cognitive requirements of the task, as able to do the activity. What these students needed help with, by virtue of its unremarkable over-specification was the organization of their workbooks.

Extract 6.5 (a)

150　*T:*　. . . What you're going to do, I'm going to give you each one of these. I'm going to give you each one of these and this is going to be for your good copy. That's why you need your rough copy book. In your rough copy book you have your have-a-go page. So you have two pages, side by side, your have-a-go page on one side, and the other side for your rough copy. On your have-a-go page you can start by writing down some animals. You don't have to write down all the animals you can think of . . .

Extract 6.5 (b)

245   *T:*   . . . now they're only little columns and it's best to have the questions and answers side by side, so when you start a new questions and a new answer, will you start on a new line please so that, leave a line, answer your question, um, ask your question and leave enough space for the answer and then, leave line before you write your next question.

Throughout the Aralia College whole class corpus, the talk made relevant precise and particular ways of setting out work – exactly where to rule lines, exactly how wide columns should be and precisely where to start and stop writing.

The Aralia College Child–Student, then, knew about the *topic* of the set task (animals and their attributes) but in the over-specification of the procedures for organizing their work books, they were accomplished as students who were in need of such detailed instruction. In comparison, St Luke's students, although similarly accomplished as having the content knowledge, were oriented to as needing tutelage, not in logistics, but in the strategies for accessing that content knowledge and in how to work with others.

In Chapter 5, we drew attention to the interactive options of primary classroom participants, for example, the teacher interrupting, the students listening to relatively longer teacher turns at talk, the students' provisional answers pending validation by the teacher – routinely accomplished by all classroom participants and exemplified below,

Extract 6.6

221   *T:*   . . . I wonder what we could say about at the front counter, now remember I want information. Pretend I don't know anything. What sort of things could you say Joel?
222   *Jl:*   You buy things there?
223   *T:*   AT THE FRONT COUNTER people can?
224   *Mg:*   Help [you
225   *T:*   [Buy what? (*points to Olivia*)
226   *Ov:*   Stamps
227   *T:*   Just stamps?
228   *Ss:*   No (*various answers*)
229   *Ch:*   [Box, the boxes
230   *Kr:*   [Envelopes
231   *T:*   Oh hands up. You can buy? Max?
232   *Mx:*   You can buy those um those book things like =
233   *T:*   / Stamp collecting kits?

234 *Mx:*   Yes
235 *T:*   Stamp collecting kits

A consideration of the way this segment of talk *continued* provides purchase on the distinctive interactive options that were made available to the students at Aralia College and, therefore, also on the distinctive features of that site's category Child–Student.

Extract 6.7

250 *T:*   All right? Things like that. You might be able to think up some other things that are at the front counter. Also at the front counter I can get information. I can get some information. If I want to know something, or I can post a parcel. Can't I?

251 *Ss:*   Yes

252 *T:*   Yes, I could take a parcel and post it.

253 *Be:*   But

254 *T:*   Yes I can, if I've got a big parcel I want to post overseas. I can't put it in the letter box

255 *Be:*   Yes you can, there's a thing, you pull down

256 *T:*   A big one like this? (*holds hands out to illustrate size*)

257 *Be:*   Yeah

258 *T:*   A big parcel?

259 *Ss:*   (*talking to other students*)

260 *Be:*   (. . .) inside it though

261 *T:*   Pardon?

262 *Be:*   (. . .)

263 *T:*   Well, I posted one, I posted one to Japan just the other day. I have a Japanese student at my house

265 *Au:*   How big was it?

266 *T:*   Max, please don't play with that, I had, it was about this, a box, this big, and she was sending some things home to Japan because her bag was so heavy that she doesn't want to have to pay excess baggage. So she took it to the post office and it was weighed and then they said, this will cost sixty-one dollars to post to Japan

267 *Ss:*   Wow

268 *T:*   Hmm. It was air mail, so that means, that's the fastest sort of mail

269 *Ov:*   Who paid for it?

270 *T:*   And then he had to stamp, she did, had to stamp it and get it sent

271 *Au:*   First class

272 *T:*   No air mail

273 *Be:*   They don't have first class mail

274 *Ss:*   (. . .)

275 *T:*   It's a bit different. I suppose it's like, I suppose it is like first class air mail
276 *Ss:* (*Ss talking to one another*)
277 *T:*   Right. So. Let's get back to what we're .
278 *Ss:* (*Ss talking to one another*)
279 *T:*   Let's get back to the front counter, so we can buy some things, that's the goods. The services are things like, we could ask information. We can post parcels and things like that. We can also . . .

Notable here are the particular interactive options afforded by and to the students. In this segment, and routinely through the Aralia College corpus, the students were accomplished as having the right to ask questions of the teacher (265 and 269), engage in two-way conversations with the teacher (252–263), talk to other students (271 and 273; 274, 276 and 278) and disagree with the teacher (253, 260, 262). The participation of the students at Aralia College, therefore, routinely looked and sounded like classroom talk (see Extract 6.6), but was also routinely peppered with other participant options – teacher as interruptee, student as questioner, initiator and evaluator. By contrast, St Luke's school talk routinely mirrored the talk-in-interaction exemplified in Extract 6.6.

Classroom Child–Student: distinctive normativities of working

It would seem likely that what is considered 'getting a task done' is an absolute rather than relative concept within primary classrooms. However, the matter of what counted as actually getting the work done in the classroom was a point of distinction between the two sites. Not surprisingly, in both sites the successful undertaking of the set task unremarkably counted as working. However, at Aralia College, perhaps paradoxically, we found that not doing the set task was also routinely nominated as acceptable, if initially troublesome. In short, not having completed the set task routinely counted as doing the work.

Extract 6.8 (a)

675 *Ml:* I didn't finish
676 *T:*   That doesn't matter. There wasn't much time was there?

Extract 6.8 (b)

49 *Bt:*   . . . I haven't wroten (*sic*) down what Jesus said
50 *T:*   Not enough room? Oh you don't have to, doesn't matter

In these excerpts, both Mitchell's and Brittany's working-products were accomplished as counting as adequate even though they were named, respectively, as not finished and incomplete. In each case, no student explanation was called for but, rather, accounts of their incompleteness were provided by the teacher: in the first excerpt, in terms of time and in the second, in terms of space on the paper. In each, therefore, the teacher alluded to practical circumstances, outside the actual task itself that rendered the work complete for the purposes of the activity.

However, for the students at Aralia College, even though *incomplete* work was acceptable as work, *not starting* the required task was routinely marked as a breach of the normativities of the classroom.

Extract 6.9

553	*T:*	. . . I will help you with it later (*walks away from the whole-class group to the teacher-desk; Bronte follows*)
554	*Br:*	I haven't started in mine
555	*T:*	Have you written the names of your animals?
556	*Br:*	No
557	*T:*	What have you been doing, Bronte?
558	*Br:*	I did do some there
559	*T:*	All this time and you've done nothing. Well, Bronte, at lunchtime could you come up, at lunchtime could you come upstairs please? And you can do this in your lunchtime. . . .

Notably, the teacher did not locate the problem, as she had done in the previous example, in a lack of resources (needing more time or paper). Nor did she locate the problem in Bronte's capacity to do the task (for example, by orienting to Bronte as, perhaps, needing teacher assistance). Rather, in Turn 557, the teacher located the problem in Bronte's choice of (in)activity. Bronte heard the teacher's question at Turn 557 as displaying the teacher's hearing that Bronte had done nothing and replied that she 'did do some there'. The teacher nominated the work that Bronte 'did do' as 'nothing' in Turn 559. This time no account was called for or provided. The teacher completed her turn and audibly closed the sequence of talk with a directive for Bronte to do the activity during her lunchtime.

In contrast to Extract 6.8 (a) and (b), in which the teacher alluded to the circumstances that rendered the students' work complete for the purposes of the activity, in this excerpt the teacher alluded to the circumstance that rendered Bronte's work inadequate and thus incomplete. That circumstance was nominated as Bronte's own choice to not even begin the task. This example illustrates the routine way in which, in the Aralia College lessons, work nominated as incomplete was accomplished as an individual work output problem and, moreover, as having individual and personal consequences for the student whose work was so accomplished (see also Freiberg and Freebody 1995: 228).

Just as what counted as completing a task might have seemed definite and pre-specified, what counts as talk relevant to a specific classroom activity may seem, at first consideration, a given. Yet the topics that were oriented to as relevant to given activities constituted another distinction between the two sites. Throughout the St Luke's corpus, personal anecdotes, information about families and talk about life outside of the parameters of the class were routinely nominated as 'non-set task talk'. Moreover, as exemplified in the following excerpt, such talk was routinely nominated as counterproductive of the current task.

Extract 6.10

189 *S:*   Mrs Milne, is Santa Claus your mum? Is your mum Santa? Mrs Milne, is your mum Santa?

190 *T:*   We'll talk about Santa at Christmas time, come on get on with this please. (20) Yes?

191 *Ha:* How do you spell disciples?

192 *T:*   Yes that's a hard one isn't it? 'd' 'i' 's' 'c' 'i' 'p' 'l' 'e' 's'. 'l' 'e' 's'. DISCIPLES. (68)

193 *S:*   Mrs Milne is Santa Claus =

194 *T:*   = Why are you on Santa Claus? Is that what you're writing about there?

195 *S:*   No

196 *T:*   Well, would you keep your mind on what you're doing there please? I think you've made a very, very wonderful start, now keep going. Don't mention Santa Claus again please, the subject is closed. Now you've made a beautiful start to your talk, keep going with it . . .

In this example, the teacher initially oriented to talk about Santa Claus as temporally inappropriate and subsequently oriented to such talk as impeding or interfering with what the student was currently writing. In line three of Turn 196, she audibly terminated the topic of Santa Claus. The teacher, therefore, heard the talk about Santa Claus as a topic shift *away* from the set task talk. Moreover, she oriented to such a shift as a breach of the normalized activity.

In contrast, in the Aralia College corpus, a variety of topics were routinely oriented to *as* relevant to and productive of the current activity, and thus achieved as 'set task talk'. In the next transcript, details of the teacher's home life are generated as logical and unremarkable facets of talk during group activities (see also Extract 6.7, Turn 263, above).

Extract 6.11

50 *T:*   I wonder how a dog laughs

51 *Be:* My dog laughs

52 *Sa:* By wagging his tail

53 *T:*   My sister had a dog

54 *Be:* Don't tell me it died

55 *T:* No, my sister had a dog and all they had to say was laugh and he would open his mouth and showed all his teeth, right across here, every single one and then he would make a funny laughing sound

56 *Be:* My dog can sit

57 *T:* I wonder, oh who has a dog

Details of students' home lives were also oriented to as relevant to the talk in and around whole class activities at Aralia College.

Extract 6.12

3 *T:* . . . Now share it with Perre please, because he wasn't here. That was when he was away overseas. Lucky boy. In Europe. For ten weeks or something

4 *Be:* No twelve weeks

5 *T:* Twelve weeks. All right. Put your hand up if you cannot see a copy . . .

73 *T:* . . . They can't just have any dog, specially trained dogs

74 *Be:* My dog's trained

75 *Wl:* My friends, they've got a duck and

76 *T:* A duck?

77 *Wl:* Yeah, (. . .)

78 *T:* Oh a goose

79 *Wl:* And it's like, everyday it can wander around the garden and one day um he was going down the drive (. . .) and they heard this crunch and then he went (. . .) and he hit him and the goose went aghh

80 *T:* A honk honk sound

81 *Wl:* And then he drove back up and then um (. . .) wing, so he took him to the vet and he had a broken wing so they had to (. . .) and they had to spend about two hundred and fifty dollars to get the wing fixed and now he looks like lopsided and he walks around all lopsided

82 *T:* Can I ask you something? So why did you think about a goose, when we were talking about dogs?

83 *Wl:* Because um the same thing happened =

84 *T:* = As in the story, what happened to the dog. So a similar thing happened to the goose, happened to the dog

In the first excerpt, the teacher marked details of Perre's European holiday as relevant to the business of sharing classroom resources. In the second, the participants oriented to the relevance of William's lengthy story about a friend's goose being run over to the current discussion of dogs. Note that in Turns 78 and 80, the teacher displayed her hearing of the propriety of the story insofar as she does not mark it as irrelevant. Moreover, in Turn 82, the teacher calls for an account of William's relating of the story and in Turn 84 elaborates William's account to designate his telling as a logical sequitur to the story which had been read to the group (about dog that was run over). The point here is not whether or not the story was in reality related to the group discussion, but that there were a number of structural moves made by the participants over ten turns at talk to accomplish William's talk *as* relevant. These excerpts illustrate the routine orientation to personal anecdote and information about family life as relevant to, and productive of, both the whole class and the student group talk in the Aralia College corpus. Such talk is therefore accomplished, in the talk, as talk relating to the activity or task, that is, as 'set task talk'.

What we have here, then, is a situation where in one site (St Luke's) actually doing the allocated activity and talking only about a range of topics described by the teacher counted as appropriate involvement in the classroom work while in the other site (Aralia) not actually completing the allocated activity and talking about a seemingly indeterminate range of topics counted as satisfactory involvement in the classroom work.

Another layer of difference was also discernible; just as what counted as doing a task and what counted as talking about a task differed, so too did what counted as being productive in the classroom. In particular, at Aralia College being productive comprised engaging in the task in the face of practical obstacles such as lack of time or space while counterproductiveness comprised choosing to do something other than the current set task and not following the teacher's directives. In contrast, productiveness at St Luke's School comprised understanding what the current task was and understanding one's own role in that task, while counterproductiveness comprised not understanding the task or one's own role in it (see Extract 5.19(a) and (b)).

Classroom Child–Student: distinctive normativities of being a worker

Working together vs working individually

The nature of the students' relationships with one another as workers differed in the two school sites. At St Luke's School, students routinely worked together on tasks whereas at Aralia College students ordinarily worked on tasks individually. At St Luke's School, end products were routinely made accountable as *one* text that was comprised of the contributions of each and every group member. End products at St Luke's were, in one instance, described by the teacher as comprising 'everything that someone in your group thinks is important' and 'the things that everyone in the group thinks are really important in life'. In contrast, the students at Aralia College in similarly routine situations were attributed with being completers of individual work. For example, in Extract 6.5 (a), Turn 150, above, the teacher oriented to the idea that the students would each be given their own activity sheet to enable them to complete the activity. She stated, 'I'm going to give you each one of these. I'm going to give you each one of these and this is going to be for your good copy.' In the same turn at talk, the teacher also made relevant the precise organization of the students' individual rough or draft writing books. Routinely in the Aralia College data, the end product was to be the work of individual students. Thus, the Aralia College Child–Student was an individual completer of his or her own work while the Child–Student operable at St Luke's was a contributing member of a small group.

The relevance of an individual student's work *to* that student was signified in the whole class talk at Aralia College with, for example, the teacher routinely exhorting the students to write their name on their work and by students unremarkably complying with this request.

Extract 6.13

157 T: . . . What's the first thing we do? (*reads from chart*) CHECK YOUR WORK. NUMBER ONE, IS YOUR NAME ON THE PAPER? So as soon as you get this sheet could you put your name on the paper and the date is the twentieth of October . . .

159 T: . . . What's the first thing you're going to do Kate?

160 Kt: Write your name

161 T: Write your name. Write your name, and the date . . .

Even in situations in which the students were working in small groups with other children, the teacher made relevant the importance of each student's name appearing on the worksheet – furthermore, set out in such a way as to indicate the major and minor contributors.

Extract 6.14

234 T: . . . And so I know whose is who, you can put your name on this line and write the name of your partner underneath. So Charlotte you will write your name here (*points*) and Susanna's below. Susanna, you will write your name on the line and Charlotte's below. That way I will know whose sheet it is and I will also know who you worked with. Okay?

The orientation by the teacher to the relevance of being able to discern which worksheet had been completed by which student effectively projected the work of individual students as the required and assessable end product.

Being responsible vs not being responsible

At St Luke's school, students clearly had responsibilities to each other as co-workers in the classroom.

Extract 6.15

94	*T:*	(*nods*) Right. Bring your work out to share it please. If you've got any sense you'll be first out here, right underneath the fan
95	*Ky:*	(. . .)
96	*T:*	Not again?
97	*Ky:*	Yes
98	*T:*	Look, I don't want to even talk to you. I'm disgusted with you. It was bad enough that you didn't bring it yesterday. How are your group getting on with you forgetting things all the time
99	*Ky:*	I've been learning what to say
100	*T:*	Yes, but what about the rest of your group? No it's not your script, it's their script. Now have it here tomorrow please, without fail. Right

In this exchange, the script was made relevant as the property of the group and not as the property of one member of the group. It therefore oriented to the rights of the group members over their working-product (i.e. the right to access it) and, as well, to the responsibilities of individual students in whose possession that group product was (i.e. the responsibility to bring it to school). Furthermore, the property of the group was made relevant as being implicated in the ongoing and future work of the group.

Various facets of being responsible for end products and works in progress were regularly over-specified at St Luke's School. The students were thereby routinely attributed with lacking knowledge about the responsibilities associated with their written work.

Extract 6.16

189	*Ar:*	Will we be allowed to type it?
190	*T:*	Well, if you want to take it home and type it up on the computer, or have you got a type-writer or something?
191	*Ar:*	Yes
192	*T:*	Well, if you want to do that, you'll have to ask the rest of the group if it's all right. Um, they might want to look it over and make sure. Excuse me. They might want to look it over and make sure there aren't any mistakes before you type it. And they will be depending on you to bring that copy back tomorrow, because they won't be able to go on with it if you leave it at home. Okay? So it's up to your group, if they think you're dependable and if they want you to do that. But that's totally up to the group . . .

In her relatively lengthy and detailed response to the question of whether students could take the script home, the teacher oriented to the relevance of a number of factors to any decision about allowing one group member to take the script home: asking the permission of the other students; ensuring all are satisfied with the work as it stands; being aware that the script will be needed the next day; and the dependability of the student who seeks to take the script home.

In this turn at talk, the teacher effectively accomplished ownership rights for all group members, and oriented to the idea that joint ownership elicits not only rights but also responsibilities. She therefore attributed the students with having the right to have their collective product protected, with having a responsibility to other group members *vis-à-vis* their relationship to the product, and with being responsible for the group product.

In contrast, students at Aralia College were not routinely accomplished as responsible for working or end products. At Aralia College, routinely, responsibility lay with the teacher.

Extract 6.17

30	*T:*	. . . Where's your rough copy book?
31	*Bt:*	You, you got it off me
32	*T:*	I've got it, have I? That's the standard answer, isn't it? If you can't find it, the teacher's got it (*in an amused tone*)
33	*Bt:*	Cause I gave you it to look at my um that um Papa Panov's special day
34	*Ch:*	(. . .)
35	*Bt:*	(. . .) (*laugh*) Right let's get to work. I better rub that out
81	*T:*	What did you do Papa Panov in last week?
82	*Bt:*	In my rough copy cause my good copy's in my desk
83	*T:*	Well, if you did Papa Panov in your rough copy book, where's your rough copy book?
84	*Bt:*	I gave it to you
85	*T:*	After Papa Panov?
86	*Bt:*	You took it up
87	*Ch:*	I got mine back
88	*T:*	I put them all back on the desks. Oh well you keep working on that. (*teacher moves away from Brittany*) How are you going, Cilla?

This segment is illustrative of the routine way in which a piece of work that was apparently lost was accomplished as no one's responsibility. In Turn 31, above, Brittany oriented to the absence of her rough copy book as the teacher's responsibility. The teacher, in facetiously orienting to it as her own responsibility in Turn 32, audibly oriented to it as, accountably, Brittany's responsibility. However, in the next Turn (33), Brittany restated that the onus for knowing where it was lay with the teacher. Similarly in the next sequence (from Turn 83), the responsibility for the absent book was audibly volleyed. Each speaker successively ascribing the responsibility to the other and neither claiming it. The relevance of this sequence to the present section is the ultimate achievement of Brittany as neither responsible nor accountable for the safe keeping of her own book.

A similar transference of responsibility occurs in the exchange presented below.

Extract 6.18

418 *Jl:*   Where'd you put my hymn book?
419 *T:*   It should be in your desk, Julia, I haven't collected your hymn books up this week (*moves to Julia's desk and rummages through it with Julia.* (3) *Picks up a book and hands it to Julia*)

In this excerpt, Julia oriented to her missing book as the teacher's responsibility, the teacher oriented to it as Julia's responsibility and provided an account of why it was not her responsibility. The teacher therefore displayed that it was normative for her to provide an account of why she didn't know where Julia's book was, that, on this occasion, she was not responsible for its absence. Note that in rummaging through Julia's desk and apparently locating the missing item the teacher instated herself *as* responsible for finding Julia's book for her. Therefore, in contrast to St Luke's School, where students were rendered always responsible for their school books and written products, at Aralia College students were routinely attributed with having little or no responsibility for the safe keeping of such materials.

Surveilling each other vs not surveilling each other

Routinely in the St Luke's corpus, the teacher publicly commented in either positive or negative terms on individual student action and interaction. She therefore made the regulation, management and, in some cases, discipline of every student relevant to each and every other student. In doing so, she oriented to the relevance to the whole class of its surveillance of individual students.

Extract 6.19

198 *T:*   . . . Ngoc? Bit disappointing to see you playing instead of thinking

Extract 6.20

76 *T:*   Joshua, I can't imagine you've put down very much. Every time I look, you're playing

In these excerpts, the teacher publicly oriented to the students' action as 'playing' and, moreover, nominated 'playing' and 'thinking', and 'playing' and 'put(ting very much) down' as mutually exclusive categories. In making such comments to the whole class, the teacher audibly accomplished Ngoc's and

Joshua's actions as breaching the normativities of the classroom practices, and, importantly, accomplishes their breaches as being of relevance to other students in the class.

In contrast, in the Aralia College corpus, although student breaches of the classroom normativities were oriented to, they occurred within private exchanges between the teacher and the given student. In doing so, the teacher oriented to the irrelevance to the whole class of the actions of individual students.

Extract 6.21

553 *T:* . . . (*walks away from the whole class group to the teacher desk; Bronte follows*)
554 *Br:* I haven't started in mine
555 *T:* Have you written the names of your animals?
556 *Br:* No
557 *T:* What have you been doing, Bronte?
558 *Br:* I did do some there
559 *T:* All this time and you've done nothing. Well, Bronte, at lunchtime could you come up, at lunchtime could you come upstairs please? And you can do this in your lunchtime. (*walks back to the whole class group with a picture-book*)

The exchange between Bronte and the teacher took place in the relatively private domain of the teacher's desk. So while Bronte was called to account for the breach, the class group were not an overhearing audience to this exchange. In the following excerpt, the teacher audibly changes the volume of her talk to accomplish the nomination of a student's work as inadequate, as a private occurrence.

Extract 6.22

549 *T:* Yes, your book and your pencil and come and sit on the mat please. (*softly to Kate*) You're a lazy girl, guess what you're going to do at lunchtime
550 *Kt:* This
551 *T:* Yes. (*loudly to the whole class*) Right listening here

In this excerpt, the teacher privately oriented to Kate's work as inadequate with the problem located in her personal attributes. That is, she was accomplished as electively or essentially lazy, rather than precluded in practical terms from doing the set task. In her unproblematic answering in Turn 550 of the teacher's question, Kate oriented to the same identity. The exchange was closed with a pre-topic shift addressed to the whole class ('Right listening here').

At Aralia College, therefore, individual student conduct was made relevant to only the student concerned and the teacher. Therefore, the rendering of any one student as unproductive in the classroom was irrelevant to the other students. By comparison, at St Luke's School, the unremarkable public ascription of individual students as, for example, playing rather than working achieved such attribution as of relevance to all of the other students.

On a similar theme, students at St Luke's also quite unremarkably made comment on the productiveness or otherwise of other students' actions. Thus, surveillance of other students was routinely afforded to the students in this site.

Extract 6.23

93 *T:*   . . . Come on, everyone down. What's the problem, Mia? When you're all sitting ready. Just have a look around for people who aren't ready. Maybe your looking at them will get them ready. (5)

This excerpt demonstrates the routine way in which all participants were accomplished as having a role in the attribution of particular students as counterproductive for any given current activity. In the excerpt below, for example, we see how the students and teacher systematically worked together to regulate the action of one of the classroom participants and to nominate that student's action as counterproductive to the work at hand.

Extract 6.24

165 *T:*   . . . Right, I'll have three volunteers to share
166 *Ss:*   (*hands raised*)
167 *T:*   (*choosing students to come to front of class to share their work*) Hoa. I'm trying to think of someone I didn't have, are you finished now Liam? All right. And Gemma. We haven't had as many girls as boys, so we'll have those three please. Right, keep your papers very still please
168 *Ll:*   Ohhhhh (*unhappy*)
169 *T:*   Excuse me, didn't you stand up and share yesterday, Lachlan?
170 *Ll:*   No
171 *T:*   Yes!
172 *Ll:*   No
173 *T:*   Yes, Mrs Milne? (*model of full response required*)
174 *Ll:*   No I didn't
175 *Ss:*   (*various*) Yes he did
176 *T:*   Excuse me, Lachlan, you did
177 *Mi:*   His was about Kieren Perkins at the pool
178 *Ss:*   Yeah, yes (*chorus*)
179 *T:*   Okay. Lachlan, you're wasting our time. Thank you, Hoa

As a response to the teacher's directive in Turn 165, many students bid for selection to speak in front of the class. The teacher selected Hoa in Turn 167, accounted for her selection of students, selected Liam and Gemma and then gave a further account for her selection in terms of gender equity and pre-topic shifted. In Turn 168, Lachlan made a noise which was heard by the teacher as complaining about his non-selection insofar as she accounted in Turn 169 (in the form of a checking question) for his non-selection in terms of the account for selection she had earlier provided. That is, she accounted for his non-selection insofar as he had 'share(d) yesterday'. This Lachlan denied at 170, the teacher maintained her position at 171, Lachlan emphatically denied it again at 172 and the teacher again maintained her position at 173, by modelling for Lachlan the response he was expected to give. Lachlan maintained his denial at 174.

Of particular interest here is Turn 175 in which a number of students self-selected as speakers to address the teacher and agree that Lachlan's answer to the question was indeed incorrect. The teacher upgraded her assertion at 176 and one turn later, at 177 Mia provided evidence that Lachlan had shared insofar as she stated what it was that he had written about. The implication was that she could only know if he *had* shared it with the class. Mia's assertion projected a chorus of agreement from many students. In the next Turn, 179, the teacher displayed her hearing that the matter had been decided and that the sequence of talk was complete: she nominated Lachlan as wasting the time of the rest of the group and directed Hoa to begin.

This sequence of talk demonstrates that, at St Luke's School, drawing distinctions among students and nominating individual students as counterproductive of the task were unremarkably the province of all of the classroom participants. Note that the point here is again not whether *in reality* Lachlan had shared the previous day, but that the participants made a number of structural moves to accomplish Lachlan as having already shared, as perhaps not clearly understanding and, therefore, as being counterproductive to the business at hand.

Conclusion

We have seen here that, although classroom sites are apparently comparable on many interactive and institutional counts, the participants enact distinctive inflections of the category Child–Student in each site. This production of difference is occasioned in and through the interactive work done in each site within routine classroom interactions. The members in the two different classrooms studied here enacted versions of the category Child–Student that were defined and driven in the talk of the local site of that particular classroom. While some of these differences may have seemed subtle and delicate, the consequences in terms of the interactive and, possibly of particular interest to educators, teaching and learning choices available to participants, are significant.

This chapter has detailed the distinctiveness of the cohorted Child–Student in terms of the distinctive accomplishment of the knowledge base of the students, their interactive options, what counted as work, and what counted as being a worker. In review, students at both Aralia College and St Luke's were routinely accomplished as knowing about the topic. Aralia College students were routinely accomplished as lacking knowledge about the management of logistics whereas St Luke's School students were routinely accomplished as lacking knowledge about the management of their own brains and bodies. Aralia College students self-selected as speakers, addressed other students and took relatively long turns at talk compared to St Luke's School students. At Aralia College, starting but not actually finishing a given task counted as satisfactorily participation, whereas at St Luke's School, only talk 'in reality' relevant to the set activity counted as contributing to that activity. At Aralia College working individually with virtually no responsibility and no concern for others' conduct counted as being a worker, whereas at St Luke's School unremarkable relevance was made of responsibly working together and surveilling others' actions.

If we consider the different constellations of the category Child–Student enacted here in light of the broad attributes of the Child–Student identified in Chapter 5, we find that it is on the matter of the characteristics of the cohort that the two groups are different. The precompetence of the students is not under issue here; this element of this category Child–Student remains. However, we saw that one of the parameters by which the business of being a Child–Student can be complicated is in the matter of what *sort* of cohort is enacted. Again, cohorting itself is achieved, but the detail of the nature and enactment of that cohort can be variously achieved by participants on the scene.

7 The child of the group

Introduction

The organization of classroom members into small groups is a familiar aspect of classroom work. Certainly, in the classrooms that we studied, students were routinely organized into small student groups to complete various activities and tasks. Our analyses of the talk of these small groups found that this way of organizing students comprised another context in which a particular inflection of Child–Student operated. We found that the attributes of the category Child–Student for the small group were not the same as those oriented to as relevant to the category Child–Student for the whole class. In short, in student groups – by virtue of the students drawing upon different interactive resources – a cohorted and competent Child–Student was accomplished.

Here we detail these two attributes of the category Child–Student for the small group as they were consistently made relevant to being a student in student groups in the two different primary school classrooms discussed earlier: Aralia College and St Luke's. Note that our analyses of the student group corpus were undertaken within the parameters set by our whole class analyses and reported in Chapters 5 and 6. Our focus here is only on those specific features that either compared or contrasted directly with what has already been documented. We acknowledge therefore that other attributes might be available in the talk; nonetheless, precompetence and cohorting remain our concern.

Student group talk compared to whole class talk

The Child–Student for student group is competent

In the student groups, we found that students mundanely and unremarkably reacted to each other as colleagues with sufficient skills with which to engage in and complete the activities and tasks required of them. Essentially, within the student groups, the students oriented to themselves and each other as competent. One way in which competence was routinely attributed to students in the student group data set was in the students' hearing of their peers' questions as real indications of some lack of knowledge.

Extract 7.1 (a)

29 *Jo:*   A little horse is a aah what's a little horse called?
30 *Ho:*   A foal

Extract 7.1 (b)

259 *Sa:*   Do sentences start with 'and'?
260 *Ch:*   No

Extract 7.1 (c)

237 *Bt:*   How do you spell horse?
238 *Sa:*   'h' 'o' 'r' 's' 'e', I mean, 'h' 'o' 'r' 's' 'e' yeah

If we compare these excerpts to those presented in Chapter 5, we find that these students did not orient to others' questions as opportunities for the display of precompetence. That is, the answering students did not ordinarily direct the questioner to, for example, 'have a go' at the spelling of the requested word or to 'try' to work out an answer for themselves. Nor did students engage in extended sequences of talk that required guessing or 'waiting and seeing'. They simply oriented to themselves and others as able to answer – using the logic, perhaps, of 'if you don't know how to spell the word "horse", and you want to spell it, you will ask someone who knows'.

The students' orientation to themselves as competent classroom participants is available in the design as well as the content of the answers. Recall that in Chapter 5 (Extract 5.2), we saw how students were achieved as precompetent in and through the design of student answers as provisional, that is, awaiting evaluation and consequent acceptance *as* answers. An example from that chapter, reproduced as Extract 7.2 below, shows that such provisionality can be signalled in the design (by a student) of answers *as* questions, most usually by uttering the response with an interrogative intonation.

Extract 7.2

68 *T:*   I'm, oh when am I writing this letter? When am I writing the letter?
69 *S:*   Today?
70 *T:*   Today. So what do I need on it?

As stated earlier, in the mundane design of and hearing of students' answers as questions, the students and the teacher together accomplished those answers as provisional, that is, as awaiting designation as valid. In contrast, in the student group corpus, the students routinely designed and heard answers to questions as *not* awaiting validation in as much the answers were unremarkably provided without an interrogative intonation (see also Extract 7.1).

Extract 7.3

31	Bt:	. . . Susi, if we go in partners will you be my partner?
32	Ch:	But we don't have to go into partners
33	Sa:	Well, if we go into partners
34	Ch:	She mightn't even put us in partners
35	Bt:	She might. I'm going with Susi if she does
36	Ch:	Oh
37	Bt:	If she says choose a partner, I'm going to say Susi
38	Sa:	(*rules line down side of page*)
39	Bt:	What did you do that for?
40	Sa:	For when she checks
41	Bt:	But, what do you do it for?
42	Ch:	What do you need it for?
43	Sa:	Well, when she checks I, she puts like 's' 'p' for spelling and that (3) (*writing*)
44	Sa:	Are we supposed to be started?
45	Ch:	Susi, do you want to see if you can come to my house? This Friday? That's tomorrow
46	Sa:	I won't be allowed
47	Bt:	Why?
48	Ch:	She has to go to bed

Note that through this excerpt student questions are audibly oriented to as actual questions (31–32; 39–43; 45–48). Note as well that the concomitant student answers were not provided in interrogative tone and the respondent did not evaluate and then either accept or reject the answers accordingly. In the design of their interaction, these students audibly orient to themselves as competent knowers and answerers – and in doing so, accomplish talk in interaction that is far more like ordinary conversation than familiar whole class classroom talk.

The extracts we have selected so far show the attributes of the Child–Student for student group as having sufficient skills and knowledge to engage in and complete the activities. Note that in these student group examples, student utterances were accomplished as reasoned, real comments. In contrast to the whole class Child–Student described in Chapter 5, we did not find instances of provisional answers, or an orientation to the students as in need of suspense, or excited or as needing to be settled. The students heard each other's talk in interaction as purposeful and reasoned and thereby accomplished themselves and others as capable and competent.

We now turn our attention away from the participant hearings within sequences of utterances to the interactive options assumed by and afforded to the students in the course of ordinary student group talk. Our interest here, then, is the system of turn-taking operable with student group talk. In particular, we document systematic differences between the turn-taking system evident in the student group talk and that operable in the whole class corpus.

In the previous two chapters, we discussed the unremarkable interactive options of the primary school students evident in the whole class corpus. In Chapter 5 we looked at the two classrooms together and found that students' turns were routinely addressed to the teacher, interruptable, provisional, that is, available for teacher evaluation, and relatively short. In Chapter 6 we compared the two classrooms and highlighted the additional interactive options that were also unremarkably afforded by and to the students in Aralia College. Our analyses in Chapter 6 revealed that for the Aralia students, although the turn-taking looked and sounded like the classroom talk discussed in Chapter 5, there was in addition an unremarked sprinkling of other interactive options, students asked questions of the teacher, engaged in two-way conversations with the teacher, talked to other students and disagreed with the teacher.

In a further variation to the interactive options available in classrooms our analyses of the student group corpus showed that at the level of turn-taking systems talk in student groups was systematically different from that in whole class situations. We did not find a two–party talk system where one participant consistently had longer turns at talk, interrupted others and initiated and evaluated the others' talk (see Chapter 5). What we did find was multi-party talk that afforded diverse interactive options, as well as more options of initiation and agency with regard to students' own contributions to the set task. In essence, the student group turn-taking systems resembled turn-taking in non–institutionalized mundane talk in interaction. As incumbents of the category Child–Student for student group, students oriented to each other, in many ways, as ordinary conversationalists.

Extract 7.3, presented earlier, illustrates the particulars of the student group system of turn-taking. Throughout this segment, turn allocation techniques were used by all participants rather than by one participant as we saw in the whole class corpus. In the student group talk, current speakers routinely selected a next speaker (31 and 45 – Susi was projected as next speaker) and participants routinely self-selected (32, 39 and 44). Taken together, Turns 43 and 44 provide a clear example of a first starter acquiring the right to a(nother) turn and transfer occurring at that place. Specifically, Susi's Turn 43 selected no next speaker and no speaker subsequently self-selected. Susi therefore unremarkably self-selected in Turn 44, at which point transfer occurred (Charlotte's Turn 45). The transitions between speakers documented in this segment and through the student group corpus are therefore directly parallel to the system of turn-taking described by Sacks *et al.* (1974) when explaining mundane talk in interaction.

If we turn our attention to the *features* of the student group talk, the same excerpt is useful in showing that Sack *et al.'s* (1974) observable features of mundane talk in interaction are clearly present. For example, turn order was varied and the relative distribution of those turns was not pre-specified; one speaker spoke at a time and the length of her or his turn varied from one word to a sentence to sequences of sentences; what the speakers said was not specified in advance; the length of the talk was not specified and the talk was continuous or discontinuous. We see, then, that the systems and features of turn-taking enacted by the students working together in groups away from the direct guidance and gaze of the teacher resembled that of mundane talk in interaction or ordinary conversation, rather than whole class classroom talk.

This is not to say that the very *idea* of the teacher – that is, the category Teacher – was not discernible in student group talk. Indeed, throughout the student group corpus, the teacher was accomplished as the person who co-ordinated what it was that the students were doing, who gave directives that were complied with by the students and was the person to whom students were accountable for doing the work. So, although the small group talk did look and sound like mundane conversation, that conversation did orient to the idea that the participants had some teacher-directed and teacher-assessable activity to do, *together*. And this brings us to the other attribute consistently made relevant to being a student in a small group within a primary school class-room – being a member of a cohort.

The Child–Student for student group is cohorted

Recall that cohorting was achieved in and through the talk in interaction in the whole class data. We found that cohorting was achieved in and through the talk in interaction in the student groups. However, a comparison of the two locations reveals that although cohorting was attributed to the students in both sites, the manner of achievement was not the same. Shared by the two locations was the naming of the students *as* a cohort ('you' in the whole class talk, as illustrated in Extract 5.12, and, as we shall see, 'we' in the student group talk) and the orientation to the notion that there was a shared purpose for them as a coterie.

Extract 7.4 (a)

238 *Jf:*   And just put a whole line across it
239 *Nc:*   Across?
240 *Ha:*   Yeah because we're supposed not to write that

Extract 7.4 (b)

46 *Bt:*   Do we have to write our own address, or?
47 *Au:*   No, we have to write our own one

Extract 7.4 (c)

330 *Sa:*   We might have to do this in the lunch hour if we don't get it done now

Although the sequences of talk do not make available whether the 'we' refers to the small group or the broader class group (all of whom are engaged in the same task), that 'we' refers to a distinct group – of which the members of the student group are incumbents – is clear.

Moreover, these sequences of talk illustrate the point that led into this discussion of cohorting. That point is that students routinely oriented to themselves as categorically different from the teacher. With respect to the three excerpts in Extract 7.4, above, our facility with classroom interactions, again as either students, teachers or analysts, allows us to hear the unnamed entity who has directed what it is that the students are 'supposed (to) write' (240), 'have to write' (47), or 'might have to do' (330) as the teacher. Throughout our student group data, student group members routinely engaged in turns at talk that oriented to the rights and responsibilities of the teacher as different from those held in common by the students (see Extract 7.3, Turns 34–44). Such talk, marking the students as a group that is other than the teacher, excludes the teacher and effectively attributes the students with being members of a cohort.

Shared, as well, was the participants' orientation to the group as a particular and current group. The excerpts below illustrate the routine way in which members of the student group compared the work of their group with the work of other groups. They oriented to themselves as not just *any* group but as particularly *that* group.

Extract 7.5 (a)

(note marked utterances)

459 *Ha:*   I'm Super-ant, you're
460 *Nc:*   Shh. Oh they've done more than us
461 *Jo:*   I'm Zono

Extract 7.5 (b)

249 *Gm:*   / A tiger lives in
250 *Jf:*   In Africa
251 *Gm:*   In Africa in the jungle
252 *Jo:*   No, a tiger lives in open grasslands like the giraffe
523 *Gm:*   Yeah
254 *Jf:*   Okay, write it down
255 *Js:*   Ours is going to be the best
256 *Ha:*   Finally, where a lion lives

Extract 7.5 (c)

458 *Ha:*   Don't, don't
459 *Jo:*   We don't do that

460 *Ha:*   Yes we do, you don't have to make it so long
461 *Jo:*   I bet ours is going to be the second worst
462 *Gm:*   What are you writing like this?

In the marked utterances we see group members referring to their group as a particular group for the purposes of completing the task. Their groupness was established in comparison with other groups and that comparison was in terms of some aspect of the set task, for example, its nearness to completion or how well it had been done.

Not available at all in the student group talk – and one major interactive resource drawn upon by participants in whole class talk that achieved the students as a cohort – was the engagement of the students in synchronized action. We found no examples of students in student groups engaging in chorused turns at talk or synchronized movement of bodies and body parts.

Therefore, in the student groups the students oriented to themselves as a cohort only insofar as it was procedural for the task at hand. Students oriented to their status as a *cohort* of students in the matters of *what* the actual task was ('Do we have to write our own address?'), *that* they were supposed to be doing it ('We might have to do this in the lunch hour if we don't get it done now'), and *that* it was assessable ('ours is going to be the best').

Perhaps as a pleasant surprise to teachers who make use of group work as a classroom organizational strategy, our analyses showed that this idea that there *was* some task to do within the small group configuration was overwhelmingly oriented to as the point of the work by the students. The student group child was accomplished as, essentially, an implementer of the set task.

But we are not proposing, here, that the students in student groups incessantly worked at their set tasks. We found that the action of 'putting the set task into operation' was accomplished by the students as involving more (or, frequently, less) than what they had been required by the teacher to do. Our analyses also showed that even though the students in the groups routinely oriented to their common activity as a set task that they were supposed to do, there was no systematic accomplishment in the student group data of the normative accountability of actually doing what the teacher required. That this was the case is most efficiently illustrated by presenting the different inflections of 'putting the set task into operation' we found operating in two different school sites. In particular, at Aralia College, telling jokes, relating stories and *not* getting any of the set task done at all were also achieved as part of the current activity. Thus, although the Child–Student for student group was accomplished as a competent student with a common set task to do, what counted as doing that set task was accomplished moment by moment by the particular interactants.

What counts as working in a small group?

Classrooms being familiar places, and group work being a common practice in many classrooms, one might think that working in a group might be, to all intents and purposes, a standard practice. Our analyses revealed, however, that there were qualitative distinctions in what counted as putting the set task into operation in the two sites. Essentially, the answer to the question 'What counts as being a productive member of a small group?' was not the same in the two classrooms.

Notably, only at St Luke's School was there an orientation by the student group members to an actual engagement in the set task as normatively accountable.

Extract 7.6

83 *Gm:*   Lollies (*snicker*)
84 *Nc:*   Um?
85 *Jo:*   What's so important about lollies?
86 *Gm:*   Nothing
87 *Jo:*   Don't say it then

In this segment, the students are compiling a list entitled 'What is important?'. Gemma humorously proposed 'lollies' as an item to be included on the group's list. In Turn 85, Julio asked her to account for her answer. In the next turn, Gemma provided an answer to Julio's question, thereby displaying her hearing of Julio's question as unremarkable. In her answer of 'Nothing' in Turn 86, she made available the fact that, in terms of the required list of important things, she had no account for her answer 'lollies'. In Turn 87, Julio names Gemma's account in Turn 86 as 'not an account', her suggestion at Turn 83 is heard then as account-less and in Turn 87 Julio directed her to not say it. Both Julio and Gemma oriented to the normative accountability of engaging in talk relevant to the set task. This sequence is illustrative of the unremarkableness of students in the St Luke's group achievement of set task talk as relevant, and non-set task talk as irrelevant and as a breach of the normativities of St Luke's School group work. Such talk in interaction was not documented at Aralia College.

The members of the student group at St Luke's School also oriented to the normative accountability of knowing what future use would be made of the group product. Moreover, what was going to be done with the product within the whole class situation was achieved as pertinent to and as having material effects for what the student group did or did not do.

Extract 7.7

199 *Ha:*   WHAT'S IMPORTANT. So how about we read this by heart.
           HELLO MY FRIENDS

200 *Nc:*   We're not going to do it by heart
201 *Ha:*   No, we have to practise
202 *Jo:*   No Hoa we (. . .)
203 *Jf:*   No
204 *Ha:*   Maybe, to say it out in front of the class
205 *Jo:*   No /
206 *Gm:*   / No
207 *Ha:*   Okay we can just read it
208 *Js:*   That's it (. . .)
209 *Ha:*   WHAT'S IMPORTANT about your life. HELLO MY FRIENDS,
           AS YOU KNOW . . .

In the first turn in this segment, Hoa suggested that the group learn by rote what they had written during the writing session. This suggestion was countered in the next turn by Ngoc, who oriented to the suggestion as something that was *not* a component of the set task. In the next turn (Turn 201), Hoa disagreed with Ngoc and displayed her understanding of what the set task was: 'No, we have to practise'. Both Julio and Jennifer rejected Hoa's statement of what they had to do in the two subsequent turns. Hoa then softened her statement of what they *had* to do to embody what they *might* or *could* do. Her construction of the set task was again rejected (Turns 205 and 206). In Turn 207, she displayed her understanding that what they had to do was to 'just read it'. Insofar as no speaker rejected Hoa's final construction of what the set task was, it was audible as accepted by the group.

In this example, and routinely in the St Luke's student group data, turns at talk that were heard as misrepresenting the set task were routinely countered and corrected. One feature of putting the set task into operation at St Luke's was therefore, each student being accountable for knowing what that set task was and executing the set task as it was supposed to be executed. Recall that this was also a feature of whole class cohorting. At Aralia College, the student group members were neither held accountable for knowing what their particular set task was nor for correctly executing it. For example, in the case of the set task of constructing a list of the names of six to eight animals, the listing of between 20 and 32 animals by the students in the group was not oriented to as in any way accountable or remarkable, say, in terms of exceeding requirements. Another example of the ordinariness of not correctly executing the set task – in this case, of retelling a known story in pictures – at Aralia College was provided in the following excerpt.

Extract 7.8

122 *So:*   That's not in the story
123 *Wl:*   I don't care. And you can see a witch in the corner
124 *Ch:*   A what?

The talk moves on and William was not called to account for his refusal to properly execute the set task of a retell; in this he was not accomplished as accountable for either being cognizant of or displaying that group's knowledge. Moreover, the excerpt illustrates the routineness of not doing the set task as a feature of 'putting the set task into operation' at Aralia College.

Therefore, while both students at Aralia College and St Luke's School were attributed with being members of a group with a particular task to do, at St Luke's School what that task actually was *was* accomplished as relevant to and having material effects for what was *actually* done. This was not always the case at Aralia College where what the students were ostensibly supposed to be doing was routinely not done.

So what were these students doing if not undertaking the required activities? At Aralia College, we found students in student groups to be routinely engaged in chatting and joking that *they* nominated as non-set task talk. The extent to which students working in groups engaged in such non-set task-related chatting and joking was documentably different at the two sites. At Aralia College, this non-set task talk included mundane talk about television programmes, their weekend activities and anecdotes about their family life. One characteristic of mundane conversation, according to Sacks *et al.* (1974) is the mundane transformation of one topic into another. This clearly occurred in the Aralia College student group talk, with the set task talk, itself, being the topic transformed into another. Our analyses revealed that the set task talk essentially and unremarkably acted as a springboard for student chatting.

While the following excerpt is not brief, it clarifies our point by providing an example of ordinary Aralia College student group talk. Our analyses of this and other transcripts allowed us to conclude that this student group talk was documentably mundane talk in interaction as identified by Sacks *et al.* (1974).

Extract 7.9

244 *Bt:*   It was Santa Claus of course. (*writes*) IT WAS SANTA CLAUS. 's' 'a' 'n' 't' 'a' CLAUS. It was St Nicholas. Do you know St Nicholas is St Nicholas and Santa Claus at the same time, those two, depends on where you live. It's true. That video we watched, um, cause my, um, my Pa, one of my Pa's live on an island and how do you reckon, um, and there's not snow around there, all there is is water, that's Jessie. And there's nowhere that Santa could land so he must go by boat.

245 *Ch:*   But where would he carry all the presents?

246 *Bt:*   Wrapped up in his, um, sack

247 *Ch:*   (. . .) goes all the way around the world. It's really only like (. . .)

248 *Bt:*   Maybe he goes whoosh

249 *Ch:*   No there's one in each country that like, how are you meant to go round all Africa, all America? There's one in each country, or Australia?

250 *Bt:* No there's not, there's only one, there's only two. There's two

251 *Ch:* [Oh but

252 *Bt:* [One does half the world and the other does the other half. Anyway there's over one hundred and fifteen countries that hardly get any presents. One hundred and fifteen, one thousand and fifteen sorry. So we're actually lucky. One hundred, one thousand /

253 *Ch:* / Like last Christmas I got about ten or eleven, ten, eleven or twelve or something, presents from Santa

254 *Bt:* I get twenty-four

255 *Ch:* I got a big lot. Quite a lot. I get sixty or more

256 *Bt:* We have, we have these sacks

257 *Ch:* I've got a big box sort of sack. It's a (. . .) sack, but when I was little I used to get these dolls in those big boxes. When I was really little, like two or three or something

258 *Bt:* I asked Santa for a porcelain doll

259 *Ch:* A what?

260 *Bt:* Do you know, um, Santa gave me a swing set with a, um, a seesaw one of those things where, you know, those bars where you go across and everything. I got one of them, a baby swing and one of those other swings

261 *Ch:* How big was it?

262 *Bt:* About from, right where the white cupboard is, to about, um? Over there

263 *Ch:* And [like

264 *Bt:* [And do you know what? And he came through, we didn't have a chimney. And do you know where, down in Melbourne we didn't have a chimney. He came through our bathroom window. My eyes are watering

265 *Ch:* Why?

266 *Bt:* They must have felt like crying. My eyes do that sometimes. Anyway, um?

267 *SG:* (25) (*writing*)

268 *Bt:* What could be next?

269 *Ch:* I know /

270 *Bt:* / One day there were (. . .)

306 *Bt:* I'm going to ask my mum and dad if we can go to where they sell, um, *Baywatch*

307 *Ch:* Can you bring me?

308 *Bt:* Yeah but you'll have to pay to get in. Bring your family

309 *Ch:* Cool

310 *Bt:* Who's in your family?

311 *Ch:* My mum, my dad and me. And my cat

That such sequences of talk at Aralia College were non-set task talk is available in the talk. Specifically, non-set task talk status is accomplished insofar as one or another group member, at some point, nominates the talk as such. For example, in Turn 266, above, Brittany pre-topic shifted by saying, 'Anyway' and re-engaging in the set task. The participants therefore oriented to the set task, as topic and 'what they were supposed to be doing' (and thus *as* the set task). Other pre-topic reinstatements documentable in the Aralia College student group corpus included 'Anyway, I'm getting on with this', 'All right let's get on with this, come on', 'I haven't even started' and 'We might have to do this in the lunch hour if we don't get it done now.' With such pre-topic reinstatements (along with the preceding and subsequent turns), the students audibly oriented to the preceding utterances as not on task and to the set task as what they should have been doing all along and what they would now proceed to do.

Essentially, the Aralia College student group corpus demonstrated that non-set task talk was accomplished as an unremarkable feature or component of putting the set task into operation in that work configuration. In contrast, at St Luke's School, extended sequences of non-set task talk – what we have termed 'chatting' within Aralia College – were not documented. Turns, audible as possible topic shifts, *were* taken by the group members. However, there were, routinely, structural moves made to achieve such talk as relevant to the set task rather than as shifting the topic.

Extract 7.10

128	*Ha:*	(*writing*) MEMORIES
129	*Nc:*	Caring for people
130	*Ha:*	Secrets
131	*Nc:*	Secrets are not important
132	*Jo:*	(*hushed tone*) Some are. My sister had a baby
133	*Gm:*	Babies are important
134	*Ha:*	Memories are important
135	*Gm:*	Caring for people

In Turn 132, Julio disagreed with Ngoc's statement that 'Secrets are not important', and then provided evidence of his argument by telling the group members – in a hushed tone – that his sister had had a baby. In the next turn, Gemma heard Julio's turn as set task relevant talk that oriented to another important thing for their list and said 'Babies are important' (rather than, for example, projecting further talk on the topic of Julio's sister's secret baby). Julio's utterance, then, was unremarkably heard as orienting to the set task rather than shifting the topic.

Similarly, joking and, in colloquial terms, joking around, in the St Luke's corpus were routinely not heard as shifting the topic away from the set task.

Extract 7.11 (a)

164 *Gm:*   And what's the planet going to be called? It could be called Jupiter, or Saturn
165 *Ha:*   No, nobody's ever been on Saturn
166 *Gm:*   Popcorn planet. No Jennifer? Jennifer-land *(laugh)*
167 *Jf:*   *(laugh)*
168 *Jo:*   Let's go to the solar system of? Saturn?

Extract 7.11 (b)

55 *Jf:*   What's next?
56 *Nc:*   Bum
57 *SG:*   *(laugh)*
58 *Ha:*   I've got to underline this, hang on

In (a), Turn 166, Gemma's laughter and Jennifer's consequential laughter accomplished Gemma's utterance as humorous. However, as no further laughter occurred, Gemma's turn was audibly not funny, after all, and the set task was reinstated as topic by Julio. In (b), Turn 56 was heard as funny by the group and the very next turn reinstated the set task talk. These segments show that the students in the student group at St Luke's School made jokes and laughed and show that such exchanges routinely resembled the adjacency pair structure. That is, a joke (as a first pair part) projected laughter (as a second pair part). At St Luke's School, these pairs of turns were not heard as topic shifts and therefore did not project more jokes or sequences of laughter. Rather, student group talk was routinely resumed after the second pair part.

Notably, in the student group talk at Aralia College joking and having fun were accomplished as component parts of engaging in the set task and set task talk routinely projected humour and jocularity.

Extract 7.12

108 *Bt:*   Look who I'm addressing it to, SO AND SO *(laugh)*. I'm addressing it to so-and-so
109 *Ch:*   I've put DEAR CHRIS, my dad's name
110 *Wl:*   I've put DEAR DEAR
111 *Ch:*   Who, dear dear? *(laugh)*
112 *S:*   Dear dumb
113 *SG:*   *(laugh)*
114 *Au:*   Dear wanker
115 *Bt:*   *(laugh)*
116 *Au:*   Dear dipulsiana
117 *So:*   Dear some bozo *(laugh)*
118 *Ch:*   No dear Mrs Willy Wonka *(laugh)*

119 *Bt:*   Dear Mr Willy
120 *SG:*   (*laugh*)
121 *Au:*   Dear Mr 'b' 'm' 'w'
122 *Bt:*   Dear Mr 'b' 'm' 'w'
123 *Ch:*   Dear Mr Gogomobile
124 *SG:*   (*laugh*)

That such sequences were fun for the students is available in their virtually continuous laughter. Fun at Aralia College was routinely organized as sequences of similarly designed turns. Other accomplished sources of humour included alliteration, references to genitals and bodily functions, and personal anecdotes. In contrast to the documentation of jokes and laughter in the St Luke's School student group, at Aralia College jocularity was not structured through adjacency pairs. Rather, it routinely comprised extended sequences of similarly designed turns (see excerpt above). In this site, therefore, jocularity was achieved as a routinely prevalent feature of the talk in and around putting the set task into operation.

Overall, at Aralia College, it was routine for the students in the student group initially to orient to the set task and, after a number of turns at set task talk, to hear some aspect of that talk as shifting the topic or orienting to fun and for the set task talk to be later reinstated. As set task talk, the reinstatements themselves were subsequently heard as making relevant new sequences of fun or non-set task talk, and so on. At Aralia College, therefore, the students accomplished alternate set task talk and non-set task talk as relevant to putting the set task into operation.

At St Luke's School, it was unremarkable for the grouped students to accomplish only talk directly related to the set task as relevant to executing that task. Possible topic shifts were routinely heard as relevant to the task and jokes were structured as two part pairs inserted into the smoothly running set task talk. It was also unremarkable for jokes and topic shifts to be achieved as outside of the normativities of the student group interaction.

In both sites, talk accomplished as set task talk was achieved as a priority in the process of putting the set task into operation. However, the analyses reported in this section demonstrate that set task talk and action are prevalent in the St Luke's student group talk, whereas in student group talk at Aralia College, both set task and non-set task talk and action prevail.

Conclusion

In this chapter, we have added another dimension to the exploration of the educational respecification of children as members of the category Child–Student by documenting the inflection of the category operable while students worked in small groups without the teacher's direct gaze or guidance. In the first section of this chapter, we documented contrasts of the student group talk with the whole class corpus that was the focus of Chapter 5. In the second section of this chapter we detailed our contrasting of the student group talk of each site, finding out that 'What counted as working?' was different in the student groups at each site.

The contrasting of the student group corpus and the whole class corpus demonstrated systematic differences between the two kinds of talk and versions of the Child–Student therein constructed. Presented in terms of the *attributes* of the Child–Student in the student group, the analyses showed that the student group Child–Student was competent and cohorted. In review the student group Child–Student had sufficient skills and knowledge to engage in and complete the activities, heard other's talk in interaction as purposeful and reasoned, was afforded diverse interactive options of initiation and agency and had a common task or purpose, was categorically different from the teacher, and was not just a member of *any* group but of particularly *that* group.

When attending to the *differences* documented between the two sites, we found that even though the student group Child–Student was shown to be comparable when contrasted with whole class Child–Student, our contrasting of the student group talk from Aralia College with that from St Luke's School highlighted distinctions in the student group Child–Student operable in each site. It was documented that the attributes of the St Luke's School Child–Student for student group included being a member of a cohort with a common set task to do and a person who routinely engaged in talk about the set task, while *not* being a person who routinely joked and chatted or a person who engaged in extended sequences of non-set task talk.

In contrast, the attributes of the Aralia College Child–Student for student group were documented as including being a member of a named cohort with a common set task who routinely engaged in extended sequences of joking and chatting which were interspersed with references to the set task.

Our main conclusion, here, is that, in contrast to the Child–Student of the whole class talk, the Child–Student of the student group at both sites was an implementer of the set task, but that there were qualitative differences in the way that the actual operation of said task was enacted in the two sites. It seems then, that the Child–Student for student group differed in terms of the *enacted relevance* of the set task to student group work. That the set task could be enacted as less than central to a student group work configuration may or may not be news to teachers! At St Luke's School the set task was accomplished in the talk *as* the student's central, current task, while at Aralia College, it was not. We could say St Luke's was a group of workers and Aralia College, a group of chatterers, who happened to be doing some work.

The membership category Child–Student has been further complicated then in this chapter by elucidating the particular constellation of the category in student group talk in the two classroom sites. Again and always, these distinctive constellations of the category Child–Student for student group were defined and driven in the local site of the student group *within* each classroom.

Readers will recall that our concern in this chapter was only the attributional work done in student group talk that either compared or contrasted directly with what had been detailed in the preceding two chapters. This approach provided us with an opportunity to continue the increasing specification of the category Child–Student that has occurred through Chapters 5 and 6. In this chapter, we were able to take advantage of our design to interrogate the category Child–Student available in student group talk and emphasize the artfulness of students' school-based interactions.

Conclusion to Part II

Because the conclusions we draw are made within the framework of ethnomethodology, the task is to draw out interpretations for which the data provide a warrant. In this Part we documented layerings of comparabilities and contrasts across school sites. For example, in the student group talk, students routinely enacted cohorting, which was attributed also to the Child–Student in whole class talk in different ways. Consider how available is the conclusion that the macro configuration (the whole class) drove the micro (the student group). That is, consider how strong the temptation is to conclude that the students at Aralia College told stories, chatted and joked while they worked in student groups *because* relating anecdotes and chatting were routinely a feature of the Aralia College whole class system of talk. However, to insinuate that hierarchies of causation were at work would be incompatible with our theoretical bases. A warrant for naming the accomplishment of an attribute in one site as the cause of the same or different attribution in some other site is provided by the participants' orientation to such causation. As Schegloff (1991) has argued, it is not provided by the observation that one situation is more macro (or indeed micro)[1] than the other. Taken together, the contrasts demonstrate that the category Child–Student is a locally driven category. Even though there were a number of presuppositions about the category made relevant *across* the sites, category attributes were shown to be qualitatively different across the varying sites. Specifically, attributes were shown to be different from classroom to classroom, from student to student, from moment to moment, and from work configuration to work configuration. The category Child–Student might be labelled more precisely, 'Child–Student for Aralia College whole class' or 'Child–Student for St Luke's School student group configuration'. These analyses are a demonstration that the social order, the rights and responsibilities and the attributes of the student participants in the classroom moments we studied were achieved through the interactive processes *of* the participants and furthermore, were made to stand as real through those same processes.

The contrasts also demonstrate, however, that in spite of qualitative differences among the enacted attributions of the broad category of Child–Student, those attributes were recognizable and audible as pertaining to schoolchildren. Therefore, what was oriented to through schooling, with regard to the Child–

Student was a multi-faceted category that was always partly a function of what resources the students knew to bring to bear on the immediate local social configuration of which the current task was a part. This furthers the idea posited by Garfinkel (1967) that people, in this case, students, are not the cultural dopes of society but reasoning participants in interaction. The contrasts we present demonstrate that the reasoning practices employed by the classroom participants in the accomplishment of the category Child–Student were multiple and, thus, there were multiple normative constellations of that category.

The contrasts also demonstrate that the resources students drew upon and the category attributes they oriented to in different kinds of local social configurations were finely tuned. An example of this is provided in the finding that precompetence was accomplished as an attribute of the category Child–Student whole class. In other words, within the material conditions of engaging in whole class talk, precompetence formed part of the working logic. The students could not participate in the whole class talk if some version of precompetence was not assumed. This finding is compatible with the work of Austin (1997), Baker and Freebody (1989a) and Speier (1976) who have worked on the centrality of precompetence to the contemporary business of being a child. In this Part we extended such work insofar as it provides the contrast of the student group configuration and found that the students *did not* orient to their precompetence. Students in student group work configurations did not spend time pretending or waiting to see, which, as discussed in Chapter 5, are some of the ways in which student precompetence was shown to be oriented to. The fact that differential manifestations of competence and cohorting were documented with respect to the work configuration of the students indicates that the students were artful in the kinds of interactive options they exercised. This finding sits comfortably beside the 'competence paradigm' (Hutchby and Moran-Ellis 1998; Prout and James 1990), an expanding body of work that explains the nature of child competencies.

The contrastive sets of data also empirically substantiate MacKay's (1974) point that, in order to interact with adults, children have to enact adult theorizations of the Child and the Child–Adult relationship. It was demonstrated that within the whole class configuration, the students competently enacted precompetence and cohort behaviour while within the student groups, they competently enacted competence and a different inflection of cohort behaviour. The fact that the whole class sessions *happened*, therefore, relied absolutely on the students already knowing what the attributes of the membership category Child–Student whole class were and on their capacity to unremarkably enact those attributes (for example, by providing chorused answers and answering teacher questions in an interrogative intonation). In the whole class sessions, the students were taught social and reasoning practices in which, in order to participate (which is what they have to do for the sessions to happen), they had to already know what they were ostensibly being taught. In short, they had to know what the prevailing theory of the Child–Student was, in order to participate. This section provides evidence that the students were knowledgeable about the normativities of the given locale's theory of the Child–Student and were good at collaborating in their own enculturation practices. While this is not a new insight, the analyses reported here provide a compelling substantiation of MacKay's point.

This Part has demonstrated that there were features oriented to as relevant to the category Child–Student in both sites' whole class talk. However, it has also demonstrated that there were significant differences between each site's category. Moreover, in the deployment of another set of contrasts (with and between student group data sets), a different perspective on the attributes of the membership category Child–Student was made available. In particular, this contrast highlighted the high degree of sensitivity to the immediate local relationships in which the students were working in order to enact highly ramified, complex and multifaceted versions of school childhood. Therefore, the students enacted a qualitatively different category Child–Student in different work configurations. What this means is that, strictly empirically, an essentialist conception of childhood and school-childhood is no longer available.

This Part, however, has presented only one facet of our exploration the school's respecification of children as members of the category Child–Student. Part II has detailed the achievement of the category Child–Student within the institutional procedures and organizational processes of different classrooms. We now turn our attention to the rendering of students as members of the category Child–Student within the *materials* of education.

Part III

Re-producing the Schoolchild

Introduction

In this Part we take our questions of what, when and how is a Child into the materials of the curriculum. The data for this Part comprise a children's novel, the classroom talk about that novel, the students' writing and the teacher's assessments of that writing. As this section revolves around a literature classroom, some discussion of the school's use of literature and of reading and writing practices of such sites may seem due. However, each of these has a rich and at times turbulent history that cannot be adequately characterized within the parameters of this project. Suffice to say that the shadowy form of each stage in this history exists alongside others in many classrooms. For example in the literature classroom we examine in Chapter 9 we find shadowy traces of the many orientations to literature over the past 200 or so years and likewise such orientations to a variety of reading pedagogies and writing pedagogies. These are not the focus of our study, however, because, while interesting, especially to the teacher, a review of this sort would not enrich our focal question. Further, ethnomethodology is not particular about its site, needing only to be set to task in a social setting, the relevancies of that setting being made available through the orientations of the participants.

It is important to note that, in keeping with the tenets of ethnomethodology, we took as the warrant for declaring something 'relevant' the participants' own orientation to the relevance (see Chapter 4). To this end, our analysis began in the classroom talk, to find the relevancies of the participants at this site, then moved to the novel (to interrogate it as the grist to the talk), asking: What is this artefact that was rendered in this way by the classroom talk, and was there anything about the novel that made this rendering possible? We then explored the students' writing and the teacher's assessments of that writing to ask whether the relevancies of the classroom talk were then re-rendered in the students' writing. The analyses are not presented in this order, however. Chapter 8 examines the novel, Chapter 9 the talk and Chapter 10 the students' writing. Of the many ways of telling this story to the reader, we chose this because it constructs a path through our ever-specifying analysis. While such an approach may seem at first review tendentious, we make no claim to definitiveness, taking a specific and particular path through this large and varied data corpus to answer specific and particular questions – the data being always available for analysis through some other set of questions or through some other analytic lens.

In Chapter 8 we examine the category Child as described *in* and *by* a children's novel. We use Membership Category Analysis (see Chapter 4) to explain the Child as described in and through the attributes assigned to the story's child characters and as described *by* the assumptions the text embodies about the version of the Child who is the child reader of the novel. We present our analysis of the classroom talk in Chapter 9. As Heap (1982) reminded us, the talk is the public display, for the teacher and students, of both the procedural and propositional content of the lesson. In the literature classroom, the teacher and the students, together, talk up how to read a given novel for a given lesson, they render it 'sense-able' in that they render what sense to make and how to make it.

In Chapter 10 we turn to the students' writing. The writing tasks were developed by the teacher and both the propositional and procedural facets of the task were routinely and comprehensively talked through in the classroom talk. Writing tasks of the nature we meet here are integral to classroom life. Most teachers will recognize and easily be able to imagine the educative reasonings that drive these tasks, whether they agree with them or not. We interrogate this writing as an artefact of the students' understanding of the novel, the classroom talk about that novel and the requirements of the task itself. As analysts we approach the writing as both an *articulation* of, and an *enactment* of, a theory of Childhood. We examine therefore the category Child as described by and enacted by the students in their writing and as enacted by the teacher's assessments of that writing.

As in Part II these chapters can be read as stand-alone analyses or together as ever enriching layers of the account of the Child at school. Each chapter concludes with a brief review of the analytic findings of that chapter, and the conclusion of Part III draws these findings together.

8 The materials of education

In schools teachers typically rely on printed and electronic materials tailored for use by children, and, often, for schoolwork. These materials are therefore already representations of some theorizations of childhood and schoolwork. As such, they are properly the objects of curiosity for scholars interested in childhood. More significant, for both educators and ethnomethodologists, are the ways in which these materials are enlivened in classroom work, the ways in which theories of the Child inform that process of 'enlivening' and the consequences of students working with, or not with, these theories.

Magpie Island (Thiele 1974) is a novel widely used in Australian schools. It is available as a cultural artifact in which the category Child is described both *in* the text and *by* the text. The category Child is described *in* the text in and through the attributes assigned to the story's child characters. The category Child is described *by* the assumptions the text embodies about the version of the Child who is the child reader of the novel, for example, the text assumes a reader who will enjoy reading illustration as well as written text. We call this the Child 'portrayed' and the Child 'assumed'– portrayed *in* the text, assumed *by* the text.

The Child *in* the text: the Child 'portrayed'

There are two ways the category Child is portrayed in the text. First, a version of Child is 'articulated', that is, appears as the *topic* of the text. The Child as topic is available in the characterization of the 'child' characters in the novel, a boy child and a juvenile bird, including their characterization in comparison to the adult characters of the novel. Second, a version of Child is inferred as a necessary circumstance or resource in making sense of the text. The Child as *resource* is available in terms of the version of the child that must be called upon to make the novel sensible (e.g. presenting the Child as carefree or naughty rather than wise).

The version of the category Child portrayed as topic and resource in this novel can be explained by Category Analysis. Recall that the Membership Categorization Devices (MCDs), described in Chapter 4, refer to the standard sets of categories (e.g. 'family') that members of a culture commonsensically organize persons into (Sacks 1974: 218; Speier 1971: 205). Category attributes refer to the sets of activities or attributes (such as feeding a baby) that are routinely associated with a certain category of person (for example, Mother) such that members of that category are normally expected to evidence those attributes or produce those behaviours (Baker and Freebody 1987: 63). Categories and category attributes can implicate each other, that is, a category can be referenced by the assignment of certain category attributes, or, category attributes can be implicated by assignment to a category. Recall also that categories are paired in Standard Relational Pairs (SRPs) – such that to mention one, say, Boy is to have the other 'programmatically present', Girl (Eglin and Hester 1992).

As in all texts, the logic of the story in *Magpie Island* is underpinned by sets of categories and category attributes 'which are implicit and non-negotiable' (Baker and Freebody 1987: 64) in the sense that they are not generally offered as an overtly interpretable feature of the meaning-making system of the text but rather as a foundation upon which to unreflectively build the meanings of the text. The category systems that make a text sensible are documentable through Membership Category Analysis. We concentrate here on the category Child and ask: 'How is the Child described?' and 'What are the category-attributes of the Child, both as explicitly referenced and implicatively referenced through the logic of SRP partnership?' We find Child described in the following sites:

- in the juvenile bird, Magpie;
- in Adult/Child SRP represented by the characters Magpie and Eagle;
- in the SRPs, Adult/Child and Parent/Child, represented by the characters, Benny and his father Benbow, each of which is briefly examined below.

Magpie: the Child

The first pages of the novel introduce the character of Magpie in the following way.

Extract 8.1

He was young and happy. He had been hatched in a wide scraggy nest made of sticks that were as hard and knotty as knuckles. His mother had laid two eggs in it; beautiful eggs they were, with spots on them, and touches of lovely colour – blue and grey and lilac. Magpie hatched out in three weeks. At first he was a disgusting sight, naked and floppy, with a big bald head and little useless wings. He couldn't even keep his balance properly when he was sitting in the nest. But he grew very quickly.

His beak was always open and pointing upwards, waiting for his mother or father to drop something into it. A beetle maybe, or a worm or a soft fat grub. His beak was a hungry, noisy beak, stretching higher than his sister's and gobbling everything quicker than a wink. When his feathers came he grew plump and strong.

(*ILLUSTRATION*)

He learnt to fly sooner than his sister did . . . Their mother and father looked on. Sometimes they fussed and sometimes they sat still with their heads to one side.

(Thiele 1974: 1–4)

From the outset, then, the magpie is described as young with the text explaining that his youth can be read in terms of two MCDs. First, Magpie can be read in the MCD 'family' because Mother and Sister are cited, thereby categorizing Magpie, in SRP, as Son and Brother. Second, his youth can be read in terms of the MCD 'stage of life' with Magpie's egghood, hatching and development described. The initial ascription then of Magpie as young, can be simultaneously heard in terms of his childness in the family and his childness in terms of his stage of life. Magpie then doubly represents the category Child in the opening of the novel.

The text does not state, 'Magpie is a child' but rather ascribes several attributes together with young, the first being happy and then elaborating with further attributes that reference the category within a 'stage of life' device: naked, floppy, bald, little useless wings, unable to balance, growing, always hungry, noisy, and gobbling. Within the device 'family', the category Child–Magpie has the category attributes of requiring feeding and attention of his parents and engaging in sibling rivalry.

The SRP partner to the magpie is represented by Magpie's parents, the SRP partner category Adult to the category Child. The parent magpies can be read as members of the category Adult because they have offspring and having offspring is an Adult attribute, unless marked, for example, 'teen mother'. The Adult attributes are laying eggs, feeding the young magpies and attending to them while they learn to fly. Note that as SRP partner, Parent, in the device 'family', the parents have the same category attributes as they do as SRP partner, Adult, to the magpie's categorization as Child.

In the first few pages of the novel, then, the category Child is portrayed as relevant within two MCDs, 'family' and 'stage of life' as described in terms of:

- vulnerability – naked, floppy, bald, little useless wings, requiring parental attention in feeding and flying;
- precompetence – floppy, bald, little useless wings, unable to balance, growing, learning to fly;
- transience – growing, always hungry, gobbling;
- activity – noisy, learning to fly, gobbling and engaging in sibling rivalry as a matter of course.

In short, the novel's opening pages, a powerful textual position especially for establishing the central meaning systems relevant to the text, represent the Child in terms of category systems.

Magpie and the eagle: the Child and the Adult

The text also characterizes Magpie's 'childness' in SRP with an eagle as Adult.

Extract 8.2

> He was a wedge-tail, a giant with a wing-span two metres wide, and he came sailing out of the Nullabor one day like a huge slow dragonship in the air. Perhaps he wanted a mate . . .
>
> (Thiele 1974: 7)

The category Adult is available in the category attributes of being large and searching for a mate. The magpie, along with other magpies, is described in the following contrasting terms, 'They gabbled and shouted like boys' (ibid.: 9).

That the eagle and magpie are to be understood as compared on the basis of age, or 'stage of life' is explicitly stated in the text.

Extract 8.3

> And all this time he was yelling and squalling at the eagle far above, like a pip-squeak school boy giving cheek to a big visitor in the distance. They seemed so small compared with the eagle in the huge empty sky: terriers yapping at a wolf hound, fighter planes buzzing a jumbo.
>
> (ibid.: 10)

Table 8.1 summarizes the contrasting descriptions of the magpie, (sometimes cohorted with several other magpies) and the eagle.

Thus, a certain version of the magpie/Child, for example, as susceptible to excited foolishness compared here to the tolerant, calm eagle/Adult is portrayed in the text. The narrative leaves the eagle and goes on to describe the predicament Magpie is in as a direct result of his excitable, childish behaviour.

Benny and Benbow: Child/Adult, Child/Parent

The interactions between the character, Benny, a 10-year-old boy, and the character, Benbow, his father, present an account of a relationship which is at once Child–Adult and Child–Parent. These two characters embody the SRP Child/Adult in the MCD 'stage of life' and the SRP Child/Parent, or more specifically Son/Father, in the MCD 'family'. This double relevance as Child/Adult and Child/Parent is pertinent as soon as they enter the text, as the fishing clipper, the *Windhover,* sails into view.

Table 8.1 Descriptions of 'Magpie' and 'the eagle'

Magpie (child)	The eagle (adult)
young	possibly looking for a mate
gabbled and shouted like boys	calm
brave, kept up their spirits with noise	serene
gabbling	silent
roused his blood, headstrong and exciting	cruising the sky in huge arcs as if he owned all heaven
eager energy	beautiful
pipsqueak schoolboy	big visitor
small compared with eagle	
terriers	wolf hound
fighter planes	jumbo
snap/slapped	ignore/treat as joke
gnats, wasps, mosquitoes	tolerant
nuisances	not angry
squawked, gabbled	silent
game	
squabble	
swooped and swung	
nagging, shouting boastful threats	
annoying bot-fly	smooth as a ship
fooling about	

Extract 8.4

It was sailed by a fisherman from Thevenard named Benbow Bates, with a crew of five and a lot of modern fishing gear such as echo sounders and radar to help find the fish. Benbow had a son, Benny, who sailed with his father whenever he was free from school, and often when he was not. Benny loved the sea and wanted to be a fisherman as soon as he was old enough.

(Thiele 1974: 20)

Benny is introduced in relation to his father (i.e. SRP Child/Parent). Later he is described as aspiring to be a fisherman. He is not a fisherman yet because of his age (i.e. SRP Child/Adult). So, although the text goes on to describe Benny's activities on the boat, certainly those of a fisherman, the logic that the narrative calls upon is that in being an incumbent of the category Child in the device 'stage of life', Benny is unable to be a fisherman because being a fisherman is an attribute of an Adult in the device 'stage of life'; Benny is thus pre-adult. The narrative does not have to explain that logic because it is part of the everyday category logic of the culture, here necessary as a resource in making sense of this statement and topicalized, that is, explicitly mentioned (ibid.: 20–21). The relation of the category and the category attribute is created and sustained by such use.

Child / Adult

The novel portrays Benny and Benbow as Child and Adult in terms of the following contrasting attributes:

- Benny is healthy and functional, Benny 'had eyes like telescopes', whereas Benbow has begun to decay, he 'adjusted focus on binoculars'.
- Benny's preoccupations are playful and frivolous, 'lazing in the sun', 'thinking about magpie', whereas Benbow's concerns are about work, that is, fishing, time and fuel. The other adults in the crew also work, 'heaving the fish aboard' and mending bait nets, and are described in terms of their worktask, for example, Harry 'the cook'.
- Benny does not pay attention to his job on the fishing boat, and his personal interests, for example, in Magpie are all consuming whereas Benbow only has a sustained interest in work matters.
- Benny experiences strong, sad emotions and is able to understand and reason a symbolic connection between Magpie and human nature and experience.
- Benbow draws on 'adult knowledge', including the economics of consuming time and fuel and propriety with respect to others' interpersonal relationships.

The Child/Adult SRP portrayed here constructs children as healthy, with capabilities essentially due to that youthful health, prone to consuming and sustained preoccupations, experiencing intense emotions and employing symbolic understanding. Adults are decaying, preoccupied with work or 'serious' rather than 'playful' matters, and possess 'adult knowledge' about interpersonal issues and resource allocation.

Child / Parent

Benny and Benbow also portray a particular Child/Parent relationship:

- Benny is a smaller version of his parent, he is named as a diminutive of Benbow.
- Benny is subject to his father's regulation. He can only do as Benbow allows him. For example, Benbow, in turn, takes Benny to the island, makes him leave the island, refuses Benny access to the island, and allows Benny to go alone.
- Benny has some fear of his father, needing to 'pluck up courage' to express his idea, finding his parenting 'tough' at times and being troubled by his father's admonition. Benny is, however, able to convince his father to engage with him in the plan and successfully 'pleads' with his father to return to the island.

- Benbow is outwardly gruff, but inwardly knowing, loving, and kind. For example, he 'knows best', participates in his son's adventure both physically, in going to the island to release a bird and anchoring the clipper for Benny to go ashore, and, to some extent, but taking care to hide it, emotionally, 'But he was really smiling just as much as Benny was' (ibid.: 30).

Benbow 'understands' the painful learning experiences his son is going through, 'His father watched Benny's gaze and understood' (ibid.: 47) and tries to be helpful by producing rhetoric aimed at comforting his son in helping him understand a wider significance to the plight of Magpie. Although not sharing his son's preoccupation, Benbow indulges Benny to the extent that he goes to the island with the bird, allows Benny to return to the island when he 'pleads', and attempts to comfort Benny when things go wrong.

The Child/Parent SRP partnership portrayed here constructs the Child as a diminutive of the parent, subject to parental regulation, echoing the precompetence and transience we met in the opening pages, but indulged by the parent, and able to 'plead' his case successfully on occasion. The parent is wise, understanding, benevolent and indulgent, although appearing otherwise at times.

The paradox of Child–Adult relations

We see above how the text of the novel builds and sustains certain versions of the category Child and the social order, that is, the child's relations with others. These are portrayed as topics in and resources for reading the text. That is, the attributes of the category Child are described as topic and at the same moment are available as an interpretive resource for a reader to make sense of the text. Children who read *Magpie Island* read a version of themselves, of Adults/Parents and of the relations between themselves and Adults/Parents. Specifically, children read that adults believe that:

- Adults/Parents know and understand children and are benevolent towards them, having the 'best interests' of the child at heart, although possibly not appearing so to the child at the time.
- Children either know this or should be told (by reading the novel).
- Adults have certain 'adult knowledges' that children do not have.
- Children either know this or should be told.

Note that this again echoes the paradox that MacKay (1974) alerted us to, namely, that children know the theories of childhood that adults construct and thus know the version of themselves they must enact in order to be a Child and become acculturated as Adults.

So we see how the text of the novel builds and sustains certain versions of the category Child and the social world it inhabits. These versions are portrayed as topic and resource in the text. That is, the attributes of the category Child are described (topic) and called upon as an interpretive resource for the reader.

The Child described *by* the text: the Child 'assumed'

All texts 'assume' particular interpretive skills of readers. *Magpie Island*, as an object that declares itself, in packaging and marketing, for example, as an object deliberately crafted for children, is evidence of how the producers of this artifact make assumptions about the sort of person that will read this, and how they will read it. The novel therefore assumes a version of the Child who is the child reader of the novel. For example, that the novel is interspersed with illustrations assumes the category Child as having the attribute of enjoying illustration, and of 'reading' illustration as auxiliary text. We can administer a 'test of recipient design' (see Chapter 2) and conclude that adult novels are not routinely illustrated in like manner. *Routinely*, because if they are, there is often a particular purpose to their being so illustrated. Children reading the novel *Magpie Island* are presented with a version of themselves as defined by the persons who make this object available to them: teachers, writers, publishers, librarians – all of whom are adult.

As a novel specifically designed for children, *Magpie Island* assumes the reader can enact the category Child, either by virtue of being a child or having some warrant for reading a child's novel (e.g. a teacher of children). What the text reveals about its reader, it thus reveals about the category Child, as the producers of this text assume it to be. The 'sense' that a text for children makes possible reveals the interpretive capacities that text assumes of the child reader, that is, the version of the Child it assumes. The 'senses', then, that *Magpie Island* textually construct provide an account of the version of the Child as 'assumed' by the novel.

Fantasy and reality

A measure of the Child this text assumes is available in the text's interleaving of reality and fantasy in certain ways. The mixing and blending of fantasy and reality is a common device in narrative, and particularly in narrative for children. Some texts unambiguously declare their fantastic nature, others subtly combine fantasy and reality, for example, embedding fantastic elements in apparently real-world events or making fantastic interpretations of real-world events (Baker and Freebody 1988, 1989a). *Magpie Island* is neither entirely realistic nor entirely fantastic: the story world intertwines fantasy and reality in the way Baker and Freebody describe: 'Child readers are expected to treat as plausible (or appear to treat as plausible) the idea that animals can talk, just as they are elsewhere expected to treat as plausible the idea that these books describe everyday life' (1987: 59).

While the Foreword begins realistically 'John Gould, the world-famous ornithologist who lived from 1804 to 1881, once said . . .' (Thiele 1974: i), it quickly becomes a mixture of fantasy and reality, 'The magpie loves the countryside, especially the fallow land and open scrub where he is a great destroyer of insect pests (ibid.: ii). In the one sentence, the magpie 'loves the countryside', a fantastic anthropomorphized rendering of animals, and 'destroys insect pests', a realistic rendering. The text then provides an eloquent description of the magpie.

Extract 8.5

> He is a fine nuggety bird with solid shoulders and a strong businesslike beak. He stands squarely and walks with dignity. He can be firm, angry and protective, but he also has a sense of fun and often seems to have a twinkle in his eyes.
>
> (ibid.: ii)

all of which is an anthropomorphized interpretation of magpie behaviour, that is, fantasy. The magpie's song is presented both realistically and fantastically.

Extract 8.6

> He sings not merely for mating or social purposes, but for the sheer joy of it, the utter exuberance of life, and the magic and wonder and beauty of the earth.
>
> (ibid.: ii)

The Foreword thus establishes the story world as the particular blending of fantasy and reality that is culturally common in fiction for children. It establishes realistic and fantastic premises that make the story logical, sensible and possible. It is significant too that this is done in the Foreword. A Foreword precedes the fiction of the story world and is, by inference, a textual non-fiction site, that is, non-fantasy. This Foreword does different work, specifically, it foreshadows the realistic and fantastic interpretive possibilities of the coming text.

The text maintains those parameters by invoking realistic and fantastic reading relevances, either alternately or simultaneously. For example, realistic descriptions of the life cycle of the magpie, the island flora and fauna, tuna fishing, and whaling stations anchor the fantasy in a realistic setting. Certain animals are anthropomorphically rendered, that is, fantastically, for example, a character is named, Magpie, and others are described realistically, almost as elements of the setting, for example, terns, penguins and other birds: 'Long-legged waders were fishing in the rock pools, petrels were diving, cormorants watched from the shore' (ibid.: 18).

The particular fantasy/reality world constructed is very specific; it is not, however, culturally unusual. The possibility of reading the novel as a sensible and coherent story attests to our cultural practice at such narrative manipulations. The Child as assumed by this text is able to make sense out of the fantasy/reality interleave. In the following we describe the complex interleaving of fantasy and reality and the complex interpretive skills this assumes in the reader in terms of the analytic concept of the 'interpretive frame'.

Interpretive frames

Readers make sense of text. This making sense is here considered in terms of its existence as an observable phenomenon, not as an assumed psychological or intellectual process. Texts, then, make certain senses possible or available to readers. Here we analyse the novel in terms of the interpretive frames it references, orients to, and thus makes available to the reader. Interpretive frames are given their boundary and definition by the resources a reader can call upon to make sense of, in this case, a particular narrative passage. The interpretive resources called upon are the sets of relevances, truths, knowledges, pertinences, sets of categories a reader must call upon, at this moment in the text, to make the text 'sense-able'. The text hails certain interpretive frames; that is, it references the sets of parameters for sensibly interpreting the fictive world. When we examined the classroom talk about *Magpie Island* (see Chapter 9) we observed that the talk fell into three categories – realistic, anthropomorphic and representational. We here recast these categories as interpretative frames and ask, at any particular moment: can this text be read as a 'realistic narrative', as an 'anthropomorphic narrative' or as a 'representational tale', or as some combination?

The Realistic Interpretive Frame

The Realistic Interpretive Frame is informed by real-world, commonsensical categories. The sense of a realistic narrative relies on the interpretive categories of the real world and its publicly endorsed reasoning practices. Common-sense resources are community resources, that which any member of the culture knows, including concepts and beliefs. Common sense is that which is apparent, observable, in the everyday world and which members operate within taken-for-granted, unconscious ways (Payne and Cuff 1982: 5).

Real-world resources, as represented in *Magpie Island,* have been introduced above as the reality of the fantasy/reality dualism, and call upon a realistic interpretive frame. Sets of relevances of the natural sciences and geography, both in the narrative present and the narrative past are present in *Magpie Island*. The interpretive categories of the natural sciences, in which the world of animals is *different* from the world of humans, is made relevant in the zoological Latin name for the magpie as cited in the foreword (*Gymnorhina tibicean hypoleuca*) and the naturalistic description of the bandicoot. The narrative is set in a real-world geographic location, Australia: 'heading back to Thevenard, or Streaky Bay, or Port Lincoln with a good catch' (Thiele 1974: 20).

Expert and technical knowledge is also hailed as a facet of the realistic interpretive frame in the present and past of the narrative, for example, the present of the narrative furnishes technical descriptions of tuna fishing.

Extract 8.7

> His father and the crewmen were heaving fish aboard as hard as they could, and Benny was supposed to be the chummer, tossing a handful of live bait to the darting tuna every now and then to keep them excited. But he wasn't . . .
>
> (ibid.: 23)

The narrative's past is presented in terms of technical knowledge of whaling,

Extract 8.8

> whale lying at the water's edge, men cutting the thick blubber into long strips with flensing knives shaped like hockey sticks, and others finally tearing it off with rope and tackle.
>
> (ibid.: 26)

and in terms of historical knowledge.

Extract 8.9

> If Magpie could have looked back a hundred years or more he would have been amazed. The edge of the very spot where he was perched would have been red hot. Fire would have been belching all around, and inside the pots blubber . . .
>
> (ibid.: 25)

Within the Realistic Interpretive Frame, then, what is (or what has really been) are the interpretive terms of reference. In the case of *Magpie Island*, 'real' incorporates common sense, the natural sciences, geography, history and technical knowledge. These realistic interpretive relevances are referenced throughout the narrative and, as briefly noted above, in the Foreword.

The Anthropomorphic Narrative Interpretive Frame

The second interpretive frame we deal with here is the Anthropomorphic Narrative Frame. In an anthropomorphized narrative, the world of animals is the *same* as the world of humans. This contrasts with the relevances of the natural sciences called upon in the Realistic Interpretive Frame, in which the world of animals is *different* from the world of humans. In the Anthropomorphic Narrative Frame, the text establishes a set of relevances, meanings and truths from the world where animals feel, think and have personalities like humans. An animal's actions, for example, might be textually represented as demonstrating an emotional state or having intent. As noted in our discussion of reality and fantasy, anthropomorphic relevances are evident in the Foreword. Recall that the magpie is 'firm, angry, and protective', 'has a sense of fun' and 'experiences joy' (Thiele 1974: ii).

The anthropomorphic rendering of the magpie in the Foreword is immediately affirmed at the outset of the narrative.

Extract 8.10

A magpie can be happy or sad: sometimes so happy that he sits on a high, high gum tree and rolls the sunrise around in his throat like beads of pink light; and sometimes so sad you would expect the tears to drip off the end of his beak.

(ibid.: 1)

Magpies are attributed with emotional states, and further, the capacity to express their emotions through song. The central animal character is thenceforth described anthropomorphically at different moments in the novel: for example, he 'loved', he sings for joy, he experiences headstrong excitement, he 'panicked', 'he was certain', he 'felt a surge of hope', and, he 'felt very lonely'.

However, the anthropomorphization in *Magpie Island* is highly occasioned, that is, it is specific and limited, for example, the Magpie is anthropomorphized both by the novel and a character in the novel; the live bait and the tuna are not.

The Representational Tale Interpretive Frame

The third interpretive frame is the Representational Tale Frame. The distinctive feature of this interpretive frame is its focus of interest, which is not in the particularization of the events and the biographies of individual characters, but in what they stand for. Within this frame, events have symbolic rather than anthropomorphic sense or common sense. Whether or not the event has narrative importance as a plot point, it is the vehicle for *representing* a parable, an allegory, or a moral tale. To declare itself readable in this way, a text references symbols and, importantly, a moral order. In *Magpie Island*, for example, an eagle is described as 'tolerant' referencing a moral order in which tolerance is virtuous. A representational tale invests characters with symbolic significance making them representative of some cultural truth or value beyond the context of the narrative itself, that is, representative of the moral order.

The character Magpie's readability as a symbol is cued early in the novel, in fact preceding the novel, in blurb on the novel's flyleaf.

Extract 8.11

A poignant haunting story, *Magpie Island* is marked by that compassionate insight into the meaning of solitude and endurance which illuminates much of Colin Thiele's writing.

The representational interpretation is again referenced in the Foreword both in symbolic representations and in references to notions of virtue, and the moral order that categorizes certain states as virtuous. Recall again the eloquent description of the magpie as fine, solid, strong, and businesslike, standing square and walking with dignity (Thiele 1974: ii); the Foreword continues by describing his singing is a symbolic expression of 'the magic and wonder and beauty of the earth'. Indeed, 'the magic and wonder and beauty of the earth' itself is founded upon an order of virtue wherein the 'natural' world holds a special claim to such things. The magpies' call is described as a chorus, a caroling and a 'carillon', the tolling of church bells being implicitly moral and symbolic in cultures with current and/or historical bases in Christianity.

On the first page of the narrative text itself a moral reading of the magpie is made plausible when wild and domestic birds are contrasted.

Extract 8.12

> birds that live locked up in cages or sit chained in backyards, where they learn to mope or screech, and maybe gabble a few words over and over loudly and harshly like an old record. This magpie was not like that. He lived high and free in the open countryside in South Australia . . . He was young and happy.
>
> (ibid.: 1)

Chaining and caging are represented as immoral by the 'screeching', 'gabbling' and 'moping' and by juxtaposition with Magpie's countryside freedom which is elaborated in terms of his youth and happiness and later his rolling 'the sunrise around in his throat like beads of pink light'. Magpie is constructed as a symbol of freedom in a moral order that values freedom and abhors captivity.

There is also a layering of symbolic and moral representations apparent.

Extract 8.13

> Even the farmers stopped munching the crusts of their home-baked bread. 'Listen to that magpie,' they said to their wives. 'The world is a happy place today.'
>
> (ibid.: 6)

The farmer, his home-baked bread and his wife are symbolic of good, natural and wholesome rural Australia. This icon of rural mythology then reads the magpie's singing as symbolic of the condition of the world.

Anthropomorphic and Representational references are often, but not necessarily, interwoven. For example, to imbue an animal with moral attributes is a distinctive anthropomorphic move. In an anthropomorphic narrative the language may describe emotional traits or characteristics of personality. A representational tale then makes a re-reading of those emotional states or personality attributes in terms of the culture's moral, allegorical and/or symbolic systems. For example, the story of talking animals in the narrative *Animal Farm* (Orwell 1954) has been widely treated as interpretable as allegorical of the nature of communism, rather than only a story about talking animals.

Slippage and manipulation of frames in the novel

We have described here three ways in which *Magpie Island* is able to be interpreted – realistically, anthropomorphically, and representationally. The novel establishes from the outset that these three interpretive frames will be salient at different moments throughout the text. Slippage from one interpretive frame to another occurs throughout the text, sometimes shifting from sentence to sentence. For example, Magpie's loneliness (an anthropomorphic rendering) is assuaged by a friendship with a bandicoot – however, the reasoning for the ultimate failure of this friendship rests on a realistic reading: 'But even Bandicoot couldn't really break the loneliness. He was a marsupial and Magpie was a bird. He had fur instead of feathers' (Thiele 1974: 26).

The species differences between these creatures is given as the self-evident hindrance to a bond of friendship between them. Bear in mind, however, that the friendship between the characters Bandicoot and Magpie is an anthropomorphic fantasy. In an entirely anthropomorphized textual world there is no reason the magpie and bandicoot could not maintain a satisfactory friendship. The logic of this story world does not allow for this, however, for the narrative would stall. In describing the friendship as inadequate on the grounds of the incompatibility of a marsupial and a bird, the text references an anthropomorphic and realistic interpretation of the textually constructed world – simultaneously (Austin 1997).

A seamless movement from the anthropomorphic frame to the realistic is evident also in Benny's concern for the magpie's unhappiness: ' "He must be sad," Benny said', which is immediately contrasted with catching and killing tuna using live bait.

Extract 8.14

> His father and the crewmen were heaving fish aboard as hard as they could, and Benny was supposed to be the chummer, tossing a handful of live bait to the darting tuna every now and then to keep them excited.
>
> (Thiele 1974: 23)

This transition from concern to carnage achieves a transition from the anthropomorphic to the realistic narrative.

The finale of the novel provides a pivotal example of the slippage between interpretive frames. In the final scene of the novel the text ambiguates its own reading possibilities. Different interpretive frames are referenced from one line to the next with the novel itself suggesting different readings but refraining from establishing one or other as definitive. Briefly, the novel concludes with Benbow and Benny returning to Magpie Island to find that the female they have bought to the island to join the stranded Magpie has died, her eggs have died and Magpie is alone again. Benny and his father sail away.

The sequence of movement between interpretive frames in this finale is as follows:

- Benny anthropomorphizes Magpie's plight: 'Benny looked back at the cove "Poor old Magpie. He looks so lonely there – worse than he was before"' (Thiele 1974: 46).
- Benbow, the adult character, explains the symbolic and moral interpretation of the narrative, that is, provides a reading from within a Representational Tale Interpretive Frame: 'Never mind, Benny. Think of what he stands for. He's a symbol, a talisman. Endurance carved into a silhouette. The everlasting picture of the one against the world. Something for people to get their inspiration from' (ibid.: 47).
- Benny, the child character, elaborates that representational reading in terms of Magpie as a symbol:

> And then, suddenly he saw what his father meant. He would live out his whole life there now, defying all the storms and thunderclaps that heaven could turn against him . . . He would become a legend as big as a mountain. He would be Crusoe for modern men. He would stir the hearts of lonely people and make stale dreams come fresh again.
> (ibid.: 48)

- the Anthropomorphic Narrative Interpretive Frame is reinstated as a relevance: 'Goodbye Magpie,' Benny whispered. 'Don't get too lonely all by yourself out there' (ibid.: 48);
- the status of the final reading is further ambiguated, with Benbow stating; 'tomorrow's going to be a bright new day' (ibid.: 48);
- however, the final line of the novel reads: 'But it was dark outside' (ibid.: 48).

It seems that although the child character Benny was able to articulate the representational reading, he has not accepted it as the *only* reading – he sees what his father meant and can read Magpie as a symbol, but he also maintains an emotional, that is, anthropomorphic, rendering of Magpie – the sadness of Magpie's plight.

So in this final scene of the novel the text ambiguates its own reading possibilities. Different interpretive frames are referenced from line to line. The novel itself does not establish the Representational Tale as its definitive interpretive frame but as one of a variety of possible interpretive frames.

Conclusion: the Child in *Magpie Island*

This chapter has interrogated the text of the novel for the category Child as textually *portrayed* and *assumed,* that is, described *in* the text and *by* the text. Category Analysis explains the Child as textually portrayed in the MCD 'stage of life' in relation to the SRP partner Adult, and in the MCD 'family' in relation to the SRP partner Parent. The novel, then, affords the possibility of interpretation in terms of the category Child both in the MCD 'stage of life' and the MCD 'family'.

The Child assumed by the text is available to us in the specifics of the distinctive, though culturally familiar, blend of fantastic and realistic pertinence. The interpretive complexity of these interpretive vacillations is accessible using the analytic concept of the interpretive frame. This novel references at least three major sets of interpretive resources; here called the Realistic Interpretive Frame, the Anthropomorphic Narrative Interpretive Frame and the Representational Tale Interpretive Frame. These interpretive standpoints, together with the slippage throughout the novel from one interpretive frame to another, afford many layers of meaning in the novel. Furthermore, the conclusion of the novel precluded the possibility of making a final or definitive interpretation, even in the face of the adult character's articulation of that interpretation.

It is significant that it is the *child* (Benny) who ambiguates the adult's instruction, to the child and the reader, to reread the events as allegory. The child confronts what is in fact an 'unhappy ending' to the events (Magpie is alone and lonely). This makes two possible readings of the category Child as portrayed available:

1   the Child as understanding the underlying allegorical meaning but resisting an adult's determination to render the events palatable by reducing them to symbols; or alternatively
2   the Child as embedded in anthropomorphism; a mature (adult) outlook on the world either refuses anthropomorphic renderings altogether, reading a 'deeper significance' into banal day-to-day events, or renders painful events survivable by overlooking the individual's reality (Magpie is alone and lonely) and attributing symbolic significance.

Crucially for our analysis here, each reading rests on a different version of the category Child. The first attributes to the Child interpretive competence and moral fortitude, that is, the ability to comprehend the symbolism but also a willingness to face events even though this might be painful. The second reading rests on a version of the Child within a developmental model which overlaps the Child/Adult developmental continuum with interpretive capacities in such a way that the child is represented as precompetent – developing through a (childlike) anthropomorphic interpretive capacity towards a (mature) representational interpretation. According to this version of the Child, Benny, the child in the novel, can be read as 'on the cusp', that is, developmentally capable of making a symbolic reading but still lingering with the anthropomorphic reading.

However, the version of the child reader, as assumed by the *structure* of the novel, that is, the slippage from one frame to another and the ambiguity of the conclusion, resists the latter construction. The Child as assumed by the text has sophisticated interpretive capabilities. The child who can make sense of this novel is assumed to be able to do the following competently:

• interpret within realistic, anthropomorphic and representational frames;
• 'slip' from one interpretive frame to another in order to read the novel as sensible and coherent;
• tolerate, or even appreciate, ambiguity in interpretation, that is, accept parallel final renderings of the story, a 'sad' ending *and* a 'symbolic' ending;
• have the emotional fortitude to sustain the 'unhappy ending' of Magpie's abandonment, loneliness and inevitable solitary death.

Therefore, even though the Child as portrayed draws on notions of pre-competence and development, the interpretive structure resists a reading of the Child only within restrictive developmental frameworks. There is, then, some tension between the Child as portrayed and the Child as assumed, this tension itself establishing grounds for reading the Child as interpreter of complex text. Student readers need to work within that tension.

The Child portrayed in this novel and the Child assumed by *Magpie Island* thus work together in interesting ways that seem at times contradictory. We saw the Child portrayed primarily in terms of attributes of vulnerability, pre-competence, transience, and activity. These attributes are expressed in many ways, for example, the baby birds requiring parental care and attention and the depiction of Benny as subject to his father's regulation, echo the Child as essentially precompetent, not quite ready to care for itself, and vulnerable, available to danger if not supervised. Quite differently, the 'slippage' from one interpretive frame to another throughout the novel and the ambiguity of the conclusion enact a complex version of the Child–Reader. So while Membership Category Analysis revealed that the text assembles the Child according to a 'stage of life' device, the structuring of the interpretive possibilities of the text challenges the very assumptions of precompetence and development that the dominant stage of life device is based upon.

Again, we recognize MacKay's (1973) point that children know the theories of Childhood that adults construct and thus know the version of themselves they must enact in order to be a Child. Specifically, to make sense of *Magpie Island* the Child–Reader, granted, like all readers, must know the theories of Childhood that underpin the novel. The significance of this for Child–Readers, however, is that their reading necessitates their enacting adult versions of *themselves*.

9 Teaching the category into being

We have explored the varying enactments of the category attributes of the Child through classroom talk. In this chapter we revisit that site, but with the particular interest of examining how the affordances of the novel discussed in the previous chapter are made available. In the context of the literature lesson, classroom talk is the public display, on the part of the teacher and students, of how to read a given novel for a given lesson, of what sense to make and how to make it. It is in the classroom talk that students learn what, of all the possible things that might be said and written about the novel, is 'sayable' and 'writable' in and for the classroom.

This chapter examines the talk of one classroom for the re-rendering of the narrative text as a text for the child in school. In order to do this, we first establish that the category Child is relevant in the talk in the classroom. We initially show how the routine categorization work of the participants established the category Child, explicitly and implicitly, as an unproblematic category in the talk. We then examine the ways that the category Child is made relevant to the classroom context. We develop the term Child–Student to describe the simultaneous category relevances of this double-incumbency. We then examine ways that the category Child–Student is made relevant to this classroom context. We therefore further refine our focus to reveal a set of concepts that are assembled to construct a particular version of the child as not only a Child–Student but, more specifically, a Child–Student of Literature.

The Child and Childhood defined

Chapters 5, 6 and 7 demonstrated particular ways that the category Child was achieved in classrooms. These chapters focused on precompetence and cohorting in the whole class and group work situations. Here we retrace some of that ground and extend our review to examine further contents of the category Child as relevant to the classroom context. A close examination of the *content* of the talk shows both how the teacher and students *construct* the category Child in their talk, and how the teacher and students *use* the category Child as a resource in making sense of their talk.

The category Child as relevant

As a matter of course, the teacher and students explicitly talked about children as an organizing category. They routinely assigned certain attributes to the category incumbents in their discussion of *Magpie Island*.

Extract 9.1

118 *T:*   . . . what sort of style does Colin Thiele have (2) Tonie?
119 *Tn:*   Umm a sort of (3) nice style? Sort of kids' style? Like he can make it really dramatic but he can make it nice sort of//
120 *T:*   What makes it nice, I know you're using that word <u>nice</u> and I
121 *Tn:*   Umm, well the way he uses animals and – like – he puts it from the animal's point-of-view and stuff [like that.
122 *T:*   [So you can] relate to it he does things that you think (2) you enjoy reading [about.

At Turn 119, Tonie articulated first of all that there can be such a category as Child, the members of which share certain characteristics such that a text can be devised specifically for those category members, and then defined what features this category would enjoy, namely 'dramatic but (still) nice'. In Turn 121, the category Child was further attributed with having an interest in animals. Note that Tonie's description at Turn 121 'from an animal's point-of-view' refers to an assumed susceptibility to anthropomorphism among this specialist readership (see Chapter 8 and Chapter 2 also).

We saw in Chapter 8 that the category Child within the MCD 'stage of life' was invoked as a sense-making resource in the text of *Magpie Island*. In the classroom talk, as well, this category Child was invoked, specifically, in Lesson 8 when the participants made relevant the category pair, Youth–Elderly.

Extract 9.2

49 *T:*   Alright, I'll pose a question. Do you think it was better – that Benny gave Magpie those moments of happiness or would it have been better to have left him alone altogether – What would you, if you were Magpie what would <u>you</u> have rather had, Janine?
50 *J:*   The other magpie?
51 *T:*   You would have rather had those moments, right?
52 *Am:*   Because you could have had happiness for a while at least . . .
53 *T:*   Right, you could have had happiness for a while.
54 *St:*   He could have thought about it afterwards (. . .)
55 *T:*   Right, Magpie was left with what?
56 *Ss:*   Memories
57 *T:*   Memories, <u>wonderful</u> memories, happy memories – that during the cold weeks, cold weeks of winter he could pull those memories out

and go over them in his mind. – What part of our community (2) tend
to do that? Some people in our community tend to look back and
look at their memories and all their good times, what part of the
community, Clinton?

58 *Cl:* Elders.

59 *T:* The elders, older people, yes. They tend to think – of all the wonderful things that happened. Why do you think older people sometimes
do that more so than younger people – Miranda?

60 *Mi:* (. . .)/

61 *An:* Because they've got more memories/

62 *T:* They've got more memories, of course they have, of course they
have, they've accumulated years and years of memories. – Yes.

63 *St:* They probably can't get out as much as younger people/

64 *T:* Right, they haven't got the same ability to get out and <u>do</u> as <u>you</u>
people. What are <u>you</u> people in the process of doing now?

65 *Am:* School/

66 *T:* Apart from school Amber, Justine?

67 *Ju:* Playing around and sport and stuff//

68 *T:* You're actually building what? –

69 *Tn:* Friends/

70 *S:* Memories/

71 *T:* Your memories, yes – you're actually living life to its absolute fullest at
the moment? – and that's what you do when you're your age, when
you're eleven or twelve? or ten?, you actually – <u>live</u> life to its its fullest.
When you get <u>older</u> and you're not as active you tend to live a lot on
what <u>happened</u> before. What <u>used</u> to be (2) And so perhaps Magpie –
is going to pull out those memories and look back.

Through the talk, the categories Elders and Young People were unproblematically evoked and described in terms of stereotypic attributes. The category attributes assembled for the category Elderly were: inactive (64, 71), wonderful
accumulated memories (59, 62), and, living in the past, remembering rather
than living (71), and not making new memories (71). The category attributes
of the category Young People were: active (64, through inference 71), living
life to the full (71), building memories (68–71), and, living in the present (71).
Importantly, the students in the class were aligned with the Young category
(64: '*you* people').

What we see above is the categorization work of all the participants in the
setting, the teacher and the students, in referencing particular categories and
category-attributes as relevant to making sense of their talk. Thus, the category
Child in an MCD 'stage of life' is evoked implicitly and explicitly as an organizing principle by these participants in this talk.

The child and the book

The child as a relevance in the school context

The relevance of the 'childness' of the students in this class is evident in the tasks the teacher requires of them. Recall the fantasy/reality interleave discussed in Chapter 8 with reference to the novel. Baker and Freebody (1989a: 71) noted this fantasy/reality interleaving as a particular child relevance. In a similar manner, the students in this class are asked to participate in an adult-defined, child-like playfulness with the text, particularly in relation to the mixture of reality and fantasy. For example, a task requiring that the students imagine a conversation between two magpies rests on an assumption that the students will engage with this reality/fantasy combination unproblematically. The task reads:

IMAGINE THAT THE TWO MAGPIES ARE ABLE TO TALK. WRITE A CONVERSATION OF WHAT MIGHT HAVE BEEN SAID BETWEEN THEM WHEN THEY FIRST MET.

As Baker and Freebody pointed out, it can be assumed that these students do know that the magpies would not, in reality, have such a conversation. The students are expected to be able and willing to participate in this playfulness, that is, as adults define children's playfulness with text to be (1989a: 70–71). The talk that ensues makes it clear that the interleaving of fantasy and reality has particular parameters – matters related to sexuality are not to be broached and the possibility that they are brother and sister is quickly and firmly denied.[1] Interestingly, later in the novel when the magpies do mate, the sexuality is accomplished in the talk as a realistic pertinence – the magpie's mate – rather than an anthropomorphic one in which they, for example, might have had a romance and made love. The interleaving of fantastic and realistic pertinences is complex.

The assumption that the students will be unproblematically susceptible to this particular reality and fantasy interleaving is available in the teacher's choice of task and in the students' participation in that task. Furthermore, the students' competence in participating in the delicate boundary work is relied upon in this interaction. This exercise simply will not work if the students are unable to manipulate the boundaries of the worlds of fantasy and reality in very particular ways.

The Child–Student: precompetence, participation and precomprehension

Precompetence

Recall that in Chapter 5 Speier's observation that the attribute of precompetence is a culturally defining feature of the category Child was taken as a kernel in examining the enactment of precompetence as an attribute of the Child–Student. We briefly revisit precompetence here, demonstrating that the interactants at this site also achieve the students as precompetent. Consider the following extracts.

Extract 9.3

10 *Rs:*   I made a few mistakes.
11 *T:*   That's the trouble, it's hard to write directly into your book but it's a skill that I really want you to learn because if you wrote a draft copy for every single thing that you wrote, you would never finish. So we've now got to press on and learn the skill of writing directly – and it's a hard skill to learn, isn't it?

Extract 9.4

45 *Tn:*   Anna's story is really good, it's really, really good but she doesn't think that it that it//
46 *T:*   Well, maybe Anna when you've written a bit more we might share it with you./
47 *Tn:*   But it's really go:od.

In the first example, the teacher recast Russell's self-proclaimed mistakes in terms of his precompetence in the skill of 'writing directly'. It is audible as precompetence rather than incompetence because the skill in question is articulated as learnable. Writing directly into a book was cast as a skill in a series of skills that are developmentally ordered. Wherein writing into a book without drafting was described as a 'hard skill', notwithstanding that for much of their schooling life this is what the students were asked to do; drafting and redrafting being a feature of storywriting, published writing, project writing or similar, rather than routine class work.

   In the second extract, the teacher formulated Anna's resistance as reported by Tonie as a prewillingness rather than unwillingness. She constructed Anna's prewillingness as founded in her precompetence, rather than incompetence. The work is not unfit to be shared, rather, it is unfinished, and, when finished, it will be competent, that is, shareable.

   Completed work is not, however, a guarantee of competence as exemplified in the teacher's response to Justine's reading of her work to the class in Lesson 2.

Extract 9.5

284 *T:*   Very good, you've tried to use some very descriptive words in your summary? Again perhaps a little too much detail but – <u>very</u> well done

Note that Justine is nominated as not having used descriptive words but rather as having '*tried* to use descriptive words'. Her writing was not evaluated as competent, but as an attempt at competence.

Participating and precomprehending

Further to the teacher and students together participating in enactments of the students as precompetent, they enacted the students as participating and as precomprehending. Participation that evidenced *striving* is a particularly valued form of participation. The teacher and students together constructed the students as participating by *striving* for competence, and *trying* to comprehend.

Extract 9.6

7 *T:*   Is there anyone else who'd like to share the *beginning* of their story not all of it (2) so that people get an idea of what other people are writing about? Clinton? What about yours?/

8 *Cl:* No/

9 *T:*   No not yet, OK. Tanya?

10 *Ty:* Alright.

11 *T:*   OK, you had your hand up.

Notice that at Turn 9 the teacher reformulated Clinton's unqualified refusal as a prereadiness rather than an unwillingness. Prereadiness does not exclude participation, whereas unwillingness is an indication of non-participation. When Tanya agreed to read her story (10), the teacher reinforced her status as participating (Turn 11), 'you had your hand up'.

In the following extract, striving as an attribute was defined as something that can be learned. That striving can be learned was tied to development in terms of the students' progression from 3rd to 6th grade which was, for these students, the final year of primary school.

Extract 9.7

53 *T:* . . . hey <u>that</u> is scarcely a page, you are <u>sixth</u> grade now, we're not in third grade, I want that story extended [please.

54 *Co:* [Yeah, it is.] That's just umm, – another bit, that's not the, yeah, there's going to be more.

55 *T:* There's going to be more, OK. (Well you just)/

56 *Co:* Cause like I (. . .)

57 *T:* Right, good. Its just you've got to learn to push yourself past the page of writing now Colin.

In this example, the inadequate length of Colin's story was not interpreted by the teacher as non-participation, incompetence or incomprehension but rather as precompetence, insofar as Colin needed to learn to write more. This particular precompetence was described as a developmental issue in terms of the changes evidenced in progression through the grades of school: not only should Colin learn the 'skill' of writing more than a page, but he should also comprehend that he is expected to write more now that he is developmentally ready, and that being able to do so turns upon 'pushing [him]self' that is, participating with renewed striving. Colin's inadequate work and his need to learn marked him as precomprehending and precompetent. The remedy for these states, as described by the teacher is to engage in renewed participation and, inferentially, continued development.

To be a successful Child–Student in the context of this classroom was to display the self as participating, and ideally, as striving. Comprehension issues were cast as matters of precomprehension rather than incomprehension. Striving to participate is overlaid with the relevance of precompetence. This precompetence is an attribute of the Child, who will 'develop' into competence and the Student who will 'strive' to become competent. Significantly, the teacher and students mutually accomplish this construction.

The Child–Student of literature

The work of accomplishing and sustaining categories is seldom an end in itself. Rather, the categories are accomplished as a contextual resource in achieving some other work. The category work is central to its achievement, but unspoken. In demonstrating this point, and adhering to our initial assertion that we will rise to Jenks' implicit challenge and examine a socially located accomplishment of the category Child, we turn to examining the interactive accomplishment in the talk of the Child–Student as specific to the classroom literature lesson. Note the articulation of the Child–Student of literature as the *topic* of the talk.

Extract 9.8

1 *T:* Let's just think about what we did yesterday, and do a quick recap. Joshua, are you right? When we do, when we work with a book a little more closely than what you people are used to with books, you have to be prepared to look back at the same words several times. You are used to – reading the book, listening to it, reading it, perhaps discussing it like we did yesterday and then leaving it – and not treating it again. We are actually going to treat this book in more detail. We're going to be going back and looking in detail at what the author has written and some of your <u>ideas</u> about what the author has written. (2) Some of what you do, you will need to actually reread certain parts of the chapter that we read, that we read yesterday. – Some of it – some of the work that we do, I'll be asking for your <u>opinion</u> – so you can write what you <u>think</u> – and that's your opinion, it's not

mine, it's not Colin Thiele's it's something that <u>you</u> think the book means to you. Ok? – Alright. Let's start off by – someone being able to tell me, just briefly what happened in Chapter One yesterday.

In this turn at talk, the teacher detailed for the students her version of what becoming a Child–Student of literature entailed. Specifically, it involved: reading the novel closely; looking back at the same words; treating the novel in detail; rereading the novel; and thinking about the novel in terms of ideas and opinions. The teacher's account for detailing this category so explicitly rests in the students' inexperience in enacting this category.

Understandings of the nature of the Child–Student of Literature are also a *resource* in making sense in this context, in making sense of the activities themselves and in making sense of doing a series of activities about a book in the first instance. Our analyses of the transcripts of talk around the novel *Magpie Island*, using the category Child as both topic and resource, revealed two broad inflections of the Child–Student of literature: the skilled and the literary. Each of these inflections was further ramified in the talk. Specifically, the Skilled Child–Student of literature was attributed with interactive skills, managerial skills and literate skills. The literate Child–Student of literature was attributed with having access to realistic, anthropomorphic and representational interpretive frameworks. Each of these sets and sub-sets is discussed in the following sections.

The skilled Child–Student of literature

The interactive skills of the Child–Student of literature

Our analyses showed that the students were routinely called upon to display the 'rules' of classroom interaction, for example, when and how to answer a question. Echoing earlier researchers on this issue (MacLure and French 1981; Freiberg and Freebody 1995), we found several features of students' contributions, such as timing, tone, pace of delivery, length and structure, were accomplished by participants as important in determining whether a given contribution was incorporated as a productive contribution to the ongoing talk of the classroom.

Extract 9.9

47 T: Right, the actual surface area of wings were bigger, if his wings are bigger then he is going to use what, less?

48 St: Energy/

49 T: Energy and effort to get through the air, his actual momentum is going to take him through the air, whereas poor old Magpie – had to use a lot of energy, a lot of flap to get where he wanted to go. Yes?

50 *St:*   Well, near our house we've got a, umm, there's paddock in, umm, across the road and when there was a fire there and the eagle left but he's come back now and the magpies always chasing it but the eagle always wins.

51 *T:*   Right. Eagle came from where, you're given information where did eagle come from.

52 *St:*   The Nullarbor

53 *T:*   From the Nullarbor, right so he was a <u>stranger</u> to?

Note that the anecdote at Turn 50 is not acknowledged in Turn 51, thereby treating Turn 50 as irrelevant to both the ongoing talk, and the routine of the interaction – teacher question, short student response, teacher evaluation – is reinstated immediately.[2] The specific criteria of the anecdote's rejection are not made explicit. In terms of content, Turn 50 relates an anecdote similar to the events in the novel. The current talk is, however, about styles of propulsion, rather than the consequences of propulsion. Further, examination of the reinstated interactive routine suggests perhaps that the anecdote was rejected not in terms of content but in terms of turn design; it was a long turn compared to other student turns. One of the skills of the Child–Student of literature in this classroom, then, is adherence to certain interactive rules.

The managerial skills of the Child–Student of literature

The management of each writing task received considerable attention in the talk with explicit instructions given on such managerial concerns as setting out the page, how many lines to write in answering each question, what sort of pen to use, where to place pictures, whether and how to draw a margin or border or picture.

Extract 9.10

237 *T:*   — Alright, – the nitty gritty of how to set it out, listening. Your setting out will vary according to you. You will have another <u>sheet</u> – with some questions on but not as many this time, so <u>allow</u> a page or half a page to put in a question sheet, it really doesn't matter where it goes. I'll bring that tomorrow for you. If you wish to start, if you're three-quarters of the way down a page and you would like to start a new page for Chapter Two, by all means do so. Otherwise, just leave a line, put a sub-heading Chapter Two and go on//

238 *Tn:*   Mrs Field, should we leave one of the pages to put, umm//

239 *T:*   Yes, you can leave a page to put your typewritten sheet on, yes, please. But I don't mind where you leave it, Okay

In this extract, where to paste the question sheet, where to start writing and whether to leave a page out, were all explained in detail. In this classroom talk, detailed instructions were often unremarkably followed by an exhortation in the nature of 'It's your book, it's your decision'.

Management of time and 'thinking' was also explicitly taught, as is the management of the body.

Extract 9.11 (a)

126 *T:*   Right, quietly please. <u>Think</u> before you <u>answer</u> your questions. <u>Don't</u> think of this exercise, kids as, I have got to get this finished, I've gotta write, I really would rather you spend – <u>time</u> before you answer each question, <u>thinking</u> out your answers so you get the best answer that you possibly <u>can</u>. (3) Try and include <u>all</u> the information that you've gained – from reading your story. (12) You may put that sheet just wherever it fits your book. (2) (*To a small group of students.*) Don't spend time decorating now please, kids, just get on to your main writing.

Extract 9.11 (b)

251 *T:*   <u>You</u> need to sit up too, that's one of the reason's your writing's so terribly, terribly untidy.

The students in no way marked their hearing of these instructions as unusual or remarkable, indicating that explicit and detailed management talk was routine and mundane to these participants.

The literate skills of the Child–Student of literature

What are often commonly called the 'skills' of literacy, for example, how to spell, read, write in sentences and punctuate, are also evident in the talk as a facet of the students' skill repertoire. In terms of specifically reading a narrative, the students are asked to refer to the text for details of the narrative such as setting, plot, character and event, and also details in the language such as vocabulary and punctuation. Instructions were again explicit and the students demonstrated practised ease with the interactive routines in which instruction takes place; that is, the students made few mistakes in their answers and the many questions they asked were heard by the teacher as unremarkable.

Extract 9.12 (a)

126 *T:*   You've got an apostrophe there have you, yes, good.
127 *Tn:*   Mrs Field, do you put the 'i' in whaling?
128 *T:*   'W' 'h' 'a' 'l' 'i' 'n' 'g' you don't put the 'e' in you miss out the 'e'.

Extract 9.12 (b)

134 *T:*   Get your book out and read that.
. . . take your book out, if you're looking at what was the island before, get your book out and read the paragraph that describes it – this isn't a memory test (2) We're looking at the book and seeing how it's been written. (6) It's not how much you can remember.

Extract 9.12 (c)

249 *T:*   . . . What do we start a sentence with Jeffrey?
250 *Jf:*   Capital letter.

In these extracts, and throughout the corpus of talk around the novel *Magpie Island*, the teacher and students routinely participated in explicit and repeated instruction in what we have here called the skills of interaction, task management, and literacy. Importantly, it is in the routine interactive procedures of classroom talk that the public display of what is taken to count in the classroom as being a skilled student is achieved.

The literary Child–Student

Recall that in Chapter 8 we made use of three interpretive frames: the Realistic, Anthropomorphic and Representational Interpretive Frames. We reported that these had been found in our analyses of the classroom talk. Here we report the analyses that brought forth these interpretive frames. Specifically, we show how the teacher and students oriented to different interpretive frames at different moments in the classroom talk.

Realistic Interpretive Frame

The Realistic Interpretive Frame comprises interpretation that refers to the real, known world (see Chapter 8 for more detail). Concern for realistic detail is apparent in stretches of talk dedicated to recounting real-world facets of the text, often in minute detail.

Extract 9.13

313 *Cl:*   How do magpies sleep, do they just roost – in trees. (2)
314 *Aa:*   Umm, but, but, don't they put their beak under their wing like ducks?
315 *St:*   Yeah they do/
316 *T:*   I think they do, yes

The common sense of the real world is another resource in sense making.

Extract 9.14 (a)

82 *T:* If it had been <u>us</u> marooned on the island would we have watched the boats with – with<u>out</u> interest?

83 *Ss:* No.

Extract 9.14 (b)

86 *T:* What would we in fact be trying to do to those occasional boats, Boyd.

87 *By:* Umm get attention/

88 *T:* Right, how could you go about getting somebody's attention if you're on an island and the boat's a speck out on the horizon, Anita.

89 *An:* You might have to get, like start a fire or get some red//

90 *St:* Jump up and down.

91 *An:* red clothes red clothing or whatever [and (.)//

92 *T:* [Yes, yes, make] make some smoke with a fire or wave some clothing or do something to attract attention. But of course the boat meant nothing to Magpie, it wasn't a <u>means</u> of escape

In Turn 82, the teacher oriented to the Realistic Interpretive Frame as relevant to that classroom moment. In subsequent turns, both teacher and students unremarkably accomplished the real world as the relevant frame within which to work, and unproblematically discussed the common–sense, assumed cultural knowledge of getting rescued from a deserted island.

Anthropomorphic Narrative Interpretive Frame

Our analyses showed that the students also engaged readily in anthropomorphic relevances, that is, worked within the interpretive framework of animals possessing human qualities. The participants' orientation to this interpretive frame is evident in the continuation of the talk about escaping a desert island (displayed in the Extracts 9.14 (a) and (b)).

Extract 9.15

98 *T:* Alright, Boyd, you've got something to contribute.

99 *By:* Umm – there, he, he probably, he probably would think that the boat's dangerous because it's got people on it on them, and where he used to live there were hunters that would shoot at them and he'd probably think that they're hunters [and stuff

100 *T:* [Yes,] I think that's a very good comment, he'd probably view human beings as a danger rather than a means of escape, definitely.

102 *T:*   . . . There are some very interesting words used in this little paragraph, which gives you an idea as to how Magpie is now feeling . . .
103 *K:*   He feels lonely?
104 *T:*   Right

In Turn 99, Boyd suggested that the magpie would 'think' that a boat is dangerous and the teacher elaborated this point in Turn 100. This is an Anthropomorphic Narrative Interpretive Frame within which the magpie is available as a thinking, and later, in Turn 102 and onward, feeling creature. The teacher and students talked as if the magpie has the same cognitive and emotional relevances as a human. Notice that this extract is just a few turns after Extract 9 in which *Magpie Island* is discussed in terms of real-world common sense.

This 'slippage' from one interpretive frame to another, in which the talk seamlessly moves from realistic to anthropomorphic references, is a feature of the talk about *Magpie Island* in this classroom. It is a permutation of the interleaving of the relevances of reality and fantasy and has direct consequences for the enactment of the Student–Reader. The students display what in this context counts as an ability to participate in the interpretive talk which slips from one relevance frame to another, sometimes sentence by sentence.

Representational Tale Interpretive Frame

The Representational Tale Interpretive Frame are interpretations that call on the relevances of symbolism, allegory and moral, that is, what the story represents rather than what it presents. In the following, the Representational Tale is introduced to a classroom discussion of the novel's conclusion.

Extract 9.16 (a)

35 *T:*   . . . Do you think that he was trying to say, not only – Magpie survived – but perhaps there was a message there for – other people? Anita?
36 *An:* That, umm, that animals have feelings too and, umm, people destroy their lifestyle and stuff?
37 *T:*   Right, so you look at it from the animals, seeing that perhaps animals do have feelings and they do feel things, and that they can feel mateship and love and and caring. Right? What about taking it the other way (2) Do you think Colin Thiele is making us think about people as well as animals. – Annette?
38 *At:* Sort of like, umm, it's kinda good to have people the same things like the feelings and like (.)/
39 *T:*   Right, perhaps people go through the same things that Magpie went through.

(Teacher reads a section from the novel)

Extract 9.16 (b)

41 T: Right, so he's saying that, he's really not talking about Magpie there is
       he? He's talking about people. – People living their life – and having to
       endure the same sorts of things as Magpie did . . .

(and again later)

Extract 9.16 (c)

114 T: — I think the author's also trying to tell us something else, that
        people? – as well as Magpie but I think he's really giving us a message
        about ourselves. That we are able to – do what?

We can note that the teacher framed the discussion in terms of the Representational Tale Interpretive Frame with the words 'perhaps there was a message
there for other people?' (35). Anita answered initially within an Anthropomorphic Narrative Interpretive Frame, 'animals have feelings too' and then a
Realistic Interpretive Frame, 'people destroy their lifestyle and stuff' (36). In
Turn 39, the teacher heard Annette's turn (38) as reinstating the relevances of
a Representational Tale Interpretive Frame, 'people go through the same
things that Magpie went through' (and see also Turn 41 'He's talking about
people'). Turn 114 is perhaps the clearest orientation to a representational reading, 'I think he's really giving us a message about ourselves'.

The teacher was, through questioning about opinions and giving her own
opinion (Turn 114), making talk about the magpie as a symbol of moral
rather than psychological personhood relevant to the discussion at hand. The
teacher asked the students to use this notion of what Magpie 'stood for' to
discuss the meanings of the novel. She adopted the author's fiction that this
character is not named, 'Before I start this story I had better tell you that he
didn't have a name' (Thiele 1974: 1) and oriented to this non-naming as a
key to reading the representational tale, that is, the key to reading Magpie as
a universal symbol, the bearer of a message – rather than a merely a character
with a story to tell.

In the next lesson, some students did indeed use the Representational Tale
Interpretive Frame. Some students were thus audible as able to read the symbolic meaning and thereby know that 'the moral' is indeed 'the lesson' and,
further, know how to draw that moral lesson from the novel.

Extract 9.17

174 Aa: Maybe he doesn't believe in calling animals names because they,
         because they might not suit that name sort of? – becaus:se/
175 T: Last week we talked about what the magpie stood for in the end. (2)
         He stood for the ability, I think you told me, to survi:ive. – Does that

help you in thinking perhaps why he didn't give Magpie a name.
This is only my feelings, it may be different to what you think, Boyd?

176 *By:* (*spoken in a slow, halting manner.*) Well, like just say you give – a dog –
a dog a name like, umm umm, Mad, Mad (Hatter) or something –
you you normally – think its – name – like, that – you might think its
name means – that he's ma:ad – a:and names/(*students start to giggle*)

177 *T:* I know what you're trying to say. Yes, Justine?

178 *Ju:* It's a bit like giving something a personality when you've hardly met
the character.

179 *T:* Does Magpie, what does Magpie <u>remain</u> at the end of the story, he is
still what?

In Turn 174, Anna introduced what could be heard as an attempt to articulate
the notion of the name as a symbol of the character. Boyd elaborated that (176)
and Justine (178) built upon the reading of a name as a symbol and called upon
a moral order in which it is improper to name, and thereby judge, a character
prematurely.

Although there is evidence that students were able to engage in representational talk, that is, talk of moral, symbol and allegory, the teacher's response to
these utterances did not validate them as being representational readings that
were possible responses to her articulated search for what the magpie 'stood
for'. At Turn 175, the teacher made no apparent response to Anna's representational interpretation at 174, but rather reminded the students to think about
what Magpie 'stood for'. Boyd's attempt (176) was overlapped with giggling
from class members and the teacher terminated his turn while Justine's reading
was met with a reformulation of the question. Therefore, none of the students'
answers were validated by the teacher as 'correct' and the episode did not audibly reach any conclusion about what it was that the magpie represented.

We can say that any interpretation is motivated in that, if there is a choice,
that which is *not* chosen is deleted from the bank of possible meanings. That
which is chosen, then, is put to work. For example, in the classroom talk
about the conclusion of the novel, wherein the central character of the novel
is left stranded and alone, with no chance of rescue, on a windswept island
far from the mainland, his mate and eggs recently killed, the students described
the emotional tenor in terms of sadness, sorrow, disappointment and depres-
sion. However, as the following example shows, the teacher worked hard to
suggest, and ultimately explicitly stated, the relevance of a symbolic reading
of the magpie as a symbol of 'hope'.

Extract 9.18

104 *T:* Sorrow? Is there another feeling other than sorrow, Tonie?

105 *Tn:* Well, at the end how it says BUT IT WAS DARK OUTSIDE and
he said it was going to be a bright new day tomorrow, well, it was
gonna like sort of begin all again? The next day?

106 T: Right. Does anyone feel that the author has left the reader

108 T: Does the author feel, do <u>you</u> think at least, does anyone feel that he's left you with perhaps a feeling of hope?

Later in the same lesson the students again used the words sorrow and sadness to describe the novel's conclusion until finally, Tonie (see Turn 105, above), echoed the teacher's word, 'hope' (164).

Extract 9.19

162 S: Depressed.
163 T: Yes?
164 Tn: Hope? – So that it might happen maybe he'll//
165 T: Maybe he'll be happy and survive. Yes.

The teacher interrupted Tonie's answer and stated her own audibly preferred version of hope: 'Maybe he'll be happy and survive'. The teacher thereby explicitly oriented to the relevance of a representational interpretation of the novel. These participants put considerable work into achieving this happy ending in the face of apparent woe. The rationality of such effort may be found in part in a prior classroom conversation that articulated the imperative that children's stories have a happy ending.

Extract 9.20

4 Tn: I thought it was going to be happy at the end like they have have, umm
5 T: Who thought it was going to have a happy ending. (3) (*some students raise hands*)
    <u>Why</u> did you think it was going to have a happy ending.
6 Ab: Because most stories do.
7 T: Because most stories do.

The teacher a few turns later reformulated Amber's response as particular to children's stories.

13 T: — It's a very interesting ending. As Amber said – a lot of books that are written, particularly for children – have a happy ending, because most people like things to end up happily —

Here the cultural convention relating to narratives for children was explicitly articulated by these members. The students' conclusion, sad and depressed, was reworked in the classroom talk as more in accord with the 'happy ending' that 'most people' like.

This section has documented the participants' orientation to realistic, anthropomorphic and representational interpretive frames in different classroom moments. Of note is that the teacher talk oriented to the relevance of the Representational Tale Interpretive Frame in understanding the novel's conclusion but in the same sequences of talk, accomplished the students as unable to participate in discussion that engages the Representational Tale Interpretive Frame. Paradoxically, the teacher then employed the Representational Tale Interpretive Frame to achieve a happy ending according to a theory which articulates the Child as requiring a happy ending, itself also articulated in the classroom talk. The consequences of this in terms of the embodiment of the Child are significant and will be elaborated below. However, there is a further interpretive skill which the Child–Student of Literature in this classroom enacts: slippage.

Slippage

These analyses show that the students engaged in interpretive talk using three sets of resources – realistic, anthropomorphic and representational. Moreover, we have shown that, quite unremarkably, the talk moved, or slipped, between interpretive frames. The teacher's turns at talk signalled the interpretive resources being referenced at any particular moment in the talk. There were interactive moments when a student's utterance revealed that the student was referencing a different set of interpretive relevances than the teacher at that moment in the ongoing talk. In these situations, participants either worked to realign the sets of relevant references (the teacher reasserting the Representational Tale Interpretive Frame in Extract 9.16, for example) or the participants unremarkably slipped between frames.

The category Child as taught into being: tensions in the Child–Student of Literature

Although the teacher's talk moved between interpretive frames and used anthropomorphism as a base camp, as it were, the representational interpretation was used as the definitive interpretation of the novel. The teacher used a representational interpretation to read the novel as symbolic and ultimately achieved for the novel and the readers a happy ending. This happy ending scenario was articulated in one lesson as having a particularly child-oriented relevance (Extract 9.20). The paradox here is that in the classroom talk, the teacher oriented to the students' inability to grasp the representational interpretation (see Extract 9.17) while at the same time, oriented to their ability to effect, in their own minds, a child-like happy ending which itself required the ability to grasp the respresentational interpretation.

Our analyses revealed that the students interpreted the novel referencing realistic, anthropomorphic, and although audibly unrecognized by the teacher, representational sets of relevances at various moments in the lessons. Importantly, however, we found classroom moments in which student talk became troublesome as it slipped from one interpretive frame to another in an apparent attempt to locate the teacher's preferred frame for any given moment in the classroom talk.

So, in summary, the tensions evident in the classroom talk are:

- a representational interpretation, deemed by a developmental theory to be beyond the capacity of many of these students because they are children, is used to achieve a 'happy ending' as considered necessary for children;
- the classroom talk supports several layers of meaning simultaneously available through the slippage from one interpretive frame to another. This is undermined, however by:
  - the naturalization of the anthropomorphic frame as the default for children;
  - the teacher's apparent failure to recognize students' symbolic renderings of narrative elements;
  - the teacher's determination to achieve a representational interpretation to establish the happy ending as a definitive one.

The classroom talk and the novel: further tensions

If we consider now the classroom talk alongside the novel, we find further lines of tension emerging. Recall from Chapter 8 that the Child as assumed by the structure of the novel is one who has complex interpretive competences that make the following possible:

- interpretation within realistic, anthropomorphic and representational frames;
- slippage from one interpretive frame to another in order to read the novel as sensible and coherent;
- tolerance of, or even appreciation of, ambiguity in interpretation, that is, accepting parallel final renderings of the story, a 'sad' ending *and* a 'symbolic' ending;
- the emotional fortitude to sustain the unhappy ending of Magpie's abandonment, loneliness and inevitable death.

Consider now this Child alongside that enacted in the classroom talk. Our analyses show that the Child as constructed in the classroom talk does the following:

- interprets within realistic and anthropomorphic frames but is constructed by the teacher as developmentally unable to interpret within a representational frame;
- slips from one interpretive frame to another in order to talk about interpretations of the novel;

- cannot tolerate ambiguity in interpretation, that is, must make a representational reading in order to achieve a happy ending for the narrative;
- cannot tolerate an unhappy ending.

The version of the Child constructed in the talk is incompatible with or, at least, reductive of, that assumed in the novel in an important way. The novel presents layers of interpretation and resists a definitive interpretation. This possibility was reduced in the classroom talk by the imperative to achieve a definitive conclusion. The definitive conclusion the teacher articulated was a representational reading. In an apparent contradiction, the possibility of students' display of the 'required' representational reading was hampered by the teacher's expectation of an anthropomorphic interpretation and her use of the representational interpretation to achieve a child-friendly conclusion. Notably, what could be described analytically as the students' displays of representational interpretations were not generally acknowledged in the teacher's talk as representational.

The 'reading' of this novel in the classroom is displayed by means of particular interactive routines. That is, of the possible ways of talking about and interpreting the novel, the classroom talk accomplishes selected accountable readings for the participants in this classroom. We saw here that the version of the novel as talked-into-being in this classroom is not definitively determined by the novel itself. The limited capacity of the novel to constrain interpretation is demonstrated particularly by the achievement of a happy ending in the classroom talk, countermanding the finale of the novel itself. In a sense we could say that the theory of Childhood enacted in the classroom, by and in the manipulation of interpretive frames, undermines the literariness of the novel. In enacting the requirements of a particular theory of Childhood, the teacher closes down interpretive possibilities apparently made readily available in the novel.

Conclusion

Ideas about Childhood are clearly both topic and resource in school lessons such as these. Moreover, the interpretive resources assumed to be at the disposal of the Student-Reader entail sophisticated displays of the manipulation of these topics and resources. But the fit here is not without apparent incongruities: the subtle interpretive affordances of the materials (in our case *Magpie Island*) including the affordances concerning the ambiguities in the relative moral and emotional capacities of children and adults are flattened out or ignored in the official (teacher-led) talk in the classroom. Similarly, the ability to slip between interpretive frames is a highly visible resource for encountering the novel and for participation in the classroom talk but nowhere developed or even mentioned as a topic. These incongruities may have a least two explanations: First, books used with children in school have adults as their target market – specifically, teachers. The subtle interpretive features of the novel may appeal to teachers but not in such a way that they are able or willing to articulate in lessons for children. Second, teachers may feel the need to pitch lessons at an interpretive level that accommodates what they consider most of their students can manage, leaving the interpretive subtleties as a domain of achievement.

Leading on directly from this last point, the talk has prospective relevance: it is the precursor to a written assessment. In that sense it sets minimally accountable criteria for acceptable engagement with the novel, affording at the same time room for interpretive 'excellence'. We explore the assessable Child next.

10 The students' writing

Introduction

One of the defining features of institutionalized education is assessment. Assessment practices have as an outcome differentiation on the basis of some criteria. Here we will show that the criteria for assessment included *being* a certain type of Child and knowing about a certain kind of Childhood. In the previous two chapters we examined constructions of the Child in a novel and in classroom talk about that novel. In further examining the achievement of the category Child–Student as a set of institutional practices, this chapter considers one additional data corpus, students' writing. Here we present a particular and selective analysis of the students' writing in terms of the questions made apparent in talk (Chapter 9) and applied to the novel (Chapter 8).

The students' writing was an integral component of the *Magpie Island* literature unit. It functioned for the teacher as a display of students' understanding of the novel, of the classroom talk about that novel, and of the literacy task that framed the writing. This writing is available to us, as analysts, as a site for both the *articulation* and *enactment* of a theory of the Child. We examined the category Child within the writing corpus from three vantage points:

- as described by the students in their writing (recall the Child as 'portrayed' in Chapter 8), both as a single category and in standard relational partnership;
- as enacted by the teacher's assessments of the students' writing;
- as enacted by the students in their manipulation of interpretive frames in their own writing.

The writing tasks and the talk–writing nexus

In most classroom activities, the parameters of writing exercises are framed in the classroom talk. In the case of the examples we draw on here each task was discussed extensively by the participants. As noted in Chapter 9, students routinely asked detailed questions about both the propositional and procedural aspects of the task (including, for example, punctuation, spelling, headings for each answer and how to set the answer on the page) and the teacher explicitly stated the importance of the talk in framing the writing exercises.

Extract 10.1

197 *T:*   Alright, last week one of the exercises I set you – was to <u>write</u> down, draw pictures of a lot of the images. – How did Colin Thiele go about, and we <u>agreed</u> that he created the most incredible amount of images. What (2) method did he use to do those images? I've got a <u>lot</u> of people not paying attention. I know we're doing a lot of talking this morning and you're soon going to be working. But this is <u>very</u> important, kids – because when <u>you</u> start to try and write maybe <u>you</u> will remember some of these methods. How did he, what, what method did he use – in all his descriptive passages, all his image making passages.

In this turn the teacher nominated what was noticeable and writable about the novel. In this and other teacher turns at talk the students heard what counted, for this classroom, as writing accountably about a novel in the classroom, both in terms of the mechanics of writing, such as punctuation and linguistic features, and in terms of the interpretive responses to the novel. What the students subsequently wrote, therefore, was mediated by the classroom talk. Consequently, in this chapter, our analyses move between the talk and writing.

Articulated theory

Recall that the novel made available a differentiation between the characters Magpie and the Eagle in terms of Childhood and Adulthood (Chapter 8). A number of writing tasks required students to focus on these two main characters, and to describe and contrast them. In this section, we present our analysis of student written responses to the following three questions:

Q6 What do you think were the main differences between the Magpie and the Eagle? Don't just think about the physical differences . . . try to think what else made them different.

Q8 Imagine that the Magpie and the Eagle were actual people . . . what sort of people do you think they would be? Give each a 'person identity' and tell me briefly about them.

Q4 Ben's dad appears to be a very grumpy fellow. Do you think this is true? Give me some reasons for your answer.[1]

We interrogate these writing tasks to explain the category-attributes of the categories of Child and Adult as assembled in the students' writing as well as the characterization of the relations between these categories. Furthermore, we examine the classroom talk that addressed these questions to explain the role of the talk in displaying the mutual construction of what was oriented to by the participants as the procedural and propositional content of the written tasks.

So what of the talk around these writing tasks? In the following three extracts, the participants discuss Q6 which required students to consider the main differences between the Magpie and the Eagle.

Extract 10.2

156 T: Number Six *WHAT DO YOU THINK THE MAIN DIFFER-ENCES WERE BETWEEN MAGPIE AND THE EAGLE? DON'T JUST THINK ABOUT THE PHYSICAL DIFFERENCES TRY TO THINK WHAT ELSE MADE THEM DIFFERENT.* What do I mean by the physical differences, (2) Kim? Ahh, Kelsy? sorry.

157 K: What they look like/

158 T: What they look like, obviously there are a lot of differences in what they looked like – but there are other differences too, and if you think about it hard what those other differences are. That's somewhere where <u>you</u> have to think and perhaps put your own opinion.

Extract 10.3

13 T: — let's have a look at Question Six. – *WHAT DO YOU THINK THE MAIN DIFFERENCES WERE BETWEEN THE MAGPIE AND THE EAGLE? DON'T JUST THINK ABOUT THE PHYSICAL DIFFERENCES TRY TO THINK WHAT ELSE MADE THEM DIFFERENT.* Now some of you have partially answered that . . . in your <u>description</u> – of Magpie and your description of Eagle. What I would like you to do there is tie that together, you will only need – again half a dozen lines. Mention the physical differences, . . . mention the physical differences, but <u>then</u> try and see if you can work out what else is different about them.

Extract 10.4

225 T: Okay, you only need one paragraph, not physical differences and just see if you can compare the other differences. Are they different in character? – Yes. Are they different, – umm, do you think in <u>age</u>? – right yes, umm, they're obviously different in size, they're different in the habitat that they – they usually occupy/

226 A: So do I//

227 *T:* You can just do them in separate sentences if you like, you don't have to tie them into a paragraph, you can just list them if you find it easier, Okay?

232 *S:* Yeah, but, what do you say, umm, how do you make the differences?
233 *T:* Well, what are, well what are some of the obvious differences? Tell me.
234 *S:* Size.
235 *T:* Size.
236 *S:* Personality
237 *T:* Personality. (6) Habitat.
238 *S:* Habitat.
239 *T:* You're told that. Flying style, there's a lot of differences.

The talk in the above extracts assembles the guidelines for the student's written answers to Question 6 in terms of content (differences between the characters' physique, appearance, age, size, habitat, flying style, and personality) and in terms of structure (six lines in length, answered together with description, one paragraph, and separate sentences, not one paragraph).

The students' written answers to this question, displayed in Table 10.1 incorporated the guidelines as described in the talk above. The task is framed as a comparison and talked as such in the classroom talk. As Table 10.1 shows, the students described the characters in terms of categorical polarities, for example, panicky–calm, impatient–tolerant, weak–strong. Six students made the age comparison suggested by the teacher (see Turn 225, Extract 10.4) while 22 made a size comparison as suggested by the teacher at (Turn 225, Extract 10.4), also repeated by a student (Turn 234, Extract 10.4). The students' answers, then, reflect the comparisons between the characters as explained in the classroom talk.

Question 8 also affords analysis in terms of the categories Child and Adult.

> Q8 Imagine that the Magpie and the Eagle were actual people . . . what sort of people do you think they would be? Give each a 'person identity' and tell me briefly about them.

In the classroom discussion, the students initially described this literacy task in terms of a Younger Child–Older Child relational category pair, and more specifically an Oppressed Child–Oppressing Child category pair, for example category Boy–category Bully. In a subsequent lesson, the teacher reformulated the discussion in terms of the category pair Child–Adult.

17 *T:* . . . Some said I think Eagle would be – a big person, a an adult.

Table 10.2 shows that students' written answers to Question 8 referenced the categories discussed in the classroom. Table 10.2 shows that in their responses to Question 8 many students employed the Child–Adult category pair or the

Table 10.1 Delineations between Magpie and the eagle in the students' writing

Student	Magpie	The eagle	Other comparisons	Comparisons age/size
Amber	squawky little baby bird	large patient strong	comparison in terms of physical prowess	age inferred size
Annette	extremely young very daring	older, tolerant	comparison in terms of flying capacity	age
Anita		larger, more patient, tolerant, leader, solitary, stronger	difference in flying style	size
Anna	small, didn't give up	gave up	difference in flying style	size
Bridget	silly, slow learning to fly	big bully, huge		size
Carmel		bigger, stronger, more tolerant		size
Janine	very cunning, sticky beak, impatient, cranky, bad temper	could put up with a lot	'they also had physical differences'	
Justine	not frightened by eagle, impatient, cunning, would not give up	tolerant, swift, graceful. large, strong, frightening		size
Karen	small, black and white, small wings, long nose	big, brown, long, long wings		size
Kim	magpie, smaller, ungraceful and flapped, more mischievous, very determined	eagle, sail and look graceful		size
Kelsy	smaller, annoying, show off, strong, fed by parents	stronger, fed himself, glide through the sky		age inferred size
Marilyn	small, weak, fly short distances, flapped	fly long distances, smart, quick-witted, big, strong, glided		size
Megan	noisy	quiet, stronger		
Miranda	scallywag	bully		

continued on next page

Sarah		bigger, stronger, tolerant	physical descriptions	size
Tanya		larger, stronger,	different colours, ages, experiences, interests	size
Tonie	magpie, quarks, loud	eagle, stronger, bigger, tolerant, silent	different areas	size
Boyd				
Clive	small, friendly, playful, young, caring	giant, friendly	size and flying style	inferred age size
Colin	determined, very active, smaller, less intelligent	bigger, more patient, calm		size
Dillon	small noisy weak panicky impatient straight beak	huge quiet powerful calm tolerant curved beak		size
Justin			voices, sizes, habitats and ages	size
Tom	flaps	bigger, glides, put up with anything, never panics		size
Lyle	younger, adventurous, eager to prove himself	tolerant, larger, smarter, patient	eagle wanted to teach magpie a lesson	age size
Joshua			sizes, voices, ages	size
Phillip	quite small, courageous, adventurous	large, strong, tolerant, patient, content, casual		size
Russell	black, white	brownish gold, bigger, more mature, more tolerant		inferred age size
Sam	flaps, has to rest	fly for hours		

Child–Bully category pair which had been nominated in the classroom talk as pertinent to the question. Two themes in the relationship between younger and older categories emerged, an 'Oppressed–Oppressor' relational partnership and a 'Harasser–Harassed' partnership. The Oppressed–Oppressor included a Child and Bully partnership and a Child and Adult partnership in which the adult is depicted as mistreating the child, such as an awful headmaster–new boy at school SRP (Kelsey's and Phillip's stories, for example). The Harasser–Harassed partnership saw the younger, whether child or adult, described as harassing the elder (Lyle's and Tonie's stories, for example).

Table 10.2 Anthropomorphic characterizations of Magpie and the eagle in students' writing

	Magpie	The eagle	Comparison partners
Amber	Mick, small but not fat, singing opera, outrageous, nickname Magpie	Professor Edward Eagle, very rich and tall, frightening	adult and adult
Anita	short, fat little man, rich, stickybeak, wanderer, sing in the shower, live in large community	important man, rich, large, eats too much, tolerate humans as 'pesky Magpies', does not like crowd	adult and adult
Anna	kindergarten child, wears glasses, teased by others	bully of the school, picked on Magpie	child and bully
Carmel	small and weak, called 'Smallian'	tolerant and big, called 'Ruffian'	small and big
Justine	cheeky little boy, sulk if in trouble, plan his revenge	like Mr West, patient, when he's had enough will get his revenge	boy and adult
Kim	a dog who annoys the butcher, patchy black and white	a butcher boasting about his meat, brown-eyed, bald but slim	dog and adult
Kelsy	new boy at school, short and thin, brown eyes, blond hair dyed black in spots	awful headmaster, long arms and mouth, big, brown evil eyes	child and adult
Megan	Bobby, loves adventure, didn't like school	Jorden, Bobby's brother, taller, doesn't annoy easily, liked school work	brothers
Miranda	playful little boy, cheeky, 5 years old, loves the beach	school bully, 10 years old, hates 5 year olds	boy and bully
Sarah	school boy, going to be a scientist, black hair, enjoys running and hurdling	school principal, watches TV, eats meat	child and adult
Tanya	from India, black beak, no bright feathers, no wife or children but still enjoys life		
Tonie	young male juvenile, loudmouth, bully, harasses old man	wise old man, tolerant and clever	child and adult
Clive	short schoolboy, brown hair, torments others	tall high school boy, brown hair, bully	boy and bully
Colin	punk, begs, annoys	rich, wrestler, bigger, stronger, king	punk and wrestler
Dillon	boy, 4 years, teases elders	62 years, hang gliding, no worries	child and adult

continued on next page

Tom	relaxed, show off	mean, tricky, school bully	boy and bully
Lyle	young, courageous, adventurous, eager, mischievous, devilish, 5–7 years, loner	older, more relaxed, like his grandfather, patient, eager to teach lessons	young and older
Joshua	young, 11 or 12 years, lunatic, always in trouble	40 years, ignores people	child and adult
Phillip	young boy, 7 years mischievous, naughty, always in trouble, adventurous, smart,	male, 35 years, wise, patient, very relaxed, headmaster, strict (illustration shows adult giving child the cane)	child and adult
Russell	school boy, mischievous and brave, dark brown eyes, could stand loneliness	adult, sensible, tolerant, businessman, big, large nose	child and adult
Sam	primary school boy, 9 years	high school bully, 14 years	schoolboy and high school bully

Another question framed in the classroom talk as relevantly referencing a category-partnership was the final question listed at the beginning of this chapter, Q4.

Q4 Ben's dad appears to be a very grumpy fellow. Do you think this is true? Give me some reasons for your answer.

Reproduced below is the initial classroom talk about Benbow (Ben's dad). This discussion occurred before the students were introduced to Q4, above, and there is no way of knowing whether the teacher developed Q4 before or after this discussion.

Extract 10.5

194 *Am:* I think he might be like Mr West (*a teacher in the school.*)
195 *T:* (*laughing voice*) I'm sure Mr West would be complimented, except that Mr West under that gruff old exterior of his is really what.
196 *Ss:* Nice/very nice
197 *T:* Very nice and very caring. I wonder if Mr Bates is under his bluff [old exterior.
198 *Am:* [He might be]
199 *T:* He might be, let's see.

This talk developed a characterization of Benbow in which his 'gruff' exterior hid a 'soft' heart. Discussion about him as impatient, uninterested and unenthusiastic was transformed by a student's suggestion that 'he might be like Mr West'. The teacher elaborated that suggestion, describing Mr West's kind and caring nature as disguised by a gruff exterior.

The writing task, Q4, was discussed in a subsequent lesson, with the teacher resisting any descriptions of Benbow that countered the 'gruff exterior/soft heart' characterization.

Extract 10.6

18 *T:* — What about Ben's dad? What does his attitude tell you, yes./
19 *D:* Oh come on get on with it./
20 *T:* Ye:es, what does that tell you about Ben's dad?
21 *S:* He's impatient? – He was impatient, he wanted to get back to (the boat/work)./
22 *T:* Ye:es, maybe. Perhaps something else, Janine?
23 *Ja:* Maybe he thinks (.) should be tough and shouldn't sort of play round and watching things should be off fishing and doing what men are supposed to do?
24 *Ss:* (*laughs*)
25 *T:* Yes, I think that's probably a very good thing. By taking the magpie and young Ben to the island, what – did Dad actually do, he showed himself to Ben as being what.

The suggestion that Benbow was an impatient man was rejected by the teacher in favour of a characterization of him as a proud man disguising his soft heart from his son and the other crew members. In the next lesson, the teacher reformulated this discussion.

Extract 10.7

172 *T:* — I think Ben's dad, we established that Ben's dad was really not such an old grouch after all and he'd have been feeling pretty upset too so maybe he was, it was his defence mechanism, umm, so that he didn't cry and look and look soppy or soft in front of the other men. I reckon the other men might have been feeling a bit sad too.

This teacher's turn posited Benbow's 'gruff' behaviour and soft inner nature as the frame for responding to Q4. For the most part, the students' writing recreated this description of Benbow, characterizing him as an essentially caring and benevolent parent. Of the twenty-eight written answers, eleven students did not explicitly frame Benbow's personality in terms of the grumpy/soft dichotomy. The remaining answers employed versions of the grumpy/soft dichotomy: describing Benbow as soft and proud; citing Benbow's temper as evidence of his industrious nature rather than his essential grumpiness, and citing a particular kind deed to demonstrate his 'non-grumpiness'.

The connection between the classroom talk and the students' writing is evident in these examples, providing material example of Heap's (1985: 252–254) explanation of classroom talk as a pivotal site in the mutual construction of what counts as procedural and propositional knowledge for the purposes of the classroom lesson. The parallels between the classroom talk and the writing indicated that the students oriented to the classroom talk as a demonstration of what counted, procedurally and propositionally, as a written response to the set writing tasks. As a hearing of the classroom talk, the students' writing re-enacted the versions of the Child, the Adult, and the Adult–Child relations as articulated in the talk. Few students interpreted the novel in terms other than those articulated in the talk. Chapter 9 demonstrated the work the teacher and students did in assembling the corpus of propositional and procedural knowledge taken to count in this context, and here we have demonstrated the students' orientation to that work as the site of knowledge production.

Children's writing: the teacher's assessments

We focus now on the teacher's assessments of the students' writing. Throughout this section, student spelling and formatting are transcribed verbatim. Examination of the teacher's assessments of the students' writing revealed that the writing was routinely assessed by the teacher in terms of suitable subject matter, story structure and vocabulary. Our interest here is in reading the teacher's written comments on the student work as the teacher's account of the ways in which that piece of writing counts (or does not count) as writing for school. The following extracts are instances wherein the teacher audibly evaluated a piece of writing as the latter, that is, as not counting as writing for school or, in other words, a breach of ordinary classroom interaction (Chapter 4). In each case, the teacher's written comments, in some instances taken together with evaluations in the classroom talk, revealed the category-attributes of the category Child the teacher oriented to in her assessments. We see that the evaluations at once sustain and create particular category attributes of the category Child.

Subject matter and story structure

Phillip's written conversation, in answer to Task 5, which was:

> Q5 Imagine that the two magpies are able to talk. Write a conversation of what might have been said between them when they first meet.

attracted teacher censure.

Extract 10.8

> 'What's your name?' asked Magpie inquiringly
> 'I don't know,' she replied.
> 'I've an idea,' Magpie spoke again.
> 'What is it? Come on out with it.'
> 'Do you want to do it?' Magpie asked.
> 'Do what,' replied the female bird.
> 'You know,' hinted Magpie with a wink.
> 'No. I'm afraid I don't.'
> 'Don't you even know what "Do it" is?'
> 'Oh, yeah, I know (~~youre~~) you're going to
> show me around – aren't you.'
> 'Yes, of course. You didn't think I (~~ment~~)
> meant anything (~~fo~~) foul did you?'

The teacher noted in the margin

> I really feel this conversation is getting out of hand, Phillip – don't you?

The final teacher comment on Phillip's work was:

> A very good unit of work Phillip – don't spoil it by careless, rude writing please!

Ana's written conversation, in which the magpies negotiate their relationship, was similarly censured.

Extract 10.9

> 'Come on I've never had a girlfriend before'
> 'I spose you wouldn't have stuck
> out here all alone my poor little
> darling'
> 'Oh'
> 'Well I'm here now and I'm hungre
> take me to some food honey bunch'
> She said kissing magpie on the cheek
> Magpie began to blush as they flew
> off into sunset to find food

The teacher's written comment read:

> Do you really think this was the sort of conversation they'd have had?

Both Phillip's and Ana's writing attract teacher reproach. The criteria upon which Phillip's writing was judged unsuitable were expressed in terms of its rudeness and its 'out of hand-ness'. The unsuitability of Ana's writing is implicit. Phillip's writing is audibly unsuitable with respect to its sexual references and we can infer similarly for Ana's writing. These teacher assessments orient to the idea that sexual references are unsuitable in this context. Member expertise suggests that the 'unsuitability' can be described as being on the basis of both the students' 'childness' and their 'studentness' – that is, the criterion of this writing's unsuitability enacts an intersection of the relevances of the Child and the public forum of the school: the Child–Student, it seems, does not broach the subject of sex.

In Carmel's response to this same task (Task 5), the participants lived 'unhappily ever after'.

Extract 10.10

So they both lived unhappily ever after.
Mate lived unhappily ever after because she hated the island and Magpie lived unhappily ever after because he hated Mate because she wouldn't be quiet.

The teacher's comment read:

Do you really think this is what would have happened?

Again, the reasoning behind the teacher's assessment is not explicit. However, the imperative that stories have a happy ending was explicitly stated in the classroom talk (Extract 9.20, Chapter 9) and recall also from Chapter 9 the considerable work the participants put into achieving a happy ending for the novel. Carmel's unhappy ending, although very much the same tone as the conclusion of the novel itself, certainly transgressed the imperative for portrayals of happiness spoken in the classroom talk.

Vocabulary

Dillon's writing in response to another task, reproduced below, was assessed unfavourably in terms of his choice of vocabulary:

Imagine you were Magpie learning to fly. Describe how you felt when you started . . . what could you see? . . . how did you feel when you actually began to fly?

Extract 10.11

> . . . to go to the thunder box' tactic when mum
> gave me a swift kick in the butt. I shot
> throw the air and felt that wonderful thing the
> ground.
> 'Trying to show off are you.'
> 'no'
> 'Oh yeah'
> 'Yeh'
> 'Here then take this' mum said handing me her
> quick cheap life insurance.
> 'So thats what this plastic hunk of crap is' but
> I took it anyway. I needed it because the next time . . .

The concomitant teacher comment nominated Dillon's vocabulary as unacceptable for school work and his writing as being 'off the track':

> Although I was happy for you to put your own feelings and opinions into answering this question I feel you have gone 'off the track' too much. I would like to see slang and swearing left out of your work please.

Exactly what the teacher meant by 'off the track' is not explained but it is clear that the writing was improper in this classroom moment. Insight into why Dillon's response failed as an answer is provided in a teacher comment to the whole class group.

Extract 10.12

5 *T:*   . . . Umm – Dillon took the liberty of – projecting his thoughts into the flying one I felt <u>too</u> far. You actually lost the thread of the story completely, and, and literally you took the idea of flying and wrote totally different story. Also, umm, some of the words that you used I don't think are suitable for using in stories. Ok, it was very, you've got a wonderful sense of humour . . .

Dillon audibly took too much literary licence in deviating from the subject matter and used unacceptable vocabulary. Note that the criterion of the unsuitability of slang and swearing marked an intersection of the Child and the school, the Child–Student uses proper language.

Critical and ironic comment

Phillip's cynicism in the following text was censured by the teacher.

Extract 10.13

> 'No!' exclaimed Freddy Froglegs, when
> Steven (a) shared his thoughts with his
> father. 'You've got to learn at school.
> I am not allowed, by law or by Darren Hinch, to
> let you stay home unless you are sick.
> And that doesn't include WORRIED SICK.'
> 'OK dad, whatever you say.' replied Steve
> miserabely. And all the time he was thinking,
> 'That's Life, good night. I'm Darren Hinch.
> 'When he came home his father was (out)
> out, but the lounge room window was open, . . .

The teacher's written comment was:

> You have some lovely ideas, Phillip, and are using good vocabulary. I feel at
> times you are trying to be too 'smart' and in so doing spoil the effect of your
> story! How many books do you read with dialogue such as . . . 'by law or by
> Derryn Hinch?' Think about it in your next story.

Note that Phillip's vocabulary is assessed as 'good' but his reference to Derryn
Hinch is nominated as unbefitting and 'too smart'. Phillip's reference is audible
as social commentary on the assumed authority of television evening current
affairs presenters ('Derryn Hinch').[2] However, the teacher did not hear it this
way. The teacher's reading of Phillip's writing as 'too smart' rather than as
competent social commentary defined, sustained and drew upon a theory of
the Child as one who does not produce such counter-readings of popular
culture.

   Recall, as well, the teacher's questioning of the unhappy conclusion in
Carmel's story (Extract 10.10). The story itself is readable in several ways: as
a bland reflection of common 'sitcom' stereotypes; as a poignant portrayal of
what she sees around her, or possibly an ironic reading of either of these.
The teacher's comment 'do you think this is what would have happened?'
gives little clue to the basis of her assessment that the writing is questionable.
However, that the teacher read the conclusion as questionable on any of
these (or any other counts) orients to the proper relevances of being a child
(i.e. preferring a happy ending) and to Carmel's breach of this relevance.

   The criteria of the teacher's assessments above (suitable subject matter, story
structure, vocabulary and absence of critical or ironic inference) describe the
category Child–Student as operant in this site and define the category Child–
Student as appropriate in this site. We can say that these category attributes
are particular to the Child–Student in that all these features might conceivably
be appropriate in adult narratives. In this sense, these students have been pre-
cocious. That is, they have enacted category attributes other, we could say,

beyond, those oriented to here by the teacher as the attributes of the category Child–Student.

Interpretive frames in the students' writing

In Chapters 8 and 9, the concept of the 'interpretive frame' was used to explain a set of text-interpreting parameters that participants drew on when interacting with text. The three frames employed were the Realistic Interpretive Frame, informed by 'real-world' categories; the Anthropomorphic Narrative Interpretive Frame informed by a set of relevances, meanings and truths from the world where animals are textually represented as feeling, thinking and having personalities like humans, and the Representational Tale Interpretive Frame wherein the text affords symbolic reading as representing a 'moral tale'.

Chapters 8 and 9 demonstrated how orientation to these interpretive frames, both as referenced by and constructed in each data corpus, worked in constructing a version of the Child. In this chapter, we extend this work to examine the students' writing in terms of the availability, in that writing, of the interpretive frames as described and enacted in the novel and the classroom talk.

Reality and fantasy – realism and anthropomorphism

Writing for children often intertwines the relevances of fantastic and realistic worlds in an unremarked way (see Chapters 2 and 8). We showed (Chapter 9) that the students involved in this literature unit readily applied both realistic and fantastic interpretive possibilities in the classroom talk. In like manner, these students displayed both fantastic and realistic pertinences in their writing. The capacity of the students to readily engage in the fantastic relevances of anthropomorphism was assumed by the questioning and the talk around that questioning. For example, the written task:

> Tell me why you think Magpie no longer sang on the island.

was specifically framed in the classroom talk as an exercise in anthropomorphism:

Extract 10.14

213 T: TELL ME WHY YOU THINK MAGPIE NO LONGER SANG ON THE ISLAND. Keep it to yourself, have a think, now we've just talked about how Magpie felt, the words the author used to describe how he was feeling, what happened when Magpie tried to sing, so I want you to tell me again – six, eight lines, half a page no more,

In this turn, Magpie's emotional response – how Magpie felt, rather than some possibly realistic reasoning was oriented to as the frame for student written responses. The discussion the teacher referred to (i.e. 'we've just talked about) described Magpie in terms of his loneliness and unhappiness. All of the students used the frame nominated by the teacher, that is, applying human emotions and thoughts to the magpie.

Extract 10.15

1) A Sad Song
Magpie is very sad, depressed and lonely
and feels there is no need to sing
because he is no longer happy and feels
rejected and along. He yearns for the
company of another magpie. There was
no-were Magpie could swoop and soar
without the fear of being driven away. If
only he could make friends with the bird
he could show them really how gentle
he was

A Sad Song!!!
I think magpie didn't sing anymore because he was sad and lonely. The other birds were different.

A further question provided for students' displays of the capacity to interleave fantastic and realistic relevance.

Extract 10.16

Magpie made one friend on the island –
a): Who was the friend?
b): Why did they become friends?
c): Do you think this was a very satisfactory friendship?

In the novel, Magpie developed a friendship with Bandicoot. We earlier (Chapter 8) discussed the novel's portrayal of this friendship as a narrative device in which the relevances of reality are used to support both the initial description of a fantastic friendship, based on shared feeding habits, and the description of its essential inadequacy, based on differences between the species. The writing task, above, referenced this interleaving of fantastic and realistic interpretive relevances. Some students wrote of the relationship between Magpie and Benny (the central child character) while others answered in terms of the relationship between Magpie and Bandicoot.

Extract 10.17

<u>Magpie's Friend</u>

Bandicoot was magpie's favourite friend. He and
magpie became friends because they were alike
in hunting for their food. They didnt look the
same, though, they <u>were</u> about the same size
but Bandicoot was crown with sharp little claws.
The friendship wasn't very satisfactory
because they also had a lot of things that were
different.

All of the students' answers blended fantasy and reality by anthropomorphizing
the magpie in terms of his capacity for friendship while using realistic reasons
(e.g. physical differences) to account for the friendship's unsatisfactoriness.

Interpretive frames in the students' narratives

The students were assigned a narrative writing task toward the end of the *Magpie
Island* literature unit. It was introduced as follows:

Extract 10.18

112 *T:*   . . . We've got three lessons left that we're going to really treat *Magpie
Island*, we may not finish the last part – during this week but we will
try to. First of all – I think we should look at – just how Colin Thiele
writes – so that you can see how he structures his book and how
interesting it can be, and how he – writes to gain a special effect,
and <u>then</u> we're going to write our own story – not a Magpie
Island story – but a story? – where an animal – is one of the main
characters in the story. So that we're going to centre it. It does <u>not</u>
have to be – anything like *Magpie Island* of course but? – Amber.

113 *Am:* Does it have to be Australian animals? (3)

114 *T:* U:um:m –

115 *Am:* Cause it could really be any animal.

116 *T:* I think we possibly <u>will</u> restrict it to Australian animals, and a setting
in Australia yes. – Because I think we'll get, I don't want us to go
back in time or forward in time. I don't want us to go back to dinosaurs or to perhaps science fiction. I want it to be fairly realistic.
Okay, if you look at the story *Magpie Island* and we have looked at
it <u>very</u> carefully over the last few weeks (3) there are many methods
that Colin Thiele uses to make his story – interesting? You can call
them strategies, you can call them – structure, you can call it <u>his</u>
writing style.

The teacher stated the task at Turn 112 ('we're going to write our own story') and referred the students to *Magpie Island* at Turn 116 ('if you look at the story *Magpie Island*') as a model for writing their narratives, specifically, for narrative 'strategies', 'structure' and 'writing style'. The students were instructed to write 'fairly realistically' with 'dinosaurs' and 'science fiction' excluded. The students' narratives are their written records of their interpretation of these instructions.

We analysed each of the twenty-three narratives produced by the students in terms of whether it afforded the possibility of:

- realistic interpretation;
- anthropomorphic interpretation as afforded by the attribution of internal state (e.g. an animal feeling or thinking);
- anthropomorphic interpretation as afforded by talking animals;
- representational interpretation as afforded by the possibility of reading a moral or symbolic content, for example, a value judgement or an implicitly moral interpretive relevance such as afforded, for example, by the consequences to animals or the environment of human destructiveness. This category is culturally specific.

Table 10.3 provides a summary of this analysis. To varying degrees, all interpretive frames were evident in the students' writing. All of the student texts (twenty-three in total) referenced a realistic interpretive frame. Sixteen anthropomorphized, fifteen of this group employed internal anthropomorphism as modelled in the novel, and three featured talking animals (anthropomorphism not featured in *Magpie Island*). Eight narratives referenced some moral or symbolic interpretation (i.e. worked within a representational framework). Six stories of the total number interwove the three interpretive frames, that is, realistic, anthropomorphic and representational (Stories 1, 3, 4, 11, 13 and 17).

Our analysis of students' narratives indicate that the students heard the teacher's classroom talk (see Extract 10.18) generally as achieving the task to be to write an anthropomorphic novel in a realistic setting. Eight of the students incorporated a representational interpretive possibility as available in both the classroom talk and the novel. Six of the students' stories afford interpretation within all three of the interpretive frames, that is, at different moments throughout the story, different interpretive possibilities were available. For example, Story 11 included the realistic relevances of pollution in Sydney, the anthropomorphic reference to a puppy's decision to make an effort to save his own life and the representational interpretation of the moral issue of polluters harming the environment and others.

Conclusion

This chapter has examined the students' writing as a site for the articulation of a theory of the Child and the enactment of a theory of the Child within the corpus of students' writing. We found parallels between the Child as described

Table 10.3 Interpretive frames employed in the students' narratives

Interpretive frame	Realistic	Anthropomorphized		Representational
Story Title		2a internal state	2b talking animals	
1 Simply Fowl	✓	knew		✓
2 Croc River	✓			
3 The Eagle's Flight	✓	knew comfort		✓
4 Her little joey	✓	celebrate dare		✓
5 Kangaroo Mouse	✓	felt sorrier than ever		
6 Kangaroo mouse may be gone	✓	didn't mind		
7 Wombat's Fever	✓	felt sorry forgotten	✓	
8 A Kangaroo	✓	love	✓	
9 Max	✓	didn't enjoy, feel enthusiastic		
10 Wally the Dog!!	✓			
11 Pollution Problem	✓	decided		✓
12 A Mothers Worst Fear	✓			✓
13 no title	✓	loved to fly, hated, scared, felt confused		✓
14 Watch out Rabits	✓			✓
15 Koala's New Home	✓	longed enjoyed		
16 Tanya	✓			
17 Captured	✓	first person animal narration		✓
18 Wilbur – The Basset Hound	✓		✓	
19 Eagle	✓	scared, had a headache		
20 The Brumby	✓			
21 Taken Seriously	✓			
22 Feathered Flight	✓	'as if to say thank you'		
23 Wombat Territory	✓	scared, curious and brave		
Total	**23**	**15**	**3**	**8**

by the students in their writing and that accomplished in the classroom talk and achieved in the novel (see Chapters 8 and 9).

Our examination of the teacher's assessments of the students' writing revealed some of the criteria of the assessment to be suitable subject matter, story structure, vocabulary and the absence of critical or ironic inference. These assessment criteria worked to both describe the category Child–Student as operant in this site and to define the category Child–Student as appropriate in this site. We identified a certain student capacity to manipulate interpretive frames in their own writing. The students produced writing that displayed the three frames described in this study: realistic, anthropomorphic and representational, and, in the same way as the novel and the talk, anthropomorphism was naturalized as a prime relevance to this group.

This chapter also examined some of the classroom talk about the students' writing tasks to explain the role of the talk in displaying the mutual construction of what is oriented to by the participants as the procedural and propositional content of the written tasks.

We have shown that the students oriented to the classroom talk as the site of the procedural and propositional display of what was to count as an assessable piece of writing in this context. The students were accountable for having heard the classroom talk *and* understood its import in the construction of knowledge in the classroom (Heap 1980, 1985).

The participants in this classroom therefore accomplished, for these classroom literature tasks, the version of the Child the students were accountable for enacting as both topic and resource. The classroom participants also achieved, for this classroom, the propositional knowledge that the students had to enact the relevances of studenthood and childhood simultaneously.

Conclusion to Part III

In this Part we have tracked across several scenes within the one site seeking answers to our core question. We found the Child as textually *portrayed* and *assumed*. The novel portrays the category Child in the MCD 'stage of life', in Standard Relational Partnership with the category Adult and in the MCD 'family', in Standard Relational Partnership with the category Parent. Representations of the Child, the Adult and intergenerational relationships in this novel can be read by children as a version of themselves and their relations with adults – as adults take them to be. For example, in the novel *Magpie Island*, children can read themselves as vulnerable, precompetent, transient and active. They can also read that they contrast with adults and parents in their excitable foolishness compared to adult serenity, their health, consuming, sustained, playful precoccupations, and possession of emotional strength and fortitude, compared to adult declining health, concern with only work matters, and possession of particular 'adult knowledge' pertaining to the economics of the world of work and interpersonal concerns. Children can also read a particular version of their intergenerational relationships; that they are a diminutive of the parent, subject to the regulation of the wise and caring parent, and indulged by the parent.

The novel also *assumes* a reader. We found complex interpretive possibilities afforded by a blend of fantasy and reality. We explained this complexity using the concept of the 'interpretive frame', showing that this novel calls up at least three major sets of interpretive resources, here called the Realistic Interpretive Frame, the Anthropomorphic Narrative Interpretive Frame and the Representational Tale Interpretive Frame. Slippage from one interpretive frame to another affords many layers of meaning in the novel. Furthermore, the conclusion of the novel precludes the possibility of making a final or definitive interpretation, even though the adult character articulates that interpretation. The tension between the interpretive frames and the possibility of simultaneous readings within many frames attests to the nature of the novel as a carefully crafted artistic work (Engell 1988). The child character maintains the events as meaningful within many possible frames, enacting a version of the Child–Reader who has the interpretive skill to read this novel on these many levels. The slippage from one frame to another throughout the novel and the ambiguity of the conclusion enact assumptions about the interpretive sophisti-cation of the Child–readership. The novel maintains that a Child–Reader has the interpretive skill to read within the many frames, the interpretive capacity to appreciate the artistic tension of the ambiguity of multiple conclusions, and, the emotional fortitude to sustain the 'unhappy ending' of Magpie's abandon-ment and loneliness.

Consider again though that *Magpie Island* is a novel *for* children, written *by* an adult. As such, it embodies a public display by an adult, to other adults, and to children, of a particular set of assumptions about the competence or precom-petence of children, in this instance in terms of the interpretive needs and capa-cities of the Child–Reader and the psychological or emotional needs and capacities of the Child–Reader. While Category Analysis revealed that the text assembles the Child according to a 'stage of life' device, the structuring of the interpretive possibilities of the text challenges the assumptions of pre-competence and development upon which the dominant 'stage of life' device is based.

The novel, however, exists in the classroom through talk. Classroom talk provides us with a crucial site, as it is the site of the accountable public display of this novel as an artifact for the classroom literature lesson. We can look there to determine whether or not, and to what extent, the version of the Child–Reader as interpretively competent and emotionally capable is sustained. That is, to what extent are the interpretive possibilities of the novel taken up in the classroom talk?

In Chapter 9 then we took a specific analytic path through the classroom talk to interrogate the versions of the Child as spoken and as at once assumed and sustained by the patterns of meanings that are validated through the lessons. It is in the talk that the students at once learn and participate in the interactive procedures that constitute displays of the propositional and procedural knowl-edges that are taken to count as 'interpretation' in the context of the classroom literature lesson.

We showed that the interactive procedures through which the category Child was assembled in the classroom talk revealed a number of tensions. Routine categorization work of the participants established the category Child as an explicit and unproblematic category in the talk in terms of the Child's essential transience, normalized child behaviours and propensities, such as the perceived need for children to read stories with a 'happy ending' and representations of Child–Adult and more specifically, Child–Parent relations. The interactive achievement or accomplishment of the student participants on this scene con-flated the relevances of the category Child and the category Student, accom-plishing a specialist category that we called Child–Student. In Chapter 9 we demonstrated the students' artful achievement of this double incumbency in talk, and in Chapter 10 we showed its relevance to classroom practice in writing and assessment. We examined the Child–Student of Literature in terms of being both 'skilled' and 'literary'; the skilled Child–Student of Literature dis-playing interactive, managerial and literate skills and the literary Child–Student of Literature displaying interpretive skills referencing realistic, anthropo-morphic and representational sets of resources.

The version of the Child as constructed in the talk by the manipulation of interpretive frames exposed a tension between the Child as constructed in the classroom talk and that assumed by the novel. The Child assumed by the structure of the novel expects an anthropomorphized narrative, but has the capacity to interpret within realistic, anthropomorphic and representational frames and has the capacity to slip from one interpretive frame to another in order to read the novel as sensible and coherent, and tolerates ambiguity in interpretation, that is, is able to accept parallel final renderings of the story, a 'sad' ending *and* a 'symbolic' ending. This Child is undermined by the Child–Reader as constructed in the classroom talk who willingly and ably engages in anthropomorphic interpretation, has the capacity to interpret within realistic and anthropomorphic frames but is constructed by the teacher as developmentally unable to interpret within a representational frame, has the capacity to slip from one interpretive frame to another in order to talk about interpretations of the novel, but cannot tolerate an unhappy ending or ambigu-ity in interpretation, that is, must make a representational reading in order to achieve a 'happy ending' for the narrative.

The version of the Child as constructed in the talk is incompatible with that assumed in the novel in an important way. The Child for the classroom is a less nuanced, flexible and emotionally street-wise Child. The version of the novel as talked into being in this classroom is not conclusively determined by the novel itself however. The possibility of a layering of simultaneous meanings is dimin-ished in the classroom talk by the imperative to achieve a definitive conclusion. The definitive conclusion the teacher articulates is a representational reading. The capacity to interpret the novel representationally is enacted by the teacher as a measure of the students' maturity as children for school. In an apparent paradox, the possibility for students' displays of maturity is hampered by the teacher's expectation of a naturalized anthropomorphic interpretation, and her use of the representational interpretation to achieve a 'child-like' conclu-sion. What could be described analytically as the students' displays of represen-tational interpretations were not generally acknowledged in the teacher's talk as representational. This illustrates Hammersley's point that maturity is highly valued, but difficult to maintain given the expectations and behaviours of others, in this case, teachers (Hammersley 1976: especially 111).

Chapter 10 demonstrated that the students orient to the classroom talk as the site of the procedural and propositional display of what is to count as an assessable piece of writing in this context. The students are accountable for having heard the classroom talk *and* understood its import in the construction of knowledge in the classroom.

We saw in Chapters 9 and 10 that the students learn from the classroom talk the version of the Child they are accountable for enacting as both topic and resource, and that, as students in this context, they must simultaneously enact the relevances of studenthood and childhood, and their enactment of this double incumbency has real consequences. For example, they can be assessed by specific criteria as 'mature' or 'immature' according to the degree of fit of their writing to the theory of the Child enacted in the talk.

One of the features that the students oriented to in their writing is what we described here as the interpretive frames. The students' writing demonstrated that they were able to produce writing that displays the three frames described in this study, realistic, anthropomorphic and representational, but that, similarly to the novel and the talk, anthropomorphism was naturalized as a prime relevance to this group.

We saw that the student participants oriented to, and participated in, adult theorizations of themselves as Child–Students in order to take part in interaction with each other and the adult at this site. This is one of our key points. In order to be a successful participant in the enculturating institution of schooling, these students already enacted institutionalized versions of themselves. We saw in Part III some of the ways in which an institutionalized version of the Child is utterly consequential to these members' enactment of their studenthood. The data here document that the category Child is not just 'a set of abstract ideas on which rhetoric is based; it is also a working category that is enacted in everyday social experience' (Freebody 1995a: 18). We saw the Child–Students' success in school as depending to some extent on their apparently natural and enthusiastic collaboration in adult theories of the Child as these theories are enacted in the subtleties of, in this case, writing about literature (Chapter 10), talking about literature (Chapter 9) and in the literature itself (Chapter 8).

Not only did students orient to the adult versions of themselves as children, but they oriented to these versions as consequential: As a case in point, Clinton produced counter-readings and interpretations in the classroom talk:

120	*C:*	Mrs Field?
121	*T:*	Yeah?/
122	*C:*	I think this story is a bit stupid because I don't think a magpie would feel all this all this, all that what we've talked about.
123	*T:*	Fair enough (*Teacher handing question sheets to students.*) (5) You think we're giving Magpie feelings that perhaps he really doesn't have.
		. . .
124	*C:*	Yeah and//
128	*C:*	Well (.) and I think the magpie probably would have drowned (. . .)//
129	*Ss:*	(*several voices protesting 'it's just a story' and similar comments, untranscribable*)//
130	*C:*	(It's not realistic) And in the story it talks about how Magpie thought//—
		. . .

132 *C:*   Oh no he's not going to get back and I don't think a magpie would
             know this. (2)

Although Clinton challenged the assumed first call of anthropomorphic readings in the classroom talk (on several occasions), he never did so in his assessable
written responses.

    Knowing about adults' versions of the Child affects children's grades; it has
consequences for their participation in lessons; it affects how well they
employ the materials they need to work with in school to get grades. Indeed,
what adults think about childhood for school is the most central topic and
resource for being a successful student, itself the core of being a good Child.

Part IV
Revisiting the production of the Child

11 The public specification of the Child

Revisiting the issue

We have revisited a number of themes throughout this discussion. One of these is a paradox observed thirty years ago by Robert MacKay who issued this complaint about how socialization was theorized and studied within sociology:

> all interaction is based upon underlying interpretive competence. This competence is not acknowledged within the normative approach [to social structure and socialization] because the study of socialization takes the views of the dominant culture (adult) and proposes them as scientific findings. It ignores the interactional nature of adult-child relationships.
>
> (MacKay 1973: 180)

Since then many researchers, especially those working within ethnomethodology, have aimed to address this complaint extending it to the notions of 'development' within psychology and 'enculturation' within anthropology. They have done this not just in the interests of the development of more fully self-conscious and equitable communities; the fact is that this complaint leads us directly to two serious paradoxes within the social sciences. The first of these applies to the social-interpretive work that young people need to do in order to 'develop', or become 'socialized' or 'acculturated'. To do this (or have it done to and with them), children need to have interpretive competence with respect to the understandings of adults, specifically those understandings that relate to children's competences. To take part competently in adult-orchestrated events designed to acculturate them into particular cognitions, attitudes, social displays and 'identities', children need to have an actionable idea of those (apparently to be learned) cognitions, attitudes, social displays and 'identities' in the first place.

A second and analogous form of this paradox applies to the study of social life by social scientists. Theories of development, socialization and enculturation pre-specify the criteria by which children will be held to be precompetent and then explore the data of social life (or of the experimental laboratory) for instances of shortfall on precisely those criteria. The potentially vast numbers

of ways in which children and adults are, could or might be in certain circumstances, the same or similar in their actions and apparent rationalities are written
out of the interest. Hence, it would be rare in most places to find a child on an
advisory group to, say, a child-abuse unit or early childhood curriculum team,
or on the council of a preschool. Social science has worked hard to produce the
object of its study, representing it as a naturally occurring phenomenon. It is the
social sciences that have most doggedly kept the generational borders patrolled
and fortified.

In this book we have argued for the denaturalization of childhood, aiming to
position the reader so that close examinations of absolutely unremarkable
everyday talk in classrooms reveal the processes of a category production that
suit the operations and rationalities of schooling. We have taken it that childhood is no more a process of massive change than other stages of life, and
that the course of childhood is neither pulled along by social imperatives nor
pushed along by the unfolding of psychic dynamisms. But social institutions
can be set up to embody the empirical reality of these pushes and pulls. For
example, schooling is apparently aimed at the 'growth, development', and all
the rest, of children. It seems to reflect and project other realities about children
and where they are headed. Most importantly, schools' existence asserts that
children are 'headed somewhere' and that this heading somewhere is what is
the essence of their stage of life, so remarkable that massive, legally mandated
and breathtakingly expensive institutional systems need to be created to help
them head off somewhere. The practices we see in schools then, from the
gaze of the naturalized child of traditional psychology, sociology or anthropology are recast as proxies or metaphors of either the sociological categories
toward which the child is being pulled, or of the internal machinery of 'unfolding' working away within the child. We have argued and tried to show that the
classroom can be studied in its own right, that the categorization work we see
accomplished there is not a proxy or metaphor for something else, but rather is
part of what is needed for the ongoing accomplishment of school life – lessons,
grades, answers, questions, and all the rest.

Results of our research

We have turned to a variety of settings in which actual and fictional children
find themselves in the nooks and crannies of school. Here we draw together
some of the main features of the performance of children that we found in
each of these settings, aiming to set out themes that are consistent and con-
vincing enough to provide a platform for some implications for theory,
method, practice and policy with which we conclude this book.

Being in the whole class

When we examined teachers working with whole classes of students, we found
that the striking features of the Child–Students of this setting were that they

were characterizable by all participants as precompetent and as cohorted – members of a knowable group, sufficiently homogeneous for the practical purposes at hand to answer and act for and as one another. We deal briefly with each of these features in this Part.

We showed in detail how precompetence was mutually achieved by teachers and students. First, we showed how to be a Child–Student was not to be simply incompetent, but rather to be moving toward competence. The practices taken to be relevant to this movement were shown to be on matters of fact, preference, motivation, morality, social behaviour and cognitive processing. On these matters, we found the collaborative foregrounding of Child–Students' 'trying' and the persistent reliance by both parties on turn design features that foreground the teacher's acceptance, confirmation or validation of the offerings of Child–Students. Answers and other contributions were heard (by all) as offerings from the group as a whole, and those offerings were at all moments possible elements of the confirmed propositional corpus of the lesson.

A second way in which the precompetence of Child–Students was established and confirmed by all was through the use of pretending and the public presentation of students' prediliction to over-believe in serendipitous events – 'aren't we lucky all these words start with "d"?' Finally, we found teachers and Child–Students publicly acknowledging Child–Students' excitability and their eagerness to be held in suspense. Teachers' frequent wondering in public and young students' gasping and ohing at revelations previously hidden create a Child–Student that is, in a prominent rather than incidental way, an innocent abroad in the classroom. The prominence of this feature of the category lies in its relevance to behavioural management ('settling down' Child–Students, rewarding 'good behaviour' with revelations, and so on). This relevance is a neat example of the apparent recruitment of a common-sensically 'natural' feature of children for learning management and the regulation of bodies and attention. Being good until lunchtime so that we can find out what our secret word is shows one's collusion in the conflation of the natural and institutionally convenient Child.

These ways of producing the precompetent person all took place within an interactional party structure that cohorted Child–Students. Teachers had group names for Child–Students in the classroom, addressed the group as a whole, and worked hard to synchronize chorused talk or actions. Teachers also reminded Child–Students of common histories, group histories. These instances often involved references to things 'we' had done earlier, or things 'we' had wanted or planned to do. Thus the coherence of the group through time is an often-used reference point for the matters at hand here and now.

We also found instances in which particular individuals were talked up as 'non-members' of the cohort. Breaches of behavioural expectations were pointed to as criteria for moment-to-moment membership, and this was sometimes accompanied by the placement of an individual in a separate place in the room to punctuate temporary non-membership.

Most significantly from a learning point of view, we found that individual students were held accountable for work done by the cohort, and that each was held accountable for displaying the knowledge in the form it was confirmed as part of the propositional corpora of lessons. On hearing and confirming an answer from a Child–Student, teachers clearly behaved as if that answer was established with the entire cohort, such that sequentially or logically enabled questions could then be asked.

Within these general observations, we found some variability in the ways in which members of different classrooms enacted the mutually contingent categories Teacher and Child–Student. In particular, we found differences across classrooms on the matter of how and when cohorting was accomplished. Cohorting was routinely done across all sites with the varying knowledge bases of the Child–Students, the kinds of interactional options they were afforded by teachers (e.g. length and placement of answers), and what counted as being engaged in the work of the classroom all relating to how, when and with what effect cohorting was performed.

Being in small groups

Without the presence, gaze or direct guidance of the teacher, we found that the attributes the Child–Students displayed, foregrounded and acknowledged in small group work in the classroom were demonstrably different in important ways from those evident in whole class work. At the most general level, we found that key attributions of the 'small group' Child–Students were competent or not and a member of the local rather than the general cohort. The Child–Students of the small group took one another and generally were taken to have the cognitive, social and moral capabilities to behave in purposeful and reasoned ways toward the management of the small group's task.

We also found differences from classroom to classroom in the ways in which these features were acted out and acted upon. For instance, the degree to which apparently off-task talk threatened membership in the group varied from site to site. Asides, jokes and extended chat carried different degrees of membership-related sanction in the sites we studied.

Even in the light of these variations, we were able to conclude that, in contrast to the Child–Student of the whole class, the Child–Student that is the topic and resource of the small group is different. This Child–Student had the option to behave as if time out from set task was an option that would not threaten adequate membership. The Child–Students variously took leads in task progress and completion, but the issue is that, even in lead positions, we found variations on the accomplishment of Child–Student, rather than, in any analytically meaningful sense, the 'adoption of a teacher role'. Young people in school can variously resource the open-textured category Child–Student; various settings and tasks hail various attributes of that category, and we have shown the responsiveness and deftness of relatively young people in mustering, nuancing and displaying these attributes, responsively in varying settings.

The child of school fiction

To illustrate the workings of the category Child in settings outside schools, we examined a novel for young people entitled *Magpie Island*. We found that, to achieve this goal with any precision, we needed to acknowledge that this particular novel calls upon three distinctive, but interleaved, interpretive frames, within each of which the category Child is worked up in slightly different ways and to different effect. These frames we termed realistic, anthropomorphic and representational. We also found that the tale slipped between these frames in unannounced ways.

For our purposes we found that this novel operated with two connected, but not always compatible, sets of resources concerning the category Child: the Child described in the story and the Child called upon as a reader of the novel. The portrayed Child (including the Magpie in question when he was a fledgling) was shown to be gullible, vulnerable, transient and active to the point of 'friskiness'. The relevance of these attributions is foregrounded as the child characters (human and otherwise) are paired with their adult counterparts.

In sharp contrast, the Child hailed as a reader of this novel is not at all an innocent abroad – linguistically, conceptually or morally. The interplay between the construction of the Child consciousness as articulated by the child character and the narrator creates an interpretive ambiguity that allows the novel to proceed toward an unsettled ending. Here again is an aspect of the paradox we described above: this novel is written for children – for members of the publicly recognizable category Child. A large part of how we know that is to do with the fact that its two central characters are of that category. The construction of that Child in the novel, however, is done in such a way that it calls upon a vastly more sophisticated, less gullible and less straightforwardly 'empirical' Child–Reader, a Child–Reader who can locate the Child status of the central characters in the book within a variety of interpretive frames – in the end, a Child–Reader with next to nothing in common with the Child characters, except for nostalgia for what it was like to be *that* kind of Child. This is a novel written for adults who can pretend to be children to read to children who are on the way toward appreciating how it is that adults read Childhood. It is therefore a novel that calls up the precompetent Child for the educative Adult, perhaps explaining its perennial popularity in Australian schools and families.

The Child of the literature classroom

It is clear that what is afforded by the interpretive multiplicities of the novel and through its narrative ambiguities makes no claim on what it is that will be oriented to by educators and students using the novel in classrooms. In fact in our case we examined the classroom talk around the novel *Magpie Island* prior to analysing the novel or the students' writing. We did this because of our understanding of the educationally prime status of teacher–student talk.

The novel, educationally, we took to be whatever collections of teachers and students could make of it in their conduct of educational work, however they could variously 'talk it into being'. While it may be rendered into other things in other settings, its relevant potentials we took to be those that could be rendered in educational talk with the Child–Student. In the classroom we examined, we found that the teacher attempted to draw out the talk on the bases of the three interpretive frames outlined above, but that most interaction oriented to the realistic and anthropomorphic frames. As in the novel, although obviously more rapidly and with less announcement, the talk slipped from frame to frame over the course of exchanges within a lesson. At times, rarer than perhaps expected, the students appeared to be answering within an interpretive frame that had recently been abandoned. Thus, one of the resources for discussing this novel as a student in this series of lessons was the ability to interleave, at a moment's notice, frameworks for making sense of literary works – realism, reportage, fantasy, allegory, fable, and so on – each putting its own particular procedural angle on the 'acceptable answer' and each referring to and drawing on the category Child in a distinctive way.

The series of eleven lessons on this novel that we examined were concluded by considerable talk concerning the interpretation of the ending. The teacher worked hard to effect a collaborative happy-allegorical ending, with characters being symbols of things, in much the same way as the human child character's father tried to interpret for him the apparently 'dark' ending. The teacher used this interpretive distinction as a gauge of 'maturity' among the students. Effectively, then, the classroom talk provides a domain that highlights the precompetence of Child–Students, allowing Child–Students to display assessable competencies and teachers to view them.

The one feature of the category Child–Students that is clear and consistent in the classroom talk, in the light of our frames of analysis of the novel, is that it is taken by the teacher and accorded by the Child–Students that the natural or at least the default interpretive frame of the Child–Student is anthropomorphism. The children in the class are taken to be attached to and knowledgeable about animals that talk, think, feel and so on like humans. They are taken to be competent at managing that frame; their 'developmental, socializing or enculturating' task, as enacted in this classroom around this novel, is to move toward competence in drawing on the other frames and moving between them in harmony with the movements of the teacher.

The Child–Student on display: writing and being assessed

These considerations we showed to be consequential for students. We showed that their success as students relied on their ability to draw appropriately on adult theorizations of Childhood, and to display key features of those theorizations in their talk. Talk, though, was not the only site wherein students' enactment of particular versions of themselves mattered. The enactment of the appropriate Child–Students mattered, also, in students' writing.

For both teachers and students, the writing exercises integral to the unit of work on *Magpie Island* were occasions for supervision and assessment of, among other things, the articulation of a theory of Childhood (as evident in or available from the novel) and the enactment of a theory of both the Child–Student reader (the reader of *Magpie Island*) and the Child–Student writer. In the students' writing we see them drawing on cultural knowledge of the categories Child, Adult and Parent singly and in relational partnerships. We see them doing this in terms of both the MCD 'stage of life' and the MCD 'family'. We find parallels between their accomplishment of this and the versions found from our analyses of the novel and the classroom talk.

As well, we found parallels between interpretive work that the students accomplished in their writing and the interpretive frames evident in the novel and the classroom talk: the anthropomorphic frame was most heavily drawn on, and some movement from frame to frame was evident. Significantly, we found that students oriented specifically to the classroom talk as the most definite authority for the inclusion of certain features in their writing. They clearly took themselves as accountable for knowing that talk and showing that knowledge in their writing, but it is equally clear that the teacher also took this talk to be authoritative as a resource for writing in school. That is, the propositional and procedural corpora marked out from within the classroom talk are doubly accountable to the students: they indicate that they themselves are accountable for knowing what those corpora contain; and they also indicate that the teacher is similarly accountable.

We found clear evidence that the students involved in this unit of work learn directly from the classroom talk which version of Childhood they would be accountable for displaying as a topic in their written work about the novel, and how they themselves are to enact this version as an interpretive resource in their writing. But clearly they write as category Student as well. What we termed the 'double incumbency' of Child and Student has very real consequences for how they are assessed, specifically in the terms of the distinction between 'maturity' and 'immaturity' as used by the teacher in her assessment of the piece. Knowledge of how to put this double incumbency to productive effect in their work is available to students from the procedural displays shown in their interactions with the teacher in and around the topic of the novel. Crucially, however, it is not a body of knowledge that is explicated *as* a body of knowledge in that talk. Rather, the adult-based contents of the incumbencies Child and Student are worked into the talk as natural attributes, common-sensically available.

What our conclusions mean

Thinking about childhood

In the most general sense, the force of our work in this book has been to show ways of de-naturalizing the Child. Both folk and official theories of the Child have foregrounded the incompetence or precompetence of this category of people, characterizing them as fundamentally on a path toward the ideal model of person – the adult. Furthermore, we have critiqued the notion that it is this movement that is the distinctive feature of children, that it is for them, but not for people who occupy other positions in a 'stage of life' programme, that this 'movement toward' is salient.

We have suggested how such a teleological version of the Child suits a number of purposes, and we have shown in detail how the purposes of schooling are furthered by such a theory. The prevalence and popularity of incompetence and precompetence theorizations of Childhood have depended to a great extent on the ways in which such accounts – from traditional psychology, sociology and anthropology – furnish an object of study. That is, they provide the theorist with a set of features of young people's activities that the researcher can focus on in their wish to study children and not just, say, people or social order or institutional interaction. The Child industry, in research as well as in public practice, needs an object of study that is commonsensically recognizable as a Child, in precisely the same ways as an economist needs objects called 'an economy', 'resources', 'employment rates', and so on. For the public practice of health, the law, and government, just as surely as for the undertaking of schooling, the Child needs to be so thoroughly accomplished that it is a commonsense categorization, even though we know that debates have always taken place about 'where to draw a line' between the Child (as precompetent, lacking in the autonomy for informed choice in their health care, their apparently criminal activity or their voting preferences) and the Adult (as publicly competent and thus accountable in these matters).

Traditional folk and official accounts of the Child foreground these contrasts with adult functioning. What is important is that we acknowledge that these accounts are not merely descriptive statements of more or less empirical validity. They also sustain a moral order that can be acted upon with apparent impunity. There is another way of making these points: When we consider the Standardized Relational Pairs – Adult–Child and Teacher–Student – we can see, as Jayyusi (1984) pointed out, that one part of each pair is the 'stable' part (Adult and Teacher) and the other we may term the 'occasioned' part. What this permits is different descriptions of the activities, motivations, capabilities and so on of each part. These descriptions are termed 'asymmetric accounts' whereby members of the stable category (Adult, Teacher) have their activities accounted for in terms of their specific biographies and/or the contingencies of the event at hand. In contrast, members of the occasioned category tend to be described in terms of their membership of that category – 'they do that because they are children'. Asymmetric accounts tend to homogenize the occasioned category members and make irrelevant, then and there in the event under consideration, both their particular biographic histories and their reasonableness. This asymmetric accounting is one of the key processes by which a culture's categorizational work enacts and sustains a set of moral relationships:

The contrastive use of attribute-specification rather than explanation-by-grounds of specific reason . . . is a feature of talk about much 'deviant' activity. . . The underlying asymmetry of perspective involved is a logical feature of such formulations, and it points directly to the normatively and morally organized character of categorization work, accounts, descriptions, predictions and discourse-interactional work in general.

(Jayyusi 1984: 28)

Of interest to us has been the ways in which folk, institutional and discipline-based accounts of children are enacted and how these accounts work together, either supporting or contradicting one another. Thus we lose the children in our studies of the Child.

This has particular consequences for educators. Schools serve clienteles that are culturally changing, presumably preparing young people to live in societies that are similarly changing in terms of vocational pathways, technologies, valued knowledges, and linguistic, cultural and moral complexity. Part of that change entails changes in versions of childhood. In many contemporary societies, this combination of changes has brought about new forms of child-hood, new activities, skills, ways and domains of relating, media exposure, and so on. Persisting with traditional curricular versions of the Child (e.g. print-literate, neighbourhood focused, morally naïve, culturally insular) and basing the organization of educational experiences for children on culturally narrow discipline-based accounts of development, socialization and encultura-tion, may mean that the object of the school's attention in effect no longer exists, if it ever did.

Studying children

For researchers, then, the task is to focus on the interpretive capabilities of people in events in which children participate, to examine how it is that certain capabilities are shown and called upon in various public and domestic settings in which children live.

In addition, researchers need to give their close attention to the ways in which both professional and nonprofessional child-carers construct the category Child for their particular purposes, patrol and fortify the borders of that category, and ascribe that category with key attributes. Policy documents relating to children and instances of their practical use are a rich source for researchers interested in how it is that cultures and sub-cultures such as educa-tors, doctors and so on produce and describe the objects of their care. If we wish to see the 'natural' social world at work, for instance, in schools, we need theories and analytic methods that keep our attention on the details of the activ-ities of the members of a culture, rather than accepting their categorizations as having explanatory status of themselves. The processes by which all members of a culture endow their purposeful categorizations with both moral, empirical and explanatory status need to remain themselves objects of study if researchers are to move beyond commonsensical accounts. Common sense itself is the bed-rock on which the validity of social practices with and for children ultimately rests. As such, it is the unremarkable that deserves researchers' most focused attention.

We have used an ethnomethodological disposition to interrogate the un-remarkable with conversation analysis and membership categorization analysis. By maintaining a focus on our specific concerns, these methods allowed fine documentations across a large and varied data corpus. This methodology allowed us to incorporate our broad theoretical questions about social order into the research design and data gathering process such that our attention stayed on the details of the apparently 'natural' phenomenon at work – Childhood.

Working with children

Commenting some years ago on the class bias of modern schooling, Bourdieu (1974) pointed out that the standard workings of classrooms were such that they allowed teachers to systematically mistake class-based cultural capabilities for academic gifts. We have made a supplementary point here, showing how it is that displays of particular versions of childhood become assessable features of students' work for school. Thereby, teachers mistake cultural-endorsed versions of displaying oneself as a member of category Child for displays of academic capability and 'mature work'.

Educators need to examine the ways in which the materials used in schools are deemed acceptable or 'good for students'. Other researchers (e.g. Baker and Freebody 1989a) have shown how materials designed for use in schools actually are tailored to fit into particular pedagogical strategies (e.g. reading books with lots of rhymes, sections ending with exercises and activities for students, and so on). More significant and generally less evident are the versions of Childhood on which many classroom materials are predicated. Their significance lies in their relevance to a child's assessment as mature or effective students. As we showed in Chapter 10, much is potentially at stake in students' working out and acting on the procedural and propositional content of adult educators' deep-seated notions of Childhood.

Making policy about and for children

We hope that the approach we have taken here at least begins a process of dissatisfaction on a number of fronts. Researchers and educators should be dis-satisfied with accounts, including policy statements, of Childhood or children that are based on some stated or assumed essential 'key' features of what it is to be a Child. How to manage children of different sorts in various sites is a matter of empirical purchase, and should be taken to be a variable task across cultures, local sites and, as we have shown within classrooms, across particular work configurations and events.

We should be impatient with accounts of Childhood – folk, discipline-based or in policy – that assume that the most interesting thing about children is the ways in which they are different from (often, not as good as) adults. Educators have long been sensitive to 'deficit' accounts of ethnic minority students and disadvantaged communities, but this sensitivity has rarely been critically applied to understandings about children.

We should be sceptical about a theory of the Child who is assumed from the start to be the Child of that theory, whose journey is then mapped along the avenues laid out by that theory, and who is then sold back to the Child as the story of the 'self'. Similarly, we should not lose sight of the fact that institutional imperatives, however benign in their intent and effect, operate in the same way as the pre-emptive theory.

We should be unimpressed by research on children that does not try to convey to us the details of their everyday activities. Much research substitutes survey statistics, interviews with adults, or even simulations for these details, and thus asks us to do the same interpretive substitution. For example, we could have simply consulted as data the teacher's grades for the written pieces she examined, or reported summary statistics of teachers' ratings of students' group work in class. Apart from not answering the questions we wished to pursue, such data has at best only a shadowy relationship to the phenomena at issue.

In many cultures, including ours, much store is put on a person's stage of life. Without knowing someone, we can feel that we know a lot about them from knowing their age (and gender, and so on). Stage of life is a productive inference machine (Sacks 1995). People are able to routinely attach moral, intellectual and interactional baggage to the category Child. Much of this baggage is negative. It is baggage to the effect, most particularly, that children cannot participate in decisions about activities that are apparently aimed solely at their well-being. These decisions may be medical, legal or educational.

We have tried to show that the Child need not be seen as a deviant or occasioned category, interesting only because of its contrast with category Adult. We have approached this by taking the example of schooling and showing how the institution of school both provides and calls for a particular set of contents for the category Child and uses those contents as yardsticks for the assessment of the effective Child–Student. The belief is that much is to be gained in the research effort, and to social practice more broadly, from the documentation and recruitment of young people's artfulness and capability.

Appendix: analytic methods

Within ethnomethodology, the analyst of social order has available the inter-actants' relevancies as shown through their talk. The key analytic methods used to inform our interpretations are Conversation Analysis (CA) and Membership Categorization Analysis (MCA). In this text, the analysis based in MCA incorporates explanation sufficient to our purposes. Further analysis using MCA can be found in, among others, Antaki and Widdicombe (1998) and McHoul and Rapley (2001). This appendix provides brief explanations of several key features of Conversation Analysis: turn-taking systems; adjacency pairs, insertion sequences; recipient design; third-turn options; retrospective hearings; and preferences. A recent and thorough account of Conversation Analysis can be found in Hutchby and Wooffitt (1998).

Turn-taking systems

It is a common understanding that in ordinary talk, the shift from one speaker to another occurs in a routine and orderly way. This systematic organization of turn-taking by speakers was explored by Sacks *et al.* (1974). The result of their investigation was, in their words, 'a simplest systematics for the organiza-tion of turn-taking for conversation' (1974: 696). A summary of their system of turn-taking is presented below.

1   For any turn, at the initial transition-relevance place of an initial turn-constructional unit.
   (a)   If the turn-so-far is so constructed as to involve the use of a 'current speaker selects next' technique, then the party so selected has the right and is obliged to take next turn to speak; no other has such rights or obligations and transfer occurs at that place.
   (b)   If the turn-so-far is so constructed as not to involve the use of a 'current speaker selects next' technique, then self-selection for next speakership may, but need not, be instituted; first starter acquires rights to a turn, and transfer occurs at that place.

(c) If the turn-so-far is so constructed as not to involve the use of a 'current speaker selects next' technique, then current speaker may, but need not continue, unless another self-selects.

2   If, at the initial transition-relevance place of an initial turn-constructional unit, neither 1(a) nor 1(b) had operated, and, following the provision of 1(c), current speaker has continued, then the rule-set (a)–(c) applies at the next transition-relevance place, and recursively at each next transition-relevance place, until transfer is effected.

(Sacks *et al.* 1974: 704)

Within this frame, a 'turn' is definable as an utterance that is heard as recognizably complete (Sacks *et al.* 1974; Taylor and Cameron 1987); 'completeness' occurs at the moment at which transition to another speaker can occur. As (1) through (2) above detail, there is an identifiable system by which the position of speaker is shifted at such 'initial transition-relevance places' to effect a change in the holder of the position of speaker. Therefore, the system of turn-taking promotes the possibility of the position of speaker being held by various speakers through the course of mundane talk-in-interaction.

What are the observable features of mundane talk-in-interaction? According to Sacks *et al.* (1974) they are:

1   Speaker-change recurs, or at least occurs.
2   Overwhelmingly, one party talks at a time.
3   Occurrences of more than one speaker at a time are common, but brief.
4   Transitions (from one turn to a next) with no gap and no overlap are common. Together with transitions characterized by slight gap or slight overlap, they make up the vast majority of transitions.
5   Turn order is not fixed, but varies.
6   Turn size is not fixed, but varies.
7   Length of conversation is not specified in advance.
8   What parties say is not specified in advance.
9   Relative distribution of turns is not specified in advance.
10 Number of parties can vary.
11 Talk can be continuous or discontinuous.
12 Turn-allocation techniques are obviously used. A current speaker may select a next speaker (as when he (*sic*) addresses a question to another party); or parties may self-select in starting to talk.
13 Various 'turn-constructional units are employed; e.g. turns can be projectedly 'one word long', or they can be sentential in length.
14 Repair mechanisms exist for dealing with turn-taking errors and violations, e.g. if two parties find themselves talking at the same time, one of them will stop prematurely, thus repairing the trouble (Sacks *et al.* 1974: 704).
15 In engaging in mundane talk-in-interaction, speakers orient to its rules and features as normatively accountable (Leiter 1980; Sacks *et al.* 1974). It follows that speakers' orientation to the system and the features makes

orderly turns at talk possible (Lee 1987). Used as a standard, these established features can be applied to other talk-in-interaction to identify the ordinary features of other types of recognizable talk.

Adjacency pairs

Adjacency pairs are pairs of utterances in which an utterance of a particular type, or either of a couple of types of second utterances, is projected by the recognisable production of a specific first utterance (Coulter 1979a; Lee 1987; Sharrock and Anderson 1986). Examples of adjacency pairs are: greetings; questions and answers; invitations and their acceptance or refusal; accusations and concomitant denials or admissions; requests and compliance or non-compliance (Freiberg and Freebody 1995; Heritage 1984; Psathas 1995; Taylor and Cameron 1987), and complaints and denial or rejection (Leiter 1980). The production of the second pair part from within the particular range of second parts is normatively accountable (Heritage 1984). Therefore, for a second speaker not to produce a projected second part can be heard by all participants as out of the ordinary and, therefore, accountable (Goodwin and Heritage 1990; Lee 1987). The management formats found in talk have the status of a 'normative order' in which all parties are accountable participants.

Insertion sequences

The ability of a second speaker to fashion an appropriate second pair part of an adjacency pair may rely upon that speaker's clarification of some part of the first pair part, or her or his collection of some further information (Wilson 1991). Therefore, sequences of talk may occur in which the second turn at talk does not function as the projected answer, but in which that projected answer is not heard as missing (Coulter 1979b; Psathas 1995). Such second turns at talk and their subsequent sequences of talk comprise 'insertion sequences'. Wilson (1991) argued that insertion sequences can be accountably uttered by speakers, even though they are recognizably *not* projected by the first pair part, only insofar as they recognizably prepare for a projected second pair part. In doing so, they orient to the fact that the second pair part is pending. Insertion sequences can be lengthy, given that an originating insertion may itself project a particular second pair part which may also be subject to an insertion sequence, and so on.

Recipient design

In producing any first pair part, 'speakers commit themselves to a range of beliefs about themselves, their co-participants and their relationships' (Heritage 1984: 270). Therefore, another feature of talk-in-interaction is that each turn characterizes and embodies the speaker and recipient/audience; each turn orients to and embodies particularly relevant membership categories and attributes of the speakers and hearers, and thus, to the rights and responsibilities of speakers. Such embodiment is referred to by Goodwin and Heritage (1990) as 'recipient design'. Examples of this include: the different relationships inherent in referring to a given group of people as 'terrorists' as opposed to 'freedom fighters' (see Jayyusi 1991); the idea that the direction of a question to one speaker by another speaker both proposes that the second speaker is knowledgeable about the information required, and that the first speaker is less informed (Goodwin and Heritage 1990; Heritage 1984); and the idea that over-specification of detail orients to the recipient as *in need of* such detail, thereby accomplishing that member as *lacking* the information (Freiberg and Freebody 1995).

Third-turn option

The 'third-turn option' refers to the idea that first speakers, in their response to a second speaker's turn, display their understanding of the adequacy of that second speaker's turn at talk. They make available, to both speakers and analysts, how any second turn was 'heard' in the sequence of talk (Drew and Heritage 1992). In third turns, speakers are able to indicate that a normatively accountable second turn is missing, inadequate or, alternatively, has been routinely produced and is thus unremarkable. Turns can be accomplished as missing or inadequate by being oriented to as accountably due, for example, by saying 'Did you hear me?', or by repeating the original turn. Routine production is indicated insofar as the second turn is not made relevant as remarkable and the talk-in-interaction is continued by all participants.

Another way in which an initial speaker can display his or her understanding of the inadequacy of a second turn is to 'restart' the original turn (Goodwin and Heritage 1990). Restarts enable the attention of recipients to be regained and allows information to be added to an original turn. They also mitigate against a response *again* being inadequate or missing.

Preferences

Directly associated with systems of turn-taking system are speakers' 'preference systems' (Goodwin and Heritage 1990; Taylor and Cameron 1987). First pair parts of adjacency pairs do not necessarily project a single second part pair, but a couple of second part pairs. For example, invitations project both rejections and acceptances, and accusations project denial as well as admission. On the whole, however, one of the two projected second part pairs is normatively 'preferred' over the other second part pair. That is, it is normatively accountable that even though two utterances may be possibly projected, one particular one will be *routinely* projected. Therefore utterances, as second parts, can be either 'preferreds' or 'non-preferreds' (Heritage 1984).

It is normatively accountable for 'preferred' responses to be produced without delay and in simple terms (Heritage 1984). By comparison, if, for whatever reason, a 'non-preferred' is produced as a second pair part, it is routinely accompanied by features that function to 'soften' the effect of hearing a 'non-preferred' but mark it as an 'out of the ordinary' utterance. In general, softeners or markers include speakers doing the following:

- pausing prior to saying the non-preferred;
- prefacing the non-preferred with 'Hmm', 'Um', 'Well', and the like;
- prefacing the non-preferred with agreement e.g. 'Yes, but . . .';
- qualifying the non-preferred. e.g. 'Now you're not going to like this, but . . .';
- providing an account or explanation for their provision of a non-preferred;
- using a mitigated 'declination component' e.g. 'Probably not, because . . .'.
 (Goodwin and Heritage 1990; Levinson 1983; Psathas 1995;
 Taylor and Cameron 1987)

Each of the 'markers' also functions to highlight speakers' awareness of the normative accountability of uttering 'preferred' responses even as they produce a 'non-preferred' response.

Solidarity

One function of the system of 'preferreds' and 'non-preferreds' is to promote the existence of solidarity, and reduce the possibility of conflict, between speakers (Heritage 1984). Thus, another systematic mechanism of talk-in-interaction is its routine promotion of solidarity and routine reduction of conflict. Inherent in the system of preferreds and non-preferreds is the prompt provision of utterances that strengthen relations between speakers, and the waivering or deferred provision of utterances which do not (see Goodwin and Heritage 1990).

Other features of mundane conversation also function to promote smooth relations between speakers. One 'family' of such features is 'prefatory comments' which includes pre-sequences (e.g., 'Can I ask you a question?', 'Do you know what?' and 'Can I get you to do something for me?'); pre-closers (e.g., 'Anyway' and 'Well') and pre-topic shifts (e.g., 'Now', 'Okay' and 'Right'). Such utterances constitute whatever it is that they 'propose to precede' as an accountable and normal 'next' option. For example, 'Anyway' can be heard as proposing that a current topic is exhausted thus making accountable ending a sequence of talk (Handel 1982). In a similar way, 'Right' audibly directs attention away from a previously projected topic or course of action (Heap 1992b), indicates that other topics are of priority, and makes changing the topic of conversation accountable. In heralding the occasion of particular utterances or types of talk, prefatory comments enable sequences of talk 'through which speakers can collaborate in forward preferred sequences or actions and avoiding (or aborting) dispreferred ones' (Heritage 1984: 278). Prefatory comments, therefore, sustain normatively accountable conversation and mitigate against 'surprise' utterances and sequences (Goodwin and Heritage 1990).

Another mechanism of talk that maintains the smooth running of an interaction is the system by which turns at talk that require explanation or accounting – for example, a person immediately and simply rejecting an invitation – have no explanation either called for or provided (Garfinkel 1967). Handel (1982) described such situations as 'letting it pass' or 'letting it stand'. When a turn at talk is 'let to stand' the discrepancy of unusually responding, for example, to an invitation is acknowledged but is accepted as reasonable for the current situation. Both speakers, in this case, would be forgiven their deviation from a routine sequence: speaker A for producing a non-softened 'non-preferred' answer, and speaker B for failing to pursue the 'preferred' answer with more alacrity.

An additional feature of mundane talk-in-interaction that contributes to speaker solidarity is formulations. Formulations are utterances that provide a summary of what a course of talk has been about, for example, what its purposes and implications are (Handel 1982). Once a formulation has been uttered and acknowledged, all participants are normatively accountable to know and accept the version of the talk-in-interaction, thus formulated. Formulations contribute to the display of 'continuously up-dated intersubjective understandings' insofar as one speaker summarizes, for all interactants, what the talk has been about. They promote smooth and efficient relations between speakers because they ensure that old ground need not be re-covered or re-summarized, conversations can continue secure in the participants' intersubjective knowledge of 'what's already happened', and there are no surprise retrospectives.

Notes

1 Framing childhood

1 For the purposes of this book, and often in works that employ Membership Category Analysis (explained in Chapter 4), capitalized words are used when referring to a category. Within this convention, Child stands for 'the category of child', Student for 'the category of student', and so forth. Chapter 4 and the Appendix explain Membership Categorization in detail but, for the moment, read the category (e.g. Child, Adult, Boy, Bikie) as the set of ideas that go together to constitute a theory of what it is to be a particular category of person, e.g. a child, an adult, a boy, or a bikie.

3 Rethinking schooling and classrooms

1 This sequence has been variously labelled, e.g. IRE (Initiation, Response, Evaluation); IRF (Initiation, Response, Feedback); QAE (Question, Answer, Evaluation); QAC (Question, Answer, Comment); and ERF (Elicitation, Response, Feedback).
2 See Appendix, 'Insertion Sequences'.
3 Although we make no claim to conclusions about differences between interactions in advantaged and disadvantaged classrooms, Chapter 6 provides the reader with examples of students' achievement of their schoolwork in one class, as relevant to the entire class-group and in other classes as relevant to only themselves, as individual students.
4 This category name is elaborated and explained in Part II.
5 Ethnomethodologists have developed an extensive body of theory and research but our description in Chapter 4 is necessarily brief and tailored to our particular aims in this book. The interested reader is referred to more detailed sources (e.g. Goodwin and Heritage 1990; Hester and Francis 2000; Heritage 1984; Hilbert 1992; Leiter 1980; Psathas 1995; Sharrock and Anderson 1986) for a more extensive introduction to this area.

4 Reconsidering social action and social structure

1 A note on notation: Membership Categorization Devices are put in 'quotation marks' and, as noted in Chapter 1, category names are capitalized.

5 The schoolchild

1 Had the interruption been problematic there might have been, for example, a student's audible insistence on finishing their turn. We cannot know with audio-taped data whether there was a non-verbal protest in a particular instance of inter-

ruption. In the body of data, however, there is no audible registration that a teacher interruption is other than routine.

Conclusion to Part II

1 Note that we might logically posit that the micro, in our example above, is driving the macro: specifically, that the teacher encouraged the students to tell anecdotes in whole class talk because that's what this group of students did when they were organized into small groups.

9 Teaching the category into being

1 Arguably the teacher's rejection is based in the future sexual relationship – the magpies do mate in the novel. At this point in the conversation the teacher knows this, having read the novel, but the students do not. Were they brother and sister the scene would be set for an incestuous relationship between the magpies, a morally problematic region in the anthropomorphized fictive world.
2 Recall Extract 6:12 in which a number of structural moves made by the participants accomplished an anecdote as relevant to the topic and thus productive to the current classroom business. The point made in Chapter 6 is pertinent; of interest to us is not whether an anecdote is or is not, in reality, relevant to the task, but that structural moves can be made by the participants that accomplish such talk as, for this group, in this moment, relevant or otherwise.

10 The students' writing

1 While the question as put here does not necessarily refer to the Adult–Child category pair, the classroom talk framed it within the relations between parents and children.
2 Phillip's reference to 'Darren Hinch' is a reference to 'Derryn Hinch' an evening television current affairs host at the time, who was known for fervently expressing his opinion. His nightly sign off was akin to 'That's Life and I'm Derryn Hinch'.

Bibliography

Alanen, L. (1998) 'Children and the family order: constraints and competencies', in
    I. Hutchby and J. Moran-Ellis (eds) *Children and Social Competence: Arenas of Action*,
    London: Falmer Press.
Alanen, L. and Mayall, B. (eds) (2001) *Conceptualizing Child-Adult Relations*, London:
    RoutledgeFalmer.
Alton-Lee, A., Nuthall, G. and Patrick, J. (1993) 'Reframing classroom research: a
    lesson from the private world of children', *Harvard Educational Review*, 63 (1): 50–84.
Antaki, C. and Widdicombe, S. (eds) (1998) *Identities in Talk*, London: Sage.
Anyon, J. (1981) 'Social class and school knowledge', *Curriculum Inquiry*, 11: 3–42.
Ariès, P. (1962) *Centuries of Childhood*, trans. R. Baldick, London: Jonathan Cape.
Atkinson, P. (1988) 'Ethnomethodology: a critical review', *Annual Review of Sociology*,
    14: 441–465.
Austin, H. (1997) 'Literature for school: theorising "the child" in talk and text',
    Language and Education, 11: 77–95.
Baker, C.D. (1991a) 'Literacy practices and social relations in classroom reading events',
    in C. Baker and A. Luke (eds) *Towards a Critical Sociology of Reading Pedagogy*,
    Amsterdam/Philadelphia: John Benjamins.
Baker, C.D. (1991b) 'Reading the texts of reading lessons', *Australian Journal of Reading*,
    14 (1): 5–20.
Baker, C.D. (1992) 'Description and analysis in classroom talk and interaction', *Journal
    of Classroom Interaction*, 27 (2): 9–14.
Baker, C.D. and Campbell, R. (2000) 'Children, language and power', in R. Campbell
    and D. Green (eds) *Literacies and Learners: Current Perspectives*, Sydney: Pearson
    Education.
Baker, C.D. and Freebody, P. (1986) 'Representations of questioning and answering in
    children's first school books', *Language in Society*, 15: 451–484.
Baker, C.D. and Freebody, P. (1987) 'Constituting the child in beginning school reading
    books', *British Journal of the Sociology of Education*, 8 (1): 55–76.
Baker, C.D. and Freebody, P. (1988) 'Possible worlds and possible people: interpretive
    challenges in beginning school reading books', *Australian Journal of Reading*, 11 (2):
    95–104.
Baker, C.D. and Freebody, P. (1989a) *Children's First School Books: Introductions to the
    Culture of Literacy*, Oxford: Basil Blackwell.
Baker, C.D. and Freebody, P. (1989b) 'Talk around text: constructions of textual and
    teacher authority in classroom discourse', in S. de Castell, A. Luke and C. Luke

(eds) *Language, Authority and Criticism: Readings on the School Textbook*, London/ Philadelphia: Falmer Press.

Baker, C.D. and Freebody, P. (1993) 'The crediting of literate competence in classroom talk', *Australian Journal of Language and Literacy*, 16 (4): 279–294.

Baker, C.D. and Perrott, C. (1988) 'The news session in infants and primary school classrooms', *British Journal of Sociology of Education*, 9 (1): 19–38.

Bellack, A., Kliebard, H., Hyman, R. and Smith, F. (1966) *The Language of the Classroom*, New York: Teachers College Press.

Bennett, N., Andreae, J., Hegarty, P. and Wade, B. (1980) *Open Plan Schools*, Slough: National Foundation for Educational Research.

Bernstein, B. (1990) 'The structuring of pedagogic discourse', *Class, Codes and Control*, vol. IV, London: Routledge.

Boden, D. and Zimmerman, D. (eds) (1991) *Talk and Social Structure*, Los Angeles: University of California Press.

Bourdieu, P. (1974) 'The school as a conservative force', in J. Eggleton (ed.) *Contemporary Research in the Sociology of Education*, London: Methuen.

Brandt, D. (1992) 'The cognitive as the social', *Written Communication*, 9: 315–355.

Breen, M.P. (1985) 'The social context for language learning: a neglected situation?', *Studies in Second Language Learning*, 7 (2): 135–158.

Breen, M., Louden, W., Barratt-Pugh, C., Rivilland, J., Rohl, M., Rhydwen, M., Lloyd, S. and Carr, T. (1994) *Literacy in its Place: An Investigation of Literacy Practices in Urban and Rural Communities*, Perth, Australia: Edith Cowan University.

Brice-Heath, S. (1983) *Ways with Words: Language, Life and Work in Communities and Classrooms*, Cambridge: Cambridge University Press.

Button, G. and Lee, J.R.E. (eds) (1987) *Talk and Social Organisation*, Clevedon: Multilingual Matters.

Calkins, L. (1983) *Lesson from a Child on the Teaching and Learning of Writing*, London: Heinemann.

Cazden, C. (1986) 'Classroom discourse', in M. Wittrock (ed.) *Handbook of Research on Teaching*, 3rd edn, New York: Macmillan.

Cazden, C. (1988) *Classroom Discourses: The Language of Teaching and Learning*, Portsmouth, NH: Heinemann.

Christensen, P. and James, A. (eds) (2000) *Research with Children: Perspectives and Practice*, London: Falmer Press.

Christensen, P. and James, A. (2001) 'What are schools for? The temporal experience of children's learning in Northern England', in L. Alanen, and B. Mayall (eds) *Conceptualizing Child-Adult Relations*, London: RoutledgeFalmer.

Cicourel, A. (1974) 'Some basic theoretical issues in the assessment of the child's performance in testing and classroom settings', in A. Cicourel, K. Jennings, S. Jennings, K. Leiter, R. Mackay, H. Mehan and D. Roth (eds) *Language Use and School Performance*, New York: Academic Press.

Clark, M. (1989) 'Anastasia is a normal developer because she is unique', *Oxford Review of Education*, 15 (3): 243–255.

Clark, M. (1990) *The Great Divide: Gender in the Primary School*, Melbourne: Curriculum Corporation.

Cleverley, J. and Phillips, D. (1987) *Visions of Childhood: Influential Models from Locke to Spock*, Sydney: Allen and Unwin.

Corsaro, W. (1981) 'Entering the child's world: research strategies for field entry and data collection in a preschool setting', in J. Green and C. Wallat (eds) *Ethnography and Language in Educational Settings*, Norwood, NJ: Ablex.

Corsaro, W. (1997) *The Sociology of Childhood*, Thousand Oaks, CA: Pine Forge Press.

Coulter, J. (1979a) 'Beliefs and practical understanding', in G. Psathas (ed.), *Everyday Language*, New York: Irvington.

Coulter, J. (1979b) *The Social Construction of the Mind: Studies in Ethnomethodology and Linguistic Philosophy*, Totowa, NJ: Rowman and Littlefield.

Cox, C. (1988) 'Scriptwriting in small groups', in J. Golub (ed.) *Focus on Collaborative Learning*, Urbana, ILL: National Council of Teachers of English.

Cree, K. and Donaldson, S. (1996) 'Co-operative learning: enhancing talking and listening', in P. Jones (ed.) *Talking to Learn*, Rozelle, NSW: Primary English Teachers' Association.

Cuff, E. and Payne, G. (1984) *Perspectives in Sociology*, 2nd edn, London: Allen and Unwin.

Danby, S. and Baker, C.D. (1998) ' "What's the problem?" Restoring social order in the preschool classroom', in I. Hutchby, and J. Moran–Ellis (eds) *Children and Social Competence: Arenas of Action*, London: Falmer Press.

Daniels, H. (1994) *Literature Circles: Voice and Choice in the Student-centred Classroom*, Maine: Stenhouse Publications.

Davies, B. (1989) *Frogs and Snails and Feminist Tales: Preschool Children and Gender*, Sydney: Allen and Unwin.

Davies, B. (1993) 'Beyond dualism and towards multiple subjectivities', in L. Christian-Smith (ed.) *Texts of Desire: Essays on Fiction, Femininity and Schooling*, London: Falmer Press.

Davies, B. and Banks, C. (1992) 'The gender trap: a feminist poststructuralist analysis of primary schools children's talk about gender', *Journal of Curriculum Studies*, 24 (1): 1–25.

Delamont, S. (1976) 'Beyond Flanders' fields: the relationship of subject matter and individuality of classroom style', in M. Stubbs and S. Delamont (eds) *Explorations in Classroom Observation*, Chichester: John Wiley and Sons.

de Mause, L. (1976) 'The evolution of childhood', in L. de Mause (ed.) *The History of Childhood*, London: Souvenir Press.

Drew, P. and Heritage, J. (eds) (1992) *Talk at Work: Interaction in Institutional Settings*, Cambridge: Cambridge University Press.

Duin, A. (1986) 'Implementing cooperative learning groups in the writing classroom', *Journal of Teaching Writing*, 5 (2): 315–323.

Edwards, A.D. and Westgate, D.P.G. (1987) *Investigating Classroom Talk*, London: Falmer Press.

Eglin, P. and Hester, S. (1992) 'Category, predicate and task: the pragmatics of practical action', *Semiotica*, 88: 243–268.

Emans, R. and Fox, S. (1973) 'Teaching behaviours in reading instruction', paper presented at National Conference of Research in English, New Orleans.

Engell, J. (1988) 'Eroding the conditions for literary study', in J. Engell and D. Perkins (eds) *Teaching Literature: What is Needed Now*, Cambridge, MA: Harvard University Press.

Epstein, D. (1993) *Too Small to Notice? Constructions of Childhood and Discourses of 'Race' in Predominantly White Contexts*, Birmingham: University of Central England.

Finney, I. (1991) *Together I Can: Increasing Personal Growth and Creating Lifelong Learning through Cooperative Learning*, Spring Valley, CA: Innerchoice Publishers.

Flanders, N. (1970) *Analysing Teacher Behaviour*, Reading, MA: Addison–Wesley.

Fleer, M. (1992) 'Teacher–child interaction which scaffolds scientific thinking in young children', *Science Education*, 76 (4): 373–397.

Frakenberg, R. (2000) 'Re-presenting the child: the muted child, the tamed wife and the silenced instrument in Jane Campion's *The Piano*', in A. Prout (ed.) *The Body, Childhood and Society*, London: Macmillan.

Freebody, P. (1995a) 'Identity and pre-competence in early childhood: the case of learning literacy', *The Australian Journal of Early Childhood*, 20 (1): 17–22.

Freebody, P. (1995b) 'Background considerations: schools, poverty and literacy', in P. Freebody, C. Ludwig and S. Gunn (eds) *Everyday Literacy Practices in and out of Schools in Low Socio-Economic Urban Communities*, Brisbane: Centre for Literacy Education Research, Griffith University.

Freebody, P. (in press/2002) *Qualitative Research Methods in Education: The Patterning of Teaching and Learning*, London: Sage.

Freebody P. and Freiberg, J. (2000) 'Public and pedagogic morality: the local orders of instructional and regulatory talk in classrooms', in S. Hester and D. Francis (eds) *Local Education Order: Ethnomethodological Studies of Knowledge in Action*, Amsterdam and London: John Benjamins.

Freebody, P., Ludwig, C. and Gunn, S. (eds) (1995) *Everyday Literacy Practices in and out of Schools in Low Socio-economic Urban Communities*, vol. 1, Report to the Commonwealth Department of Employment, Education and Training, Melbourne: Curriculum Corporation.

Freiberg, J. and Freebody, P. (1995) 'Analysing literacy events in classrooms and homes: conversation-analytic approaches', in P. Freebody, C. Ludwig, and S. Gunn (eds) *Everyday Literacy Practices in and out of Schools in Low Socio-economic Urban Communities*, vol. 1, Report to the Commonwealth Department of Employment, Education and Training, Melbourne: Curriculum Corporation, pp. 185–372.

Garfinkel, H. (1952) 'The perception of the other: a study in social order', unpublished PhD dissertation, Harvard University.

Garfinkel, H. (1967) *Studies in Ethnomethodology*, Englewood Cliffs, NJ: Prentice-Hall.

Garnica, O. (1981) 'Social dominance and conversational interaction: the Omega child in the classroom', in J. Green and C. Wallat (eds) *Ethnography and Language in Educational Settings*, Norwood, NJ: Ablex.

Gilbert, P. (1997) 'Discourses on gender and literacy: changing the stories', in A. Musprat, A. Luke and P. Freebody (eds) *Constructing Critical Literacies: Teaching and Learning Textual Practice*, St Leonards, NSW: Allen and Unwin.

Gilbert, P. and Tayor, S. (1991) *Fashioning the Feminine: Girls, Popular Culture and Schooling*, Sydney: Allen and Unwin.

Gilles, C. and van Doven, M. (1988) 'The power of collaboration', in J. Golub (ed.) *Focus on Collaborative Learning*, Urbana, ILL: National Council of Teachers of English.

Goodwin, C. and Heritage, J. (1990) 'Conversation analysis', *Annual Review of Anthropology*, 19: 283–307.

Goodwin, M.H. (1990) *He-Said-She-Said: Talk as Social Organization among Black Children*, Bloomington: Indiana University Press.

Graff, H. (1995) *Conflicting Paths: Growing Up in America*, Cambridge, MA: Harvard University Press.

Greig, A. and Taylor, J. (1999) *Doing Research with Children*, London: Sage.

Gumperz, J. and Field, M. (1995) 'Children's discourses and inferential practices in cooperative learning', *Discourse Processes*, 19 (91): 133–147.

Haas-Dyson, A. (1987) 'The value of "time off talk": young children's spontaneous talk and deliberate text', *Harvard Educational Review*, 57: 396–420.

Haas-Dyson, A. (1991) 'Viewpoints: the word and the world – reconceptualising written language development or do rainbows mean a lot to little girls?', *Research in the Teaching of English*, 25 (1): 97–123.

Haas-Dyson, A. (1992) 'The case of the singing scientist: a performance perspective on the "stages" of school literacy', *Written Communication*, 9 (1): 3–47.

Halperin, D. (1986) 'The changing perceptions of the nature of the child in early childhood education', unpublished EdD thesis, Nova Scotia University.

Hammersley, M. (1976) 'The mobilisation of pupil attention', in M. Hammersley and P. Woods (eds) *The Process of Schooling: A Sociological Reader*, London and Henley: Routledge and Kegan Paul in association with the Open University Press.

Hammersley, M. (1990) *Classroom Ethnography*, Buckingham: Open University Press.

Handel, W. (1982) *Ethnomethodology: How People Make Sense*, Englewood Cliffs, NJ: Prentice-Hall.

Heap, J.L. (1980) 'What counts as reading: limits to certainty in assessment', *Curriculum Inquiry*, 10: 265–292.

Heap, J.L. (1982) 'The social organization of reading assessment: reasons for eclecticism', in G. Payne and E. Cuff (eds) *Doing Teaching: The Practical Management of Classrooms*, London: Batsford Academic and Educational.

Heap, J.L. (1983) 'Dialogue: interpretations of "What do you mean?" – frames and knowledge in a science lesson: a dialogue with Professor Heyman', *Curriculum Inquiry*, 13: 397–417.

Heap, J.L. (1985) 'Discourse in the production of classroom knowledge: reading lessons', *Curriculum Inquiry*, 15: 245–279.

Heap, J.L. (1992a) 'Normative order in collaborative computer editing', in G. Watson and R.M. Seiler (eds) *Text in Context: Contributions to Ethnomethodology*, Newbury Park, CA: Sage.

Heap, J.L. (1992b) 'Seeing snubs: an introduction to sequential analysis of classroom interaction', *Journal of Classroom Interaction*, 27 (2): 23–28.

Heritage, J. (1984) *Garfinkel and Ethnomethodology*, London: Polity Press.

Hester, S. and Eglin, P. (eds) (1997) *Culture in Action: Studies in Membership Categorization Analysis*, Lanham, MD: University Press of America.

Hester, S. and Francis, D. (eds) (2000) *Local Education Order: Ethnomethodological Studies of Knowledge in Action*, Amsterdam and London: John Benjamins.

Hilbert, R. (1992) *The Classical Roots of Ethnomethodology*, Cambridge: Polity Press.

Hull, R. (1985) *The Language Gap: How Classroom Dialogue Fails*, London: Methuen.

Hunter, I. (1993) 'The pastoral bureaucracy: toward a less principled understanding of state schooling', in D. Meredyth and D. Tyler (eds) *Child and Citizen: Genealogies of Schooling and Subjectivity*, Brisbane: Institute for Cultural Policy Studies.

Hutchby, I. and Moran-Ellis, J. (eds) (1998) *Children and Social Competence: Arenas of Action*, London: Falmer Press.

Hutchby, I. and Wooffitt, R. (1998) *Conversation Analysis: Principles, Practices and Applications*, London: Polity Press.

Jackson, S. (1982) *Childhood and Sexuality*, Oxford: Basil Blackwell.

James, A., Jenks, C. and Prout, A. (1998) *Theorizing Childhood*, Oxford: Basil Blackwell.

James, A. and Prout, A. (eds) (1997) *Constructing and Reconstructing Childhood: Contemporary Issues in the Sociological Study of Childhood*, 2nd edn, London: Falmer Press.

Jayyusi, L. (1984) *Categorization and the Moral Order*, Boston: Routledge and Kegan Paul.

Jayyusi, L. (1991) 'Values and moral judgement: communicative praxis as moral order', in G. Button (ed.) *Ethnomethodology and the Human Sciences*, Cambridge: Cambridge University Press.

Jenks, C. (1982) 'Introduction: constituting the child', in C. Jenks (ed.) *The Sociology of Childhood: Essential Readings*, London: Batsford.

Jenks, C. (1989) 'Social theorizing and the child: constraints and possibilities', in S. Doxiadis (ed.) *Early Influences Shaping the Individual*, NATO Advanced Study Workshop, London: Plenum Press.

Jenks, C. (1994) 'Historical perspectives on normality', in P. Lindstrom and N. Spencer (eds) *The European Textbook of Social Paediatrics*, London: Oxford University Press.

Jenks, C. (1996) *Childhood*, London: Routledge.

Johnson, D. (1981) 'Student-student interaction: the neglected variable in education', *Educational Researcher*, 10 (1): 5–10.

Johnson, D. and Johnson, R. (1985) 'Student-student interaction: ignored but powerful', *Journal of Teacher Education*, 36 (4): 22–26.

Johnson, D. and Johnson, R. (1992) 'Encouraging thinking through constructive controversy', in N. Davidson and T. Worsham (eds) *Enhancing Thinking through Cooperative Learning*, New York: Teachers' College Press.

Johnson, D. and Johnson, R. (1994) 'Learning together', in S. Sharan (ed.) *Handbook of Cooperative Learning Methods*, Westport, CT: Greenwood Press.

Kamler, B. (1993) 'The construction and reconstruction of gender in classroom discourse: disciplining the student body', paper presented at the 83rd Annual Convention, National Council of Teachers of English, Pittsburg, Pennsylvania.

Kamler, B., Maclean, R., Reid, J. and Simpson, A. (1994) *Shaping up Nicely: The Formation of Schoolgirls and Schoolboys in the First Month of School*, report to the Gender Equity and Curriculum Reform project, Department of Employment, Education and Training, Canberra.

Keogh, J. (1999) 'The role of texts and talk in mediating relations between schools and homes', unpublished PhD thesis, Griffith University, Queensland, Australia.

Kerry, T. and Sands, M. (1982) *Handling Classroom Groups: A Teaching Skills Workbook*, London: Macmillan.

Lawlor, E. (1974) 'Who listens? A problem and a solution', *Science Education*, 58 (1): 3–6.

Lee, J.R.E. (1987) 'Prologue: talking organization', in G. Button and J.R.E. Lee (eds) *Talk and Social Organisation*, Clevedon: Multilingual Matters.

Lee, J.R.E. (1991) 'Language and culture: the linguistic analysis of culture', in G. Button (ed.) *Ethnomethodology and the Human Sciences*, Cambridge: Cambridge University Press.

Leiter, K. (1976) 'Ad hocing in the schools: a study of placement practices in the kindergartens of two schools', in M. Hammersley and P. Woods (eds) *The Process of Schooling*, London: Routledge and Kegan Paul.

Leiter, K. (1980) *A Primer of Ethnomethodology*, New York: Oxford University Press.

Levinson, S.C. (1983) *Pragmatics*, Cambridge: Cambridge University Press.

Lewis, A. and Lindsay, G. (eds) (2000) *Researching Children's Perspectives*, Milton Keynes: Open University Press.

Luke, C. (1989) *Pedagogy, Printing and Protestantism: The Discourse on Childhood*, Albany, NY: State University of New York Press.

Luke, C. (1990) *Constructing the Child Viewer: A History of the American Discourse on Television and Children*, New York: Praeger Press.

Luke, C. (1991) 'On reading the child: a feminist poststructuralist perspective', *Australian Journal of Reading*, 14: 109–116.

Lyle, S. (1996) 'An analysis of collaborative group work in the primary school and the factors relevant to its success', *Language and Education*, 10 (1): 13–31.

McHoul, A. (1978) 'The organization of turns at formal talk in the classroom', *Language in Society*, 7: 183–213.

McHoul, A. and Rapley, M. (eds) (2001) *Analysing Talk in Institutional Settings*, London: Continuum International.

MacKay, R.W. (1973) 'Conceptions of children and models of socialization', in R. Turner (ed.) *Ethnomethodology: Selected Readings*, Harmondsworth: Penguin Education.

MacKay, R. (1974) 'Standardized tests: objective/objectified measures of "competence"', in A.V. Cicourel, K.H. Jennings, S.H.M. Jennings, K.C.W. Leiter, R. MacKay, H. Mehan, and D.R. Roth (eds) *Language Use and School Performance*, New York: Academic Press.

MacLure, M. and French, P. (1981) 'A comparison of talk at home and at school', in G. Wells (ed.) *Learning through Interaction*, Cambridge: Cambridge University Press.

Malcolm, I. (1979) 'The Western Australian Aboriginal child and classroom interaction: a sociological approach', *Journal of Pragmatics*, 3: 305–320.

Mannheim, K. (1952) 'On the interpretation of "Weltanschauuung"', in P. Kecskemeti (ed.) *Essays on the Sociology of Knowledge*, New York: Oxford University Press.

Mayall, B. (1994) *Negotiating Health: Children at Home and Primary School*, London: Cassell.

Mayall, B. (1996) *Children, Health and the Social Order*, Milton Keynes: Open University Press.

Mehan, H. (1978) 'Structuring school structure', *Harvard Educational Review*, 48 (1): 32–64.

Mehan, H. (1979) *Learning Lessons. Social Organization in the Classroom*, Cambridge, MA: Harvard University Press.

Mehan, H. (1986) '"What Time is it Denise?": asking known information questions in classroom discourse', in M. Hammersley (ed.) *Case Studies in Classroom Research*, Milton Keynes: Open University Press.

Mishler, E. (1972) 'Implications of teacher strategies for language and cognition: observations in first grade classrooms', in C. Cazden, V. John and D. Hymes (eds) *Functions of Language in the Classroom*, New York: Teacher's College Press.

Orwell, G. (1954) *Animal Farm*, London: Martin, Secker and Warburg.

Payne, G. (1976) 'Making a lesson happen: an ethnomethodological analysis', in M. Hammersley and P. Woods (eds), *The Process of Schooling: A Sociological Reader*, London and Henley: Routledge and Kegan Paul with the Open University Press.

Payne, G. and Cuff, T. (1982) 'Introduction: some theoretical considerations for practical research', in G. Payne and T. Cuff (eds) *Doing Teaching. The Practical Management of Classrooms*, London: Batsford Educational.

Payne, G. and Hustler, D. (1980) 'Teaching the class: the practical management of a cohort', *British Journal of Sociology of Education*, 1 (1): 49–66.

Payne, G. and Ridge, E. (1985) '"Let them talk" – an alternative approach to language development in the infants school', in E. Cuff and G. Payne (eds) *Crisis in the Curriculum*, London: Croom Helm.

Perrott, C. (1988) *Classroom Talk and Pupil Learning: Guidelines for Educators*, Sydney: Harcourt Brace Jovanovich.

Place, B. (2000) 'Constructing the bodies of ill children in the intensive care unit', in A. Prout (ed.) *The Body, Childhood and Society*, London: Macmillan.

Polakow, V. (1989) 'Deconstructing development', *Journal of Education*, 171 (2): 75–89.

Polakow-Suransky, V. (1982) *The Erosion of Childhood*, Chicago and London: The University of Chicago Press.

Pollard, A. (1984) 'Coping strategies and the multiplication of differentiation in infant classes', *British Educational Research Journal*, 10 (1): 33–48.

Pollock, L.A. (1983) *Forgotten Children: Parent-Child Relations from 1500–1900*, Cambridge: Cambridge University Press.

Poynton, C. (1985) *Language and Gender: Making the Difference*, Melbourne: Deakin University Press.

Prout, A. and James, A. (1990) 'A new paradigm for the sociology of childhood? Provenance, promises and problems', in A. James, and A. Prout (eds) *Constructing and Reconstructing Childhood: Contemporary Issues in the Sociological Study of Childhood*, 1st edn, London: Falmer Press.

Psathas, G. (1995) *Conversation Analysis: The Study of Talk-in Interaction*, Thousand Oaks, CA: Sage.

Reid, J., Forrestal, P. and Cook, J. (1989) *Small Group Learning in the Classroom*, Rozelle, NSW: Primary English Teachers' Association.

Sacks, H. (1972) 'On the analyzability of stories by children', in J.J. Gumperz, and D. Hymes (eds) *Directions in Sociolinguistics: The Ethnography of Communication*, New York: Rinehart and Winston.

Sacks, H. (1974) 'On the analysability of stories by children', in R. Turner (ed.) *Ethnomethodology*, Harmondsworth: Penguin.

Sacks, H. (1995) *Lectures on Conversation*, vols 1 and 2, ed. G. Jefferson, Oxford: Blackwell.

Sacks, H., Schegloff, E. and Jefferson, G. (1974) 'A simple systematic for the organization of turn-taking for conversation', *Language*, 50 (4): 696–735.

Schegloff, E.A. (1991) 'Reflections on talk and social structure', in D. Boden and D. Zimmerman (eds) *Talk and Social Structure: Studies in Ethnomethodology and Conversation Analysis*, Cambridge: Polity Press.

Schegloff, E.A. (1995) 'Parties and joint talk: two ways in which numbers are significant for talk-in-interaction', in P. Ten Have and G. Psathas (eds) *Situated Order: Studies in the Social Organization of Talk and Embodied Activities*, Washington, DC: University Press of America.

Schutz, A. (1964) *Collected Papers*, Amsterdam: Martinus Nijhoff.

Sharan, Y. and Sharan, S. (1992) *Exploring Co-operative Learning Through Group Investigations*, New York: Teacher's College Press.

Sharan, Y. and Sharan, S. (1994) 'Group investigation in the cooperative classroom', in S. Sharan (ed.) *Handbook of Cooperative Learning Methods*, Westport, CT: Greenwood Press.

Sharp, R. and Green, A. (1984) 'Social stratification in the classroom', in A. Hargreaves and P. Woods (eds) *Classrooms and Staffrooms: The Sociology of Teachers and Teaching*, Milton Keynes: Open University Press.

Sharrock, W. and Anderson, B. (1986) *The Ethnomethodologists*, Chichester/London: Ellis Horwood/Tavistock Publications.

Simpson, B (2000) 'The body as a site of contestation in school', in A. Prout (ed.) *The Body, Childhood and Society*, London: Macmillan.

Sinclair, J. and Coulthard, M. (1975) *Towards an Analysis of Discourse: The Language of Teachers and Pupils*, London: Oxford University Press.

Singh, P. (1995) 'Discourses of computing, competence, evaluation and gender: the case of computer use in the primary school', *Discourse: Studies in the Cultural Politics of Education*, 16 (1): 81–110.

Smith, C. (1988) 'In the primary classroom', in J. Hickman and K. Kimberley (eds) *Teachers, Language and Learning*, London: Routledge.

Smith, D.E. (1987) *The Everyday World as Problematic: A Feminist Sociology*, Boston: Northeastern University Press.

Smith, D.E. (1999) *Writing the Social: Critique, Theory, and Investigations*, Toronto: University of Toronto Press.

Speier, M. (1971) 'The everyday world of the child', in J.D. Douglas (ed.) *Understanding Everyday Life: Toward the Reconstruction of Sociological Knowledge*, Chicago: Aldine.

Speier, M. (1976) 'The child as conversational interactions between adults and children', in M. Hammersley and P. Woods (eds) *The Process of Schooling*, London: Routledge and Kegan Paul.

Taylor, T. and Cameron, D. (1987) *Analysing Conversation: Rules and Units in the Structure of Talk*, Oxford: Pergamon Press.

Thiele, C. (1974) *Magpie Island*, Ringwood, Victoria: Puffin Books.

Turner, G. (1973) 'Social class and children's language control at age five and age seven', in B. Bernstein (ed.) *Class, Codes and Control*, vol. II, London: Routledge and Kegan Paul.

Tyler, D. (1993) 'Making better children', in D. Meredyth and D. Tyler (eds) *Child and Citizen: Genealogies of Schooling and Subjectivity*, Brisbane: Griffith University Institute for Cultural Policy Studies.

Walker, R. (1991) 'Classroom identities', in I. Goodson and R. Walker (eds) *Biography, Identity and Schooling: Episodes in Educational Research*, London: Falmer Press.

Walkerdine, V. (1990) *Schoolgirl Fictions*, London: Verso.

Watson, G. and Seiler, R.M. (eds) (1992) *Text in Context: Contributions to Ethnomethodology*, London: Sage.

Watson, R.D. (1992) 'Ethnomethodology, conversation analysis and education: an overview', *International Review of Education*, 38 (3): 257–274.

Webb, N. (1982) 'Student interaction and learning in small groups', *Review of Educational Research*, 52: 421–445.

Weeks, B. (1990) 'Watching children teach themselves to write', in L. Badger, P. Cormack and J. Hancock (eds) *Success Stories from the Classroom*, Rozelle, NSW: Primary English Teachers' Association.

Wells, G. (1985) 'Preschool literacy-related activities and success in school', in D.R. Olson, N. Torrance, and A. Hildyard (eds) *Literacy, Language, and Learning: The Nature and Consequences of Reading and Writing*, Cambridge: Cambridge University Press.

West, M. (1988) *Children, Culture and Controversy*, Hamden, CT: Archon Books.

Willes, M. (1983) *Children into Pupils: A Study of Language in Early Schooling*, London: Routledge and Kegan Paul.

Wilson, S. (1984) 'The myth of motherhood a myth: the historical view of European child rearing', *Social History*, 9 (2): 181–198.

Wilson, T. P. (1991) 'Social structure and the sequential organization of interaction', in D. Boden and D. Zimmerman (eds) *Talk and Social Structure. Studies in Ethnomethodology and Conversation Analysis*, Cambridge: Polity Press.

Zeiher, H. (2001) 'Dependent and independent relations: children as members of the family household in West Berlin', in L. Alanen and B. Mayall (eds) *Conceptualizing Child-Adult Relations*, London: RoutledgeFalmer.

Index